Thomas Hewitt Key

Philological Essays

Thomas Hewitt Key

Philological Essays

ISBN/EAN: 9783742801883

Manufactured in Europe, USA, Canada, Australia, Japa

Cover: Foto ©Andreas Hilbeck / pixelio.de

Manufactured and distributed by brebook publishing software (www.brebook.com)

Thomas Hewitt Key

Philological Essays

PHILOLOGICAL ESSAYS

BY

T. HEWITT KEY, M.A., F.R.S.,

FORMERLY PROFESSOR OF MATHEMATICS IN THE UNIVERSITY OF VIRGINIA, U.S.;
THEN OF LATIN IN UNIVERSITY COLLEGE, LONDON;
NOW OF COMPARATIVE GRAMMAR IN THE SAME,
AND HEAD MASTER OF THE SCHOOL.

LONDON:
BELL & DALDY, YORK STREET, COVENT GARDEN.
1868.

PREFACE.

THE following Papers are in part now published for the first time, in part reprinted from the 'Transactions of the Philological Society,' but with many changes or additions. In the selection I have passed over several papers, because I wish to reserve them for a systematic treatise on language, the greater part of which is already ripe for publication.

I fear that some traces of haste will be visible in what I am now putting out; but I have two pleas in excuse: first, that the head-master of a school of nearly four hundred boys has little leisure for other work; and secondly, that such leisure cannot now be expected to be very productive for one who has entered his seventieth year.

I take the present opportunity of enumerating the various philological papers which have proceeded from my pen during the forty years or so in which I have been connected with University College, first as Professor of Latin (thirteen years) and then as Professor of Comparative Grammar (nearly twenty-seven years).

A. Quarterly Journal of Education, published by the Society for the Diffusion of Useful Knowledge :—

Vol. i. p. 89, Review of Zumpt's Grammar, in which I first put forth several of the new ideas which appear in my Latin Grammar.

Vol. ii. p. 143, Review of Sallust's Catiline and Jugurtha, as edited (1) by the Rev. W. Trollope, M.A.; (2) by Professor Charles Anthon, of New York.

Vol. ii. p. 344, School Editions of Terence, where (pp. 349-364, &c.) I first give my theory of Terentian metres.

Vol. iii. p. 312, Review of Crombie's 'Gymnasium.'

Vol. iv. p. 134, Review of Allen's Treatise 'On Latin Particles.'

Vol. iv. p. 336, Review of Carey's 'Latin Prosody made Easy.'

B. Various articles in the Penny Cyclopædia, chiefly bearing on language. Among these papers was one on Terentian metres, in agreement with the article already mentioned as published in the Journal of Education. These papers were for the most part collected in a little volume entitled :—

C. 'The Alphabet, Terentian Metres, &c.;' with a new paper on 'Good, Better, Best, Well,' &c. 1844. To this was prefixed 'A Prefatory Letter' (to Mr. Long), with 'Remarks on the Varronianus of the Rev. J. W. Donaldson, 1844,' where I brought against him several distinct charges of plagiarism. The first published copy of this book was sent to him August 23d.

In 1849 there was a 'second issue' of this book, with a paper 'On the Pronouns of the Third Person.'

D. The publication of the above-mentioned 'Prefatory Letter' led to a controversy with Mr. Donaldson, which took the shape of four additional pamphlets: first from him what he was pleased to call, 'A Reply to the Calumnies and Misrepresentations of Professor T. H. Key.' A copy of this I received on the 20th of November 1844. I at once wrote, and on the 30th of the same month sent him a printed copy of

A Rejoinder to the Reply of the Rev. J. W. Donaldson, B.D., in a second 'Letter to G. Long, Esq. M.A. &c.;' to which I attached a paper on

The Formation of the Latin Perfects *amavi*, &c.

On the 13th of December I received his second pamphlet, entitled 'A Brief Examination of Professor Key's Rejoinder;' and on the 8th of the following January I sent him again in print—

Comments on Mr. Donaldson's Brief Examination of a Rejoinder, &c.

All the five pamphlets in the year 1845 I had reprinted, and distributed in private circulation nearly five hundred copies, which produced from him a threat that he would apply to the Court of Chancery for an injunction,—a threat however that ended, as I expected, in nothing; for although of course I had no legal right to print what he had written, yet I felt justified in so doing, because he had implied that I looked forward to a verdict in my favour in the sole hope that my readers might not see his replies.

E. In 1846 I published—

A Latin Grammar on the System of Crude Forms; and in 1862 what I may call a third edition of the same, 'corrected and somewhat enlarged.'

F. Proceedings of the Philological Society, vol. ii.

p. 50 : On the English Verb *do* and the Latin *dare;* and On the Formation of the English Weak Perfects.

Ibid. p. 143 : On the Relations which exist between the Preterite *went* and the Verb *go ;* and also between *va* and the Verbs *aller* and *andare.*

Ibid. p. 180 : The Lapp and Finn Tongues not unconnected with the Indo-European Family.

Ibid. p. 249 : On the Origin of certain Latin Words.

Ibid. vol. iii. p. 45 : On the Misuse of the Terms Epenthesis and Euphony.

Ibid. p. 57 : On the Origin of the Demonstrative Pronoun, the Definite Article, the Pronouns of the Third Person, the Relative and the Interrogative.

Ibid. p. 115 : On the Names of the Parts of the Human Body, as common to the several Families of the Indo-European Language.

Ibid. p. 130 : On apparent Exceptions from the Triliteral Form of Monosyllabic Roots.

Ibid. p. 136 : On the Chronology of the Catilinarian Orations.

Ibid. p. 205 : On the Origin of certain Latin Words.

Ibid. vol. iv. p. 25 : On the Pronouns of the First and Second Persons.

Ibid. p. 87 : An Attempt to prove the Identity of the Roots *is, was,* and *be.*

Ibid. vol. v. p. 51 : On the Nature of the Verb, particularly on the Formation of the Middle or Passive Voice.

Ibid. p. 89 : On the Derivation and Meaning of certain Latin Words.

Ibid. p. 103 : On the Etymology of certain Latin Words.

Ibid. p. 191 : On Vowel-assimilation, especially in relation to Professor Willis's Experiment on Vowel Sounds.

Ibid. vol. vi. p. 63 : On the Imperfect Infinitive, Imperfect Participle, and those Substantives which fall under the definition 'Nomen actionis.'

Ibid. p. 93 : Miscellaneous Remarks on some Latin Words.

Ibid. p. 117 : On some alleged Distinctions in Languages believed to be without foundation.

Ibid. p. 127 : On the Etymology of ἁπλοος, διπλοος, &c.

Ibid. p. 138 : On the Etymology of στοα.

Ibid. p. 139 : Some Remarks on the Speech 'Pro Plancio.'

Ibid. p. 152 : On the Etymology of *circumforaneus, circulator, cento.*

Ibid. p. 155 : A Translation (from the German) of Ahren's Paper, 'On Feminines in α and ως; and on the word γυνη.'

Ibid. p. 188 : A Translation (from the Italian) of Dr. G. Henzen's Paper, 'On the Inscription of Sora.'

G. Transactions of the Philological Society—vol. for 1854, p. 26 : On the Derivation of *maritimus, aeditimus, finitimus, legitimus, miles,* and *diues.*

Ibid. p. 29 : A Search in some European Languages after the Representatives of the Greek Preposition ανα as prefixed to Verbs.

An unfavourable review of this paper appeared in Kuhn's 'Zeitschrift für vergleichende Sprachforschung,' vol. iv. pp. 217—219; but the editor, with somewhat unusual courtesy, gave admission to a reply from me (zur Erwiederung) in vol. v. pp. 72—80.

Ibid. p. 72 : On the Meaning of *adaequare*.

Ibid. p. 85 : On the Prepositions *en*, *in*, and related Words.

Ibid. p. 131 : On the Etymology of the Verb *obsolescere* (but see pp. 200, 220).

Ibid. p. 199 : On the Use of the Reflective form *deuerti*.

Ibid. p. 206 : On Metathesis.

Ibid. vol. for 1855, p. 1 : On the Latin Verb *mittere*, its Origin and Affinities; and generally on Verbs signifying 'to *go*' in the Indo-European Family.

Ibid. p. 96 : On the Derivation and Meaning of the Latin Verb *usurpare*.

Ibid. p. 119 : On Greek Accentuation.

Ibid. vol. for 1856, p. 219 : On Diminutives.—I. English.

Ibid. p. 195 : (On Diminutives—II. Latin ; or) On the Representatives of the Keltic suffix *agh* or *ach* ' little,' in the Latin Vocabulary.

Ibid. vol. for 1857, p. 115 : On the Word *Inkling*.

Ibid. vol. for 1859, p. 136 : On the Derivations of *duntaxat*, *tranquillus*, and *si* in *si dis placet*.

Ibid. p. 140 : On the Derivation of the Gothic *hanfs* ' one-handed.'

Ibid. p. 143 : On the Derivation of the Word δημος.

Ibid. p. 145 : On the Convertibility of *n* and *d*.

Ibid. p. 273 : A Supplemental Paper on the Keltic Suffix *agh*, &c. as occurring in Latin, Greek, and other Languages.

Ibid. vol. for 1860-1, p. 172: Miscellaneous Remarks suggested by Ritschl's Plautus, especially on the Formation of the Latin Perfect.

Ibid. vol. for 1862-3, p. 1: Miscellaneous Papers: (A) On *altero-* and its Analogues; (B) On Words which denote 'Waterfowl' and 'Swimming;' (C) On ετ of ειπειν (*inquit*) and επ of επομαι (*sequor*); (D) On *alaceri-* and some related Greek Words; (E) On *uiuere*, &c.

Ibid. p. 113: The Sanskrit Language as the Basis of Linguistic Science, and the Labours of the German School in that Field—are they not over-valued?

Ibid. p. 213: On *titillare* and τικτειν.

Ibid. p. 216: The Anglo-Saxon Language called in aid to support the Doctrine which attributes a Suffix *agh* or *ag* to Latin Verbs.

Ibid. vol. for 1865: On the so-called 'A privativum.'

Ibid. vol. for 1866, p. 1: *Daughter* and *Fille*, are they connected?

Ibid. p. 25: On the Latin Words *temere* and *temerare*.

Ibid. p. 30: On the Latin Prepositions *re* and *pro*; their Origin and Primitive Meaning.

Ibid. p. 49: The Latin *et*, *que*, *atque* (*ac*), and the Greek και, τε, all of one Origin.

Ibid. vol. for 1867, p. 1: On the Formation of Greek Futures and First Aorists.

II. Bell's English Journal of Education. Thirteen papers on Latin Etymology, signed 'Claudius,' viz.: I. July 1850, p. 254; II. August, p. 292; III. September, p. 310; IV. October, p. 354; V. November,

p. 402; VI. January 1851, p. 1; VII. March, p. 69; VIII. April, p. 109; IX. May, p. 149; X. June, p. 196; XI. July, p. 240; XII. August, p. 281; XIII. September, p. 313.

I. A Review of Smith's Latin Dictionary in the *Westminster,* July 1855.

As my arguments touched upon moral questions as well as matters of scholarship, I was the more unwilling to take shelter under the anonymous, and accordingly gave him formal notice that I was the writer.

J. Knight's English Cyclopædia, article 'Language.'

One object in entering into these particulars has been to correct some errors which have appeared in certain classical publications, and are believed to prevail somewhat widely. In an edition of the Adelphi by the Rev. Wharton B. Marriott (formerly Fellow of Exeter College, Oxford, and late Assistant Master of Eton), 1863, the second part of the Introduction deals with the metres of Latin comedy, and to the views of Bentley are opposed those of 'more recent scholars' (p. 13); and he then proceeds to discuss 'the main ground these "recent scholars" take up,' adding a note,—

'See particularly the article on Terentian Metres in the Penny Cyclopædia, evidently by Professor Donaldson; and the chapter of the same author's Varronianus (xiv.), on the Constitution and Pathology of the Latin Language.'

Soon after, in § 5, he speaks of 'the three kinds of

evidence they adduce in support of (their) view;' and then says, 'The two first of these arguments have already been stated by Donaldson (Varron. pp. 433, 437, *sqq.*) in a way that leaves nothing for others to add.'

Again, his notes (vv. 688 and 899) on the pronunciation first of *item quidem modo*, and then of *student* and *facere*, refer to Donaldson's 'interesting chapter' as the source of his information.

On my first seeing Mr. Marriott's book, I wrote a note to him in which I pointed out that he had fallen into a very natural mistake in ascribing to the author of the Varronianus the paternity of the article Terentian Metres in the Penny Cyclopædia, for this article and the corresponding chapter in the Varronianus evidently proceeded from the same pen; but that the simple fact was that the article in the Penny Cyclopædia was written by me, and dishonestly appropriated by Donaldson. He at once favoured me with a courteous reply, in which he admitted his error, and at the same time assured me that the mistake he had made was one of general currency.

And in fact I find that the editor of Terence in the 'Bibliotheca Classica' shares the error, for he also commences his Introduction on the Metres of Terence (p. xxviii.) thus :—

'This subject has been noticed by the author of the Varronianus (chap. x.), who refers to the Journal of Education (vol. ii. p. 344, &c.), where it is treated generally in a manner which leaves nothing for others.'

When he wrote these words, I have little doubt that, in his own mind, Mr. Parry ascribed to Dr. Donaldson the authorship of the article in the Journal of Education, for in his preface (p. ix.), after saying that 'the question of Terentian language and metre is a subject which has till lately lain fallow in England since the time of Bentley and Hare,' he adds in a note, 'When I wrote this sentence, I had not seen Mr. Key's Essay on the Metres of Terence and Plautus. My only acquaintance with his researches was through the Varronianus.' Now the whole of the chapter of the Varronianus in question is, with two petty exceptions, an unmitigated plagiarism by Donaldson from my two articles on Terentian Metres, that in the Journal of Education and that in the Cyclopædia. One exception is the doctrine that *homines* (in the Phormio, v. 1, 37) is a monosyllable (!). The honour of this is all his own. The other is that *puellam* in Haut. v. 5, 16 is to be pronounced *pullam*. It must have been somewhat grating to Dr. Donaldson's conscience to find that Mr. Parry, amid his general approval of his chapter on the comic metres, selects this one remark for disapproval (p. xxxv. note).

I confess that it is not satisfactory to me that my views should come to the knowledge of scholars through the medium of Donaldsonian writings; and I have deemed it a duty to print these pages, although the offender has now passed away. I never thought it necessary to notice the abusive or contemptuous terms in which I have been habitually alluded to in the later editions of the Cratylus and Varronianus, for such abuse I heeded as little as I did the flattery he bestowed upon me in the first edition of the former work.

CONTENTS.

	PAGE
PREFACE	v
I. On the Representatives of *ava* in Allied Languages	1
II. On the Prepositions *ava*, *in*, and related Words	57
III. On the Latin Prepositions *re* and *pro*	74
IV. On the German Prefix *ver* and Allied Forms	101
V. *Post* and *after* the same Word	117
VI. On the so-called 'a privative'	127
VII. The Latin *et*, *que*, *atque* (*ac*), and the Greek *ουν*, *τε*, all of one Origin	149
VIII. On the Latin Particles *aut*, *an*, *nē*	170
IX. On Plural Forms in Latin with a Singular Meaning, and especially on Virgil's use of *menta*	185
X. Excrescent Consonants	204
XI. On False Division of Suffixes	225
XII. Qvaeritvr: The Sanskrit Language as the Basis of Linguistic Science; and the Labours of the German School in that Field—are they not over-valued?—First Part	248
XIII. Qvaeritvr—Second Part	270
XIV. Postscript to Qvaeritvr	309
Addenda, Corrigenda, &c.	317
INDEX	323

PHILOLOGICAL ESSAYS.

I.

ON THE REPRESENTATIVES OF ava
IN ALLIED LANGUAGES.

The little syllables which are prefixed or affixed to roots in the process of word-building were probably at the outset possessed of an importance equal to that claimed for the roots to which they are attached; in other words, they also are roots; but, supporting for the time an inferior part, are of course subject to be treated with some indignity beside the greater personage on whom they wait. Thus it will be often found that both prefixes and suffixes are curtailed of their fair proportions. But among such secondary syllables, none perhaps suffer more abridgement or alteration than the prepositions used in the composition of verbs, especially those which fall under the class called by German grammarians inseparable. Grimm has particularly noticed this liability (Deutsche Grammatik, ii. 865).

'The doctrine,' says he, 'which holds true generally of particles, that they become obscure in signification and disguised in form, is specially applicable to the inseparable particles. The notion which they express wavers between increased intensity and a privative character, or occupies an intermediate position. The form again passes commonly through all the vowels, and at last fades away into an unaccented *e*, while the consonants either drop off or are modified by the influence of the initial consonant of the word which is brought into contact with them. One particle indeed (our *ge-*), in the vulgar dialect, has sunk down into an almost imperceptible breathing. The more this corruption of a particle develops itself, the less capable does it become of maintaining the independent and separate character which it first possessed.'

Greek scholars in this country will probably give a ready assent to the power which Kühner assigns to the preposition *ἀνα* in the etymological portion of his grammar (§ 365, 2): '*ἀνά*, auf (hinauf).' At any rate *up* is the notion which distinctly presents itself in a large number of the verbs compounded with *ἀνα*.[1] But German authors have allowed themselves to be biassed by the tempting similarity between the Greek *ἀνα* and the Gothic and old German preposition *ana*, which in modern German takes the shorter form of *an*, the equivalent of our *on*; and hence in his syntax, § 602, Kühner writes: "Ἀνά [old Germ. *ana*, and as still written *an* with the dative and accusa-

---

[1] It is a somewhat strange fact that Matthiae, in his large grammar of more than a thousand pages (at least in the English translation), gives not a word which can lead his readers to the true sense of *ἀνα*. His examples are limited to such as he translates by *on, in, throughout, against, with*, or by phrases of *distribution*. On the sense which *ἀνα* brings to verbs in composition he is utterly silent.

live]. The fundamental signification of the preposition ἀνά is *on, up* (*an, auf*).' In justification of the sense *on*, Kühner gives no examples but ἀνὰ σκήπτρῳ, ἀν' ὤμῳ, ἀνὰ Γαργάρῳ ἄκρῳ in Homer, and εὗδει δ' ἀνὰ σκάπτῳ Διὸς αἰετός in Pindar. Now in all these examples elevation is a prevailing idea; and the English translation '*upon*,' or rather '*up* on the sceptre,' duly represents the first of the above phrases, where ava contributes no more to the sentence than the English *up*, for the second preposition *on* represents what the Greek expresses by the dative case-ending.

In the course of this paper the real representative of the Greek ava on German ground will be pointed out, together with the arguments necessary to establish its claim. For the present I must deal with ava alone. Now the chief meanings which belong to this preposition are the following: 1, *up*, as ava τον ποταμον, ava ροον πλειν; ava ρωτα θεουσα; 2, it is often convenient to fancy an acclivity, where none may actually exist, and thus on the most level ground we may speak of going up this line and down that. Hence we get the meaning of *along, through*, as ava νηας, αστυ, πεδιον. 3, from *through in place* we pass readily to *through in time, during*, as ava νυκτα 'all night long,' ava τον πολεμον 'throughout the war.' 4, that the idea of *distribution*, which is so common in this preposition, is in immediate relation with that of *along* or *through*, is often seen physically; for example, when a postman distributing his cargo of letters passes along the streets as he leaves them at the successive houses. So an epidemic passes through a camp, attacking one soldier after another. I purposely pass over the statement that ava with numerals signifies *up to, full*, as is stated in a lexicon of repute, or *auf* (*circa*) as Kühner would translate it, because in the passages (Hom. Od. ix. 209, Herod. iv. 101) quoted or referred to, the distributival sense seems to prevail;[1] but of course, when more decisive instances are produced, I shall readily welcome a usage which is perfectly consistent with the sense of the preposition, as our own construction, '*up* to three hundred,' serves to show.

I next pass to what more concerns me, the use of ανα in composition with verbs; and here the important bearing of the subject upon the future arguments must be my apology for entering into fuller detail.

1. The sense of *up* is, as I have already said, too evidently exhibited in the compound verbs to render a collection of instances necessary to establish it. Still, with a view to matter which will subsequently come under consideration, I would draw attention to certain classes of verbs in which this sense of *up* is prominent; as, *a.* verbs with the idea of *flame, heat, &c. ascending*: αν-αιθ-, -αιθυσσ-, -άττ-, -αυ-, βρασσ-, -δαι-, -ζε-, -θυμια-, -και-, -καχλαζ-, -λαμπ-, -πρηθ-, -πυρο-, -φαιν-, -φλεγ-, -φλυ-; *b.* verbs of *searching* or *investigating*, in which ανα seems to signify *up to the very sources*: αν-ειρ- (r.), -ερευνα-, -ερωτα-, -εταζ-; ανα-ζητε-, -κριν-, -μανθαν-, -μαστευ-, -πηλο-, -πυνθαν- (r.), -σκοπε-;—*c. loud noise*, where the loudness is attributed to ανα, just as we ourselves say 'speak up, raise your voice, you speak too low to be heard.' Under this head Liddell and Scott's Lexicon furnishes some thirty or forty

---

Of the phrases ανα στομα, ανα θυμον εχειν; and ανα τους πρωτους ειναι, mention is made below.

examples, some of which however perhaps belong to § 6.

2. As downward motion, by the law of gravity, is the natural course of most visible bodies, the idea of *up* is connected with reversed action. Hence the sense of *back* is found in more than thirty compounds in the same lexicon.

3. But to go back is to go over the same ground again. This idea, *again*, occurs as frequently as the last. I will only quote the examples ανα-γιγνωσκ- and ανα-γνωριζ- 'know again, recognise'; and ανα-μιμνησκ-, 'remind.'

4. But to retrace one's steps is another phrase for the *reversal* of some preceding action, where the English prefix is commonly *un-*. Hence αν-απα- (r.) 'recall a curse,' ανα-διδασκ- 'unteach,' -ελισσ- 'unroll,' -ευχ- (r.) 'recall a prayer,' -καλυπτ- 'unwrap,' -κλωθ- 'untwist (what has been spun),' -κολυμβα- 'come to the surface again after diving,' -κυπτ- 'raise (the head) again after stooping,' -μαντευ- (r.) 'make an oracle invalid,' -πτυσσ- 'unfold,' -σκευαζ-[1] 'dismantle,' -σφαλλ- 'rise up after a fall,' -σφραγιζ-'unseal,' -τυλισσ-' unroll.'

5. Sometimes the simple verb already in itself expresses the idea of *loosening, stripping, opening*; and then the prefix appears only to strengthen the idea of relaxation: and yet there will often be found some-

---

[1] Ανασκευαζ- we are told means 'strictly to pack up the baggage (τὰ σκεύη), Lat. vasa colligere, and so to carry away, Xen. An. vi. 2, 8: usu. in Med. to break up, march away.' Why not 'dismantle' here, as in the other uses of the word? This would be in agreement with the phrase just quoted from the lexicon, 'break up;' and indeed it is usual for a series of acts to take their collective name from the first in the series.

thing more than this, viz. a reference to a previous act of binding, &c. This in English is the case with 'to unloose,' not so with 'to loosen;' and similarly τηκ- 'melt' is applicable to things which in their natural condition are solid, whereas ανα-τηκ- implies a return to a former condition, and can only be used of thawing congealed fluids. Examples of such words are ανα-γυμνο-, -δερ-, -οιγ-, -παυ-, -τηκ-, -χαλα-, αν-ιημι, and ανα-πεταν-νυμι.

6. The idea of *opening* or *discovery* is also seen in other compounds with ανα, where the simple verb denotes some means by which the opening is effected. Here again not unfrequently our own language also consistently expresses the idea by *up*: αν-ευρισκ- 'find out,' -ευρυν- 'widen,' ανα-σκαζ- 'split up,' -κλιν- 'bend back (a door) and so open,' -ξαιν- 'tear up or open a wound,' -ῥηγνυμι 'break up or open,' -σχιζ- 'split up,' -τεμν- 'cut up,' -χαιν- 'gape open.'

7. From the idea of opening we readily pass to that of *commencing*, where again *up* is at times used in English. Thus we say: 'open a ball, open fire, strike up a tune.' To this head perhaps belong the following words, where the translation is borrowed from the lexicon already named: -ανα-κοκκυ- 'begin to crow,' -κρεκ- (r.) 'begin to play (a tune),' -κρου- (r.) 'strike up (a tune) or begin a speech,' -μελπ- 'begin to sing,' -βαλλ- (r.) 'begin (anything), -οδυρ- (r.) 'break into wailing,' -φυσα- 'begin to blow,' -ραψωδ- 'begin singing;' and perhaps we should not be wrong in translating ανα-γελα- 'burst out laughing, set up a laugh.'

8. The idea of *back* is in close connexion with those of *escaping, removal, away*: ανα-κομιζ- (r.)' get safe

away, escape,' -φευγ- 'escape,' -φοβε- 'frighten away,' -ρυ- (r.) 'rescue.'

9. Indeed the idea of removal also connects itself directly with the idea of *up*, inasmuch as motion upward is in many cases a convenient or even essential preliminary. Thus in Latin *ferre, tollere, sustuli* have for their first sense 'to raise,' and only in a secondary way signify 'carry off.' Examples are αν-αιρε- 'take up and so carry away,' αν-αρπαζ- 'snatch up and carry off,' ανα-καθαιρ- 'clean up or clear up,' -σπογγιζ- 'sponge up,' -ψα- 'wipe up,' -πετ- (r.) 'fly away.'

10. As the idea of *through* is often expressed by ανα in company with nouns, so we have ανα-πειρ- 'pierce through, spit,' -τιτρα- 'bore through,' -πηγνυμι 'transfix.'

11. Hence we may perhaps deduce *thorough distribution, an act pervading all parts*, as seen more or less in: ανα-διδωμι 'distribute,' -ζυμο- 'leaven thoroughly,' -κεραννυμι, -κιρναμαι, -μιγνυμι and -μισγ-, -φυρ-, 'mix thoroughly, mix up.' But very possibly a better interpretation, so far as regards the verbs of mixing, may be obtained directly from the idea of upward movement, seeing that the process of mixing is a constant battle with the heavier ingredients which persist in sinking. The truth of this will be felt by any one who has mixed a bowl of salad or a powder containing calomel.

12. The idea of *completeness* or *thoroughly* might well be expected in compounds with ανα, and accordingly we find this meaning attributed to αν-αρμοζ-, -αισιμο-, -ελεγχ-; ανα-βιβρωσκ-, -ζωγραφε-, -πρι-. Even of these some may be doubted, and at best the list is very short. The explanation of the paucity may perhaps

be this. It was noticed above that ανα obtained its sense of 'through' from the notion of a fictitious acclivity, where a person goes up this line and down that. Hence κατα 'down' would be entitled to share the privilege, and accordingly this preposition is equally used in distributival phrases, as κατα φυλα 'by tribes,' κατ' ανδρα 'man by man,' &c. On the same principle it is well calculated to express 'thoroughness' with verbs. This office it performs in the Greek vocabulary to a great extent, being in much higher favour for the purpose than ανα, whereas with us the word *up* is more in vogue. Hence κατ-εσθι- 'eat up,' κατα-πιν- 'drink up,' κατα-χρα- (r.) 'use up.'[1]

In a few instances the idea of *on* or *at* is said to be the signification of ανα, as in αν-ειρ- 'fasten on,' ανα-κολλα,- 'glue on,' αναρραπτ-, 'sew on.' But here we seem to have a totally different preposition, the analogue of the Gothic *ana*, German *an*, signifying 'on.'

I find that I have spent many more words upon this preliminary matter than I had intended. My apology must be, that I knew of no grammar or dictionary in which the subject was handled in sufficient detail. Nor indeed is there any part of language more commonly neglected in grammars, for to them the question properly belongs, than the power of prepositions as prefixed to verbs. At the same time, what I have said seems necessary for the just appreciation of the evidence I shall have to adduce; and I have now

---

[1] It should be stated that, in drawing up these lists of compound verbs, I have relied almost exclusively on the excellent lexicon of Liddell and Scott, an acknowledgment I am the more bound to make, as I have ventured at times to criticise some of their statements.

the satisfaction of knowing that Pott in his new edition of the Etymologische Forschungen (p. 305), has adopted my distribution of the meanings of ανα.

After this preface, the first problem is, whether the Latin language has any representative of ανα. My answer is, that it has at least one, and, as I believe, no less than three, or even four representatives. That ανα should appear in Latin without a final vowel is what is to be expected when we compare the cases of απο and ab, επι and ob, παρα and per in perjurus, ενι and in. Further, in Greece itself ανα was reduced to αν in some forms and dialects, just as κατα, παρα, ενι were to κατ, παρ, and εν, and this especially in those dialects which have the closest affinity to Latin, the Doric, and Æolic. Now in three words, *ancisus*, (Lucr. iii. 660), *anquir-*, and *anhela-*, the form *an* has been preserved; but for all of these a word of remark seems necessary. Lucretius is speaking of a snake suddenly divided into many parts, and yet in these several parts still exhibiting signs of vitality for a while:

"Omnia iam sorsum cernes ancisa recenti
 Volnere tortari."

Here therefore *ancisa* is no compound of *am*, as Forcellini would make it; but clearly means 'cut off, or cut through.' *Anquir-* seems to have for its meaning 'search up to the sources,' and indeed αναμαστευ- is explained by Liddell and Scott as = *anquir-*. *Anhela-* is used of those violent up-blowings which follow volcanic action, as in Cic. *anhelitus terrae*, and Ovid, Fast. iv. 491; also of the flame driven out by a furnace-blast, or from the nostrils of Colchian bulls. Comp.

ἀνα-φυσα-, whence ἀνα-φυσησ-σι- 'the blow-hole of a crater,' and ἀνα-φυσια- 'blow as a dolphin.' At any rate such an explanation of *anhela-* seems more satisfactory than what we find in Andrews's Lexicon, who gives as the 'literal' sense: 'to draw the breath from around the whole body.' This translation no doubt proceeded on the assumption that the word contains the prefix *am* 'round,' although in this case it should have been *am-hela-*, if we may judge from *am-ici-*. But besides this, *an-hela-* clearly means an expiration rather than an inspiration.

Of course before a labial *an* would pass into *am*, and accordingly we have *am-puta-* 'cut off,' *am-mone-* 'remind' ἀναμιμνησκ-, *am-bur-* 'begin to burn, singe,' *am-bed-* 'begin to eat,' 'nibble at.' Cf. our own *burn*, *bite*. The notion of *am* 'round,' is inconsistent with the meaning of both *am-puta-* and *am-mone-*; and the form *ammone* is that which for Ovid's Fasti has by far the best authority, if we may take for our guides those MSS. which Merkel himself collated.

Assimilation also accounts for the forms *alleva-* 'lift up,' *alliga-* 'tie up,' and the impersonal *allubescit* of a commencing love, for in all these the notion of *ad* 'to,' seems out of place. The first has for synonyms in Forcellini, 'sublevo, in altum tollo, sursum levo.' As for *alliga-*, it is enough to quote the phrase *alligare vulnus*, and to note that Pliny, when he has occasion for the idea 'tie to,' or rather, 'tie up to,' uses *adalliga-*; but a verb twice compounded with the same preposition would be something strange. *Alloqui* too is very insufficiently translated by the verb 'address.' It means to 'console, cheer up,' and so is clearly a compound of *an*.

Again, before *s* an *n* would of course be silent; and so we have an explanation of such forms as *assicca-* 'dry up' = ἀναξηραιν-, *assudesc-* 'burst out into a sweat,' and *assurg-* 'rise again.' In such phrases as *majoribus natu assurgere*, both the notion of *ad* and that of *ava* are intelligible, but in all other uses of this verb, that of *ava* alone is admissible, especially in sentences where the notion of 'get up again' after a fall is implied, as in '*Galli neque sustinere se prolapsi neque adsurgere (assurgere ?) ex voraginibus poterant*' (Liv. xxii. 2); and again: '*Tetra ibi luctatio erat . . . . in prono citius pede se fallente ut seu manibus in adsurgendo seu genu se adjuvissent, ipsis adminiculis prolapsis* (or *prolapsi*) *iterum corruerent*' (xxi. 36).

I next take cases where in place of *an* I find but a simple *a* to represent the prefix. Here again we have what is parallel to the usage of Greece. In the Doric and Æolic dialects (see Ahrens, De Dialectis), if the simple verb began with a σ, followed immediately by another consonant, the fuller form ἀν, or its equivalent, ὀν, dropped its nasal. Accordingly we find in Latin *a-scend-* opposed to *de-scend-*, *a-spira-* 'exhale' ('pulmones se contrahunt aspirantes,' Cic.), *a-stru-* 'build up,' opposed to *de-stru-*; *a-sta-*, as used in Plautus without any meaning of *ad*, e.g. '*Haut ineusceme* (for so the MSS. = ἀνευσχημως,) *astiterunt*,' 'no inelegant *pose* that' (Trin. iii. 1, 24). On the same principle we have *a-gnosc-* 'recognise,' = ἀνα-γιγνωσκ-.

Thus already we have a respectable stock of words in which an assumed *an*, = *ava*, has all in its favour alike as to form and meaning. But I also venture on the assertion, that a visible *ad* in Latin compound verbs not unfrequently stands as a substitute for our *an*; so that the language had in fact for the composition of verbs two prepositions of this shape, which it is important to distinguish. The interchange of an *n* and *d* is what most philologers will readily admit, and indeed the relation between these letters is precisely the same as that between *m* and *b*, and as that between the nasal *ng* and *g* (of *go*). Only when the nasal passage is in communication with the wind-pipe, have we *m*, *n*, and *ng*: but the moment this passage is closed by the *velum palati*, these respectively pass into *b*, *d*, and *g*. (See Mr. Weymouth's paper on this subject, in the 'Transactions of the Philological Society' for 1856, page 21, and the work of Blindeisen, to which he refers.)

But I cannot now stop to discuss this point at any length. Assuming that a preposition *an* may well take the form *ad*, I request attention to the following: *acclivi-* 'up-hill,' opposed to *de-clivi-*, 'down hill;' *accresc-* 'grow up,' by the side of *de-cresc-* 'grow down;' as in 'Valitúdo mi decréscit, accrescit labor' (Plaut. Curc. ii. 1, 4); *acced-* 'rise as the tide,' and *deced-* 'ebb;' *ad-olesc-* 'grow up,' but *ab-olesc-* 'cause to grow down;' *ad-aestua-* 'boil up,' *apprehend-* 'take up,' *accumula-* 'heap up,' *agger-* 'heap up,' *ad-imple-* 'fill up, *ad-aequa-* 'raise' to a level (with),' *ad-operi-* 'cover up,' *atting-* 'begin to touch, lay a finger upon,' *ad-juva-* 'lift up,' and *accumbo* 'I lie with the body raised,' as on a dinner couch, = ανα-κειμαι.

---

[1] In Livy i. 29 we ought to read, *omnia tecta solo aequavit* (not *adaequat*).

Secondly, the notion of 'again' has already been seen in *a-gnosc-* and *ammone-*, which by some are written *adgnosc-* and *admone-*.

Thirdly, the *reversal of an act* was common with *ava*, but for *ad* I can only produce *acquiesc-* 'rest after labour,' identical in sense and perhaps in form with *ava-παυεσθαι*, seeing that the Latin loves to have *q* as the analogue of a Greek π.

Fourthly, *ad-aperi-* bears a close analogy to *αν-οιγ-* ; and as in discussing the powers of *ava* I deduced from the idea of opening that of *commencement*, so in Latin I find *ad-ama-* 'fall in love,' *ad-mira-* (r.) 'be suddenly seized with wonder,' *affle-* 'burst into tears,' *ad-dormisc-* 'fall asleep,' *ad-hinni-* 'set up a loud neigh,' *accend-* and *ad-ole-*¹ 'set on fire,' *ad-gem-* 'all at once sigh,' *ad-vesperasc-* 'begin to be dusk,' *ad-esuri-* 'be seized with a fit of hunger.'

The physical notion of *through* clearly resides in *ad-ig-* 'drive through, pierce, transfix.'

Again, the sense of *removal* growing out of the sense of upward movement, as seen in compounds of *ava*, § 9, has its counterpart in *ad-im-* 'take up and so take away' (comp. *αν-αιρε-*), *ad-aresc-* 'dry up' (intrans.), *ad-bib-* 'drink up.'

With the class of *ava-μισγ-*, *ava-φυρ-*, I unite *ad-misce-*, as also *assicca-* already quoted.

To the lists already given I am not sure but that I

---

¹ This *adole-* is virtually one with *ndolese-*, the root-syllable of being only a variety of *al* of *alere*. In both the notion of 'upward' prevails, only in *adole-* we have that special sense which occurs in the familiar *al-ere flammam*. *Ard-ere* and *ard-uus*, of the same stock, also unite the two meanings.

ought to add many others. Thus *ad-i-*, *aggredi-* (r.), *ad-equita-*, *accurr-*, *acced-*, *acci-* invite me as it were to the translations, 'go up, march up, run up, ride up, step up to any one, call up;' at any rate, these phrases are quite in agreement with the idiom of our own language. Again, *admin-iculum* 'a prop,' seems to imply a verb *ad-min-* 'prop up;' and *ad-juva-* in its preposition claims affinity with *ava*, partly because verbs of assistance are very apt to appear with a preposition signifying *up*, as *sub-leva-*, *sub-veni-*, *succurr-*, *subsid-ium*, and partly because the simple verb *juva-* seems in itself to have had for its first sense 'to lift or elevate,' which will at once explain its double power 'to delight' and 'to assist.' I think, nay, I suspect the root to be identical with that of the verb *lev-a-* and adj. *levi-*, and our own *lift*, for an initial *j* in Latin raises the suspicion of a lost *l*; thus *jecur* and ἧπαρ are brought into connexion with our *liver*, *jocus* with our *laugh*. The close connexion between *l* and the *y* sound (of the Latin *j*) is well seen in the '*l*' *mouillé* of the French.

I am fully aware that some of the compounds with *ad* to which I have laid claim might admit of an explanation from the power of the ordinary preposition *ad*. Thus the first element in *acclivis* might have been justified by the prefix of the Greek προσαντης. Yet in many instances this preposition *ad* fails utterly, while the senses of *ava* are all-sufficient, so that I still adhere to what I have said, the doubtful instances receiving a borrowed light from the non-doubtful.

With all this I in no way deny that *ad* 'to or near' has contributed its compounds to the Latin language, so that it may often be difficult to adjudicate between the conflicting claims of the prepositions; and at times a just judgment will perhaps make a division between the two rivals, assigning some uses of the same word to the one, some to the other, as in the case of *acced-*. Or possibly the *ad* = *ava* may have been at first the only prefix admitted to composition with verbs, and subsequently compelled to submit to invasion of its domain, when the Roman, no longer alive to the sense of *up*, may have allowed himself to be unduly biassed by the meanings of the familiar preposition *ad* 'to.' Be this as it may, there will be seen in the sequel not a few instances of independent prefixes sinking into an identity of form.

I proceed to yet another variety. It is a peculiarity of Latin notation that it often prefers a weak vowel to the stronger vowels of other languages. Thus, to the Greek ομβρο- and δακτυλο- stand opposed the Latin *imberi-* and *digitulo-*, to the Sanskrit *agni-* the Latin *igni-*; and again the Latin *sine* and *lingua* are represented in French by *sans* and *langue*. But the most valuable instance for the present question is that of the so-called privative particle *av* of Greek = *in* of Latin. It will presently be seen too, that the preposition *ava* takes in German a form in which the first *a* gives place to *i* or *e*. Am I not justified then in expressing a suspicion that the Romans in such distributival phrases as *in-dies, in-horas,* &c., employed a preposition *in* = *ava* ? But the present dealings are rather with compound verbs, and here I first throw together—*intumesc-* 'swell up,' *ingrandesc-* 'grow up,' *incresc-* 'grow up,' *inhorre-* 'bristle up,' *institu-* 'set up,' *insurg-* 'rise up,' *innutri-* 'bring up by nursing,' *infla-* 'puff up,' *incita-* 'rouse up,' *incandesc-* 'blaze up,' *inardesc-* 'blaze up,' *incend-, inflamma-* 'set on fire,' *indaga-, investiga-* 'trace up to the sources;' to which we should probably add the adjective or rather participle *insolenti-* 'swelling up with pride,' from a lost verb *sole-* 'swell,' so that it corresponds to the German participle *anschwellend*.

Then with the notion of back: *in-hibe-* 'hold up or back = av-εχ-*, and *in-flect-* 'bend back.'

For 'again' I find two clear cases: *in-staura- = restaura-* and *in-gemina-* 'redouble.'

But the most striking use of *ava* is in the sense of 'reversing.' Now the Latin *inconcilia-* in some current dictionaries is said to have the two somewhat opposite meanings of 'to win over to one's side, to conciliate,' and 'to make an enemy of.' *Concilia-* also is for the most part mis-explained. But Forcellini had already given the right view as to both these verbs. Thus of *concilia-* he says: '*Verbum est fullonum*,' quoting Varro, '*Vestimentum apud fullonem cum cogitur conciliari dicitur;*' and supporting this view by Scaliger's derivation of the word, '*a ciliis, h. e. pilis.*' The word in fact means to felt cloth, as we still do in making drugget or wide-awakes. The metaphorical use of the word in the sense of promoting the union of friendship is sufficiently intelligible; and of course *inconcilio* is correctly explained in the same work: '*Contrariam significationem habet* τῷ *concilio;*' in other words it means (to invent a new verb) 'to unfelt (cloth),' or separate again the woolly fibres which had been previously united in the process of felting. Thus we have a most expressive metaphor, somewhat like our own 'unravelling,' and available generally for the idea of breaking up, dissolving, what had been closely united. The word occurs in at least four passages of Plautus, and in all this idea is most appropriate, due allowance being made for this comic poet's love of bold metaphors. The process of felting is no longer carried on under our eyes, as it was under the eyes of Romans in the age of Plautus; we shall therefore have a more intelligible, yet at the same time equivalent metaphor, if we use in its place the phrase 'to make oakum' of him or it, 'to tear to rags.' In the Trinummus i. 2, 99, and the Mostellaria iii. 1, 85, the accompanying accusatives are persons, and the idea is breaking them up as regards their property. In the Baccides iii. 6, 22—*inconciliare copias omnis meas*—the idea is substantially the same; and in the Persa v. 2, 53, *non inconciliat quom te emo* may be rendered by 'he does not tear up,' that is 'annul my purchase of you,' *quom* in the older writers often having the power of *quod*. C. O. Müller indeed, in his edition of Festus, v. *inconciliasti*, finds an objection to the doctrine that this verb is the opposite of 'concilia-' in that the prefix *in*, which denotes negation (*abnuitionem*), is never attached to verbs, except in the participial form. This difficulty vanishes so soon as we make the *in*, not the negative prefix, but a variety of *ava*.

A second example is *i-gnosc-* (for *in-gnosc*) 'unknow,' to invent another word, that is 'forget,' from which the idea of 'forgive' readily flows.

Insimula- is on all sides maltreated. But all will be smooth if we start from *simula-re-* ' to make oneself like (what one is not),' or 'put on a mask;' for then *insimula-re* is 'to unmask (a rogue),' 'to expose him,' that is 'to accuse.'

Infitias ire is in the lexicons translated 'to deny;' but the incorrectness of this is at once seen in the Plautian phrase, '*neque nego neque infitias eo.*' But if we derive this substantive from a theoretic *infari*, 'to unsay,' i.e. 'to eat one's words,' 'to retract what one has already admitted,' the sentence in Plautus has a meaning.

For the idea of opening I offer *in-ara-* 'plough up,' *in-find-* 'cleave open,' 'plough up;' and for 'beginning,' not only *in-cipi-* 'take up,' 'begin' (and perhaps *in-coha-*), but also *in-calesc-* 'begin to get hot,' and *in-tepesc-* 'begin to get warm.' And here I come across some verbs the meaning of which deserves consideration. In Forcellini there is a mixture of what is sound with what is unsound, yet even in this latter case his articles supply the data for safe conclusions. In *informa-re* he is wholly right; and yet recent dictionaries wholly wrong. Thus his words run: '*Primam et rudem alicui rei formam induco;*' and under *informatus* his first quotation is: '*His informatum manibus iam parte polita fulmen erat*' (Aen. viii. 426), while Furlanetto in his edition of the great lexicon adds: 'Varr.' (Verr. is a misprint) 'ap. Gell. iii. 10: *Quarta hebdomade caput* (of a male foetus) *et spina quae est in dorso, informatur.*'

As to *imbuo*, what appears to me to be the correct starting-point is what we read near the end of Forcellini's article: '*Re intacta adhuc uti incipere.*' But the word is probably only a Latin variety of the Greek αναδυ-ω, or in another dialect ανδυ-ω. At any rate 'imbue' is the translation given by Liddell and Scott for the one passage which they quote. The change of consonants is parallel to what is seen between the German *lende* 'loins,' and Latin *lumbi*; and again between the Italian *anda-re* and the Latin diminutival verb *ambula-re*. I would therefore translate *imbu-* 'wet for the first time;' and it may have got its metaphorical meanings from the military idea of wetting a hitherto maiden sword in the enemy's blood. Those who translate *imbutus* 'steeped in,' 'thoroughly imbued with,' wholly mistake the power of the word as understood by Cicero and Catullus.

The verbs *imminu* and *impell-* are usually treated as though the preposition were superfluous. But here we should give a preference to the translation 'begin to impair,' *i.e.* 'impair what was previously entire,' and 'begin to drive,' or, in other words, 'give to that which has hitherto been quite firm its first movement,' 'start' it.

The notion of 'removal,' 'away,' is to be seen in the verb *incid-* in the sense of 'cut off,' which will thus be a different word from *incid-* 'cut into,' and in *infring-* 'break off,' *intabesc-* 'melt away.'

In dealing with the Celtic languages, I shall be very brief. The Welsh has a representative of *ava* in its inseparable prefix *ad-* signifying 'back,' 'again,' 'reversal of an act.' Thus from *nofio* 'to swim,' *brynu* 'to buy,' *nabod* 'to know,' *gwna* 'to do,' and *gwisg* sb. 'dress,' there are compounds *ad-nofio* 'to swim back,' *ad-brynu* 'to redeem,' *ad-nabod* 'to recognise,' *ad-gwneud* 'to undo,' *ad-wisg* sb. 'undress, disarray.' Of verbs alone compounded with this *ad* there exist above one hundred and seventy.

The Gaelic form corresponding to the Welsh *ad-* is commonly *ath-*, sometimes *as-*. Thus *snámh* 'to swim,' *ath-shnâmh* 'to swim back;' *buail* 'to strike;' *ath-bhuail* 'to strike back or again;' *loisg* 'to burn,' *ath-loisg* 'to burn again, burn deeply;' *obair* 'work,' *ath-obair* 'work done over again;' *casta* or *caiste* 'twisted,' *ath-chasta* 'strongly twisted;' *beum* 'a wound,' *ath-bheum* 'a second wound;' *ainm* 'a name,' *ath-ainm* 'a surname or nickname;' *eirigh* 'rising,' *ais-eirigh* 'resurrection.'

In the Breton the particle takes the shape of *ad-* or *as-*, as *ober* 'faire' (I quote from Legonidec), *ad-ober* 'refaire;' *kouéza* 'choir, tomber,' *as-kouéza* 'retomber.' But even *ana-* in its fullest form has left its trace in this language. The verb *ana-out* has also the dialectic varieties *ana-vout* and *ana-vezout*, and is in fact a compound of the simple verb *gouzout*. These verbs are of great irregularity, *gouzout* in particular changing the radical syllable *gouz* to *gwez* or *gwi* when the following syllable has one of the weak vowels (*i* or *e*). But the relation of the two verbs to each other becomes indisputable, when we place some of the tenses, as for example the futures, alongside of each other:—*gwez-inn* 'je saurai,' *gwez-i* 'tu sauras,' &c. *ana-vez*[1]*-inn* 'je connaîtrai,' *ana-vez-i* 'tu connaîtras,' &c. I take this from the grammar of Legonidec; in his dictionary the verb is also translated, and perhaps more correctly, *reconnaître*. This example is the more interesting, because not merely is the prefix identical with the Greek ανα, but the root of the verb also is but a variety in form of the Greek root Fισ or Fιδ- as seen in ισημι οιδα, the Latin *vid-* of

---

[1] This loss of a *g* is but an instance of a general law in the Celtic languages. See another example in *ad-wisg* from *gwisg*, a few lines above.

vide-, and our own *wis-* or *wot-*, whence *wisdom, wise, wit*, and the obsolete verb *wit* or *wot*. It is also worth while to note, that in the ordinary form *anaout*, all trace of the root syllable has vanished, just as, to quote an example of Bopp's, is the case with the German *im* for *in dem*, where we have a remnant of the preposition, and a remnant of the case-suffix, but not a particle of the pronoun signifying 'the.' We also find in the Breton, both *kouna* 'to remember' and *an-kouna* 'to forget,' where, besides the original form of the prefix, we have in its signification what reminds us of one of the most important uses of *ana*, the reversal of an act.

In Irish there are some three or four prefixes which have a claim more or less certain to represent *ana*. 1. *ath-*, as *cruinnighim* 'I collect,' *ath-chruinnighim* 'I collect again;' *rioghaim* 'I rule,' *aith-rioghaim* 'I dethrone.'—2. *adh-*, as *molaim* 'I praise,' *adh-mholaim* 'I praise warmly.'—3. *an-*[1], which unites the two very different powers of *intensity* and *reversal: sgairtim* 'I cry out,' *an-sgairtim* 'I cry out loudly;' *glearaim* 'I follow' (sequor), *ain-ghlearaim* 'I pursue' (insequor); *aithnim* 'I know' (ich kenne), *an-aithnim* ('ich kenne nicht,' says Leo, perhaps rather 'I forget'); *icim* 'I help,' *ain-icim* 'I help zealously;' and a verb of the same form *icim* 'I count or reckon,' *ain-icim* 'I pass over in counting, I save.'—4. *amh-*, 'which negatives (or rather reverses) like the German *un-*,' as *garaim* 'I gladden,' *amh-garaim* 'I torture;' *réidhim* 'I arrange,' *amh-réidhim* 'I disarrange.'

---

[1] Leo sees in this the Latin prefix *in*; but his criticism is damaged by his treating the preposition *in* and the privative *in* as one word.—*Ferienschriften*, 1852.

I cannot leave this part of the subject without drawing attention to the light which some of these Celtic examples throw on the Latin *ignosc-*. It is a common practice, I believe, to consider the prefix in this verb as being the privative *in*. But to this there is the all but insuperable bar that this negative prefix is attached solely to adjectives and participles. The apparent exception *ignora-re* is none, as it is immediately formed from the adjective *ignaro-*. But if *in-* of *ignosc-* represents the Greek ἀνα with the sense of reversal, we have what we desire, 'forget,' which readily takes the sense of 'forgive;' and now the Celtic languages confirm this view by the Breton *ankouna* 'to forget,' and the Irish *an-aithnim*. Nor is it a grave objection that I am here assigning an identity of origin to words so different in meaning as *ignosc-* and *agnosc-*. For example, ἀνα-σκευαζ- commonly means 'to dismantle,' but in Strabo and Dioscorides 'to build again or to repair;' ἀν-ειλε- 'roll up' in Thuc. and Arist., but 'unroll' in Plut.; ἀν-οικιζ- 'rebuild' Paus., 'restore to (his) home' Strab., but 'cause to leave a home' Aristoph. The only difference between these cases and that of *agnosc-* and *ignosc-* is, that the Romans very wisely availed themselves of the variety in form to mark the variety in meaning.

In the Teutonic family I shall first note that the form *an-* was preserved for a while in one verb of old English, viz. *anhang*, as in Chaucer's 'Doctoures Tale' (v. 12,193 of Tyrwhitt's ed.)—

'He had to take him and anhang him fast.'

See also Coleridge's Glossarial Index.

So again in modern German we must distinguish

from the compounds with *an-* 'to,' those in which the notion of commencement resides. Of these, to place the meaning beyond doubt, I quote thirty, and might quote perhaps twice as many:—*an-bahnen* 'to break a path;' *an-beissen* 'to bite the first piece;' *an-blasen* 'to blow the first note;' *an-bohren* 'to broach;' *an-brennen* 'to begin to burn;' *an-brüten* 'to begin to hatch;' *an-faulen* 'to begin to rot;' *an-feilen* 'to begin to file;' *an-geben* 'to begin to give;' *an-hacken* 'to begin to hack;' *an-hauen* 'to begin to cut;' *an-hetzen* 'to begin hunting;' *an-jagen* 'to begin to chase;' *an-klingen* 'to begin to sound;' *an-laufen* 'to begin to run;' *an-pflügen* 'to begin ploughing;' *an-platzen* 'to begin to crack;' *an-raspeln* 'to begin to rasp;' *an-reissen* 'to begin to tear;' *an-reiten* 'to ride for the first time;' *an-rennen* 'to start;' *an-säen* 'to begin to sow;' *an-sägen* 'to begin to saw;' *an-saugen* 'to begin to suck;' *an-schaben* 'to begin to scrape;' *an-schälen* 'to begin to peel;' *an-scharren* 'to begin to rake;' *an-scheren* 'to begin to shave;' *an-schiessen* (*eine flinte*) 'to try (a gun);' *an-schmelzen* 'to begin to melt.'

Still more complete is the similarity of the Gothic *ana-kunnan*, 'to read,' which thus preserves one of the meanings of the Greek ἀναγιγνώσκ-; and of *ana-kumbj-an* in the sense of lying on a dinner-couch, so that the word is one in meaning with the Greek ἀνακειμαι, and the Latin *accumbo*. But not rarely this language follows its habit of adding to the *n* an excrescent *d*, so as to produce the forms *anda*, *and*, or *und* in place of *ana* and *an*; and indeed even within the limits of the Greek language we find the preposition ἀνα itself taking a δ. As from the adverb αἶψα 'quick,' comes an adjective αἰψηρο- 'quick,' so from ανα 'up,' the adjective ανδηρο- 'raised,' whence ανδηρον, 'a raised bank, dyke, or levée beside a river or canal.' This derivation seems more satisfactory than those proposed from the verbs αναδεω or ανθεω.

In old German a *t* is preferred to a *d*; and besides this we find a substitution of weak vowels for the *a*, as in *ind-*, more commonly *int*, sometimes *in*; but old Saxon *ant*, middle German *ent* or *en*, modern German *ent*, Dutch *ont*, old Frisian *ond*, *ont*, *on*, as well as *and*, *ant*, *und*; Danish and Swedish *und*. Lastly, in Anglo-Saxon we find, what might be expected in a language to which a great variety of immigrants contributed, not only *on* but *oŏ*, *œt*, and *ed*. The evidence about to be given is drawn chiefly from Grimm; but it is right to observe that this scholar connects these prefixes for the most part with the Greek αντι (not ανα), moved thereto in some measure by the appearance of the *d* or *t* in so many of the forms. But this seems to be a very insufficient basis for his argument; and the meanings of ανα are far more suitable in the cases where both afford a tolerably satisfactory explanation, while in many the notion of αντι utterly fails. Thus we find the Gothic *anda-bahht-s*, 'ransom,' *anda-set-s*, German 'ent-setzlich,' *anda-stathjis*, 'adversary;' *and-bindan*, 'ent-binden,' 'unbind,' *and-hamon*, 'ent-kleiden,' *and-huljan* = 'enthüllen,' *and-hruskan* = 'unter-suchen,' *and-kvithan* (*krith* = our *quoth*), 'ent-sagen,' *and-letnan*, 'ent-lassen werden,' *and-standan*, 'resist,' *and-thaggkjan sik*, 'ent-sinnen sich,' *and-vasjan*, 'ent-kleiden.'

Having thus paid the Gothic, what is due to it as the oldest record of the Teutonic languages, the compliment of a separate consideration, I proceed to the allied dialects; but for brevity will mass the evidence, taking for my guidance the series of meanings; and in the quotations I shall not unfrequently attach the Latin equivalent as supplied by Grimm.

1. The idea of 'up' is visible in Old Germ. *int-habén*, 'sustinere, suffulcire,' *int-hefan* 'sustentare,' *in-rihten* 'erigere,' *in-bláhan* 'inflari (be puffed up), turgere;' Old Sax. *ant-hebbian* 'sustinere;' Ang.-Sax. *on-bláwan* 'inflare,' *on-hebban* 'elevare,' *on-hréran* 'incitare (rouse up),' *on-standan* 'adstare (stand up),' *on-stellan* 'incitare,' *on-vacan* 'expergisci (wake up);' Mid. Germ. *ent-haben* 'sustinere,' *ent-springen* 'oriri,' *ent-wérfen* = 'aufstreben;' Mod. Germ. *ent-stehen* 'arise, originate,' &c.

2. As we found among the Greek compounds with *ava* many verbs of 'flaming up or taking fire,' so also here we have Old Germ. *in-liuhtan* 'illuminare,' *in-prëhtan* 'illucescere,' *int-prennan* 'accendere,' *in-prinnan* 'exardescere,' *in-scînan* 'illustrare,' *in-zundan* 'incendere;' Mid. Germ. *en-blazen* and *en-brennen* 'accendere,' *en-brinnen* 'accendi,' *en-pfengen* 'accendere;' Ang.-Sax. *on-âlan* 'accendere,' *on-bernan* 'accendere,' *on-tyndan* 'accendere;' Mod. Germ. *ent-flammen, ent-glimmen, ent-zünden*, &c.

3. But if the two classes, which have just been given, repudiate all connexion with ἀντί, and favour the cause of *ava*, still stronger evidence in support of *ava* is found in the extensive series of words, where the prefix carries with it the peculiar power of 'reversing' the action of the simple verb. An enumeration would be idle. The verbs of this class constitute the great bulk of Grimm's third division, yet he has

given but a small fraction of the whole, for the Modern German contains a full hundred examples of such compounds with *ent-*, the Dutch lexicons contain at least a hundred and fifty such compounds with *ont-*; and our own language might furnish a rich supply, as *untie, unbind, unloose*, &c. In confirmation of the view that this sense of reversing a previous act naturally associates itself with the idea of 'up,' I may observe that the German and Swedish languages at times avail themselves of the prepositions, which in form as well as in sense correspond to our own *up*, in the formation of such verbs, for example, *auf-decken* and *upp-täcka* 'to uncover,' *auf-lösen* and *upp-lösa* 'to unloose.'

I may here be permitted to draw attention to a prevalent error among our own writers on grammar, who assume, it must be confessed very naturally, that *un-* as used before verbs (*unbind*, &c.) is identical with *un-* as used before adjectives and participles (*unwise, unseen*). Grimm has carefully noticed the distinction (p. 816); but the error still stands in Thorpe's translation of Rask's Ang.-Sax. Grammar and elsewhere. The evidence to the fact that the prefix *un* in verbs and the prefix *un* in adjectives and perfect participles are wholly unconnected, consists of two parts. In the first place the meanings differ. The *un* before adjectives is, for the most part,[1] a simple unqualified negative. Thus *unwise, unseen*, are no more and no less than 'not wise,' 'not seen;' the Latin *indicta causa* is 'causa non dicta.' On the other hand, *to unfix* is a positive act; the loosening of that which was previously fixed. Had the English language possessed

---

[1] See, however, the paper on *av* 'not.'

the verb *to unknow*, like the Latin *ignosc-ere* and the Breton *an-kouna*, 'not to know' would have been a mistranslation; it should have been 'to forget,' a word of different import; for although he who forgets is now in the position of one who does not know, yet the expression carries with it a distinct reference to a knowledge once possessed. Still more clearly does the difference in the power of the prefix come out, when we regard such verbs as *unloosen*, ἀναιτηκειν, which cannot for a moment be held to be equivalents for 'not to loosen,' 'not to melt.' At the same time it is true that now and then the two prefixes may lead to a common result. Thus our own *to unman* is a pretty correct translation of ἀνανδρο-ειν, and yet this Greek verb is derived from the adjective ἀν-ανδρ-ο- 'unmanly.' So much for the distinction of sense. The difference of form is best seen in a table:

Eng. *un* before adj. =

Greek	Welsh	Goth.	Old Sax.	Old Germ.	Germ.	Ang.-Sax.	Dutch.	Dan.	Swed.
ἀν	an	un	un	un	un	un	on	u	o.

Eng. *un* before verbs =

ἀνα	ad	and	and	int	ent	on	ont	und	und.

Thus English and Latin stand almost alone in confounding the two prefixes under an identity of form.

4. In p. 813 Grimm dwells at some length on the fact, that the compounds with our prefix often denote an incipient sense, as Germ. *ent-schlafen* 'to fall asleep,' Ang.-Sax. *on-drædan* 'to shudder.' This sense, peculiar as it is, was marked in the compounds of *ava* (§ 7). To this division of course belong the large family of German compounds with *an-*, of which I have already given abundant instances (p. 23).

5. The notion of 'escaping, driving back or off, away,' is also common to *ava* and the Teutonic prefixes. Thus I find in Grimm's list: Old Germ. *int-lázan*, Ang.-Sax. *on-lætan* 'to let off,' Old Germ. *int-cán* 'evadere,' *ind-rinnan* 'effugere,' *int-sltfen* 'elabi,' *in-slingen* 'evadere,' *int-sagên* and *int-rahhôn* 'excusare,' *int-fallan* 'elabi,' *in-pharan* 'dilabi,' *infliohan* 'effugere;' and the list might easily be extended from existing German languages.

6. 'Opening' is a sense found in: Old Germ. *in-brëstan* 'rumpi,' *in-kinnan* 'aperire,' *in-geinen* 'findere.'

7. For 'again,' the evidence of the Ang.-Sax. *on-cnáwan* 'know again, recognise,' would be most valuable even if it stood alone; but the already quoted Gothic *and-thaggkjan*, translated by Grimm 'cognoscere,' Old Sax. *ant-kennjan*, translated by him 'intelligere,' should probably go with it; and at any rate the modern German *ent-sinnen sich* 'remind oneself, remember.'

8. And this brings me to a special consideration of other verbs which Grimm translates by 'intelligere.' The notion of mental perception is very commonly expressed in language by words which when analysed literally signify 'take up.' Thus we often hear such a phrase as: 'Did you pick up anything at the lecture?' for those who unite attention to fair ability, seize what they hear, and make it their own, while the stupid or inattentive let the words fall unnoticed. Hence the Latin phrase *non me praeterit*, 'it does not escape me.' So again the Scotch have the expression *gleg at the uptake* for 'quick of apprehension.' The word which has just been written shows

that the Latin *apprehendere* was with reason included
in the list where *ana* simulates the form of *ad*, the
more so as this interpretation equally suits that other
use of *apprehendere*, viz. 'to take up or apprehend
in the sense of arresting a prisoner;' and of course
with *apprehendere* must go the French verb *ap-
prendre* 'to learn.' To this head belong also the
Old Germ. *in-kêzan* 'cognoscere,' and its representative the Ang.-Sax. *on-gëtan* or *on-gitan*, 'intelligere,' with its subst. *and-gët* or *and-git* 'intellectus,'
and adj. *andgitol* 'intelligibilis.' As for the Gothic
verb *and-standan* 'resistere,' Old Sax. *and-standan*
'intelligere,' Old Germ. *in-stantan* 'intelligere,'
Modern Germ. *ent-stehen* 'arise,' various as their
powers are, they all admit of satisfactory explanation
if we start from the notion of 'standing up.' To
stand up in spite of difficulties well calculated to
weigh down the weak, or in other words 'not to
succumb,' is a notion which the Gothic *and-standan*
shares with the Latin *sub-sistere*. The same metaphor applied to the mind gives us the idea, 'to be
equal to a mental task, parem esse negotiis, to be
strong enough for one's place, to understand one's
work.' Lastly, the German *ent-stehen*, Dutch *ont-
staan* 'to arise,' express the action, not the mere
state of 'standing up.'

9. The verbs which carry with them the idea of
'beginning or undertaking' have frequently an identical origin with that which in the last paragraph was
assigned to verbs of perception. 'To take a thing up,'
'to take a thing in hand,' are phrases with ourselves
for 'beginning;' and 'to take a thing upon one,'
means 'to take the responsibility of an undertaking.'

The Latin *suscipere* acquires its notion of 'undertaking' in this way, and hence it is well calculated to translate so many of the compounds in Grimm's list: Goth. *and-niman* 'suscipere,' Old Germ. *en-nĕman*, Old Germ. *int-fâhan*,[1] Old Sax. *ant-fâhan* 'suscipere,' corresponding to Ang.-Sax. *on-fangan* or contracted *on-fon* 'undertake,' Germ. *an-fangen* 'to begin,' Old Germ. *in-kinnan*, Ang.-Sax. *on-ginnan*[2] 'incipere.' I may here observe that Grimm seems to have included in his lists not a few verbs which belong to compounds with *an* 'on' or 'to,' and its representatives, especially in the Ang.-Sax. series, as *on-clifjan* 'adhaerere,' *on-féallan* 'incidere,' *on-irnan* 'incurrere,' *on-settan* 'imponere.' On the other hand, by a most unsatisfactory compensation, in his list of compounds with the Gothic *ana* = our *on*, there are some which must be claimed as compounds with *ana* = *ava* 'up,' viz: *ana-fang* 'initium,' *ana-saga* 'objectio.'

In dealing with the German compounds I have passed over three which have an initial *emp-* before an *f*, *emp-fehlen*, *emp-fangen*, *emp-finden*. In the first we have a deceitful form, corrupted, as it seems to me, from *an-befehlen* 'to recommend to.' The argument for this lies in the Dutch and Danish forms of the word, viz. *aan-bevelen* and *an-bevale*. But in the others, *emp-* is but a modification of *ent*, caused by the following lip-letter. The Old Germ. *int-fâhan* 'suscipere,' and *int-findan* 'sentire,' give bail for *emp-fangen* and *emp-finden*; and the precise meaning of the latter was probably 'all at once to become sensible of,' for

---

[1] *Suspicere* is merely a misprint in Grimm.

[2] *Ginnan*, the simple verb, is obsolete. Grimm holds that its sense must have been 'capere, complecti' (p. 811).

'to feel' is an older meaning of the verb *finden* than 'to find,' in our English sense. The Scotch indeed still possess the verb with this power. 'You don't mind what I say,' says the angry mother to her boy; and giving him a smart box on the ear, she adds, 'D'ye find that.'[1] It is easy to see how from the idea of feeling that of discovery or finding would arise.

As regards the Anglo-Saxon, the quotations in which the senses of 'again' and 'away' have entered, have been few. I might indeed make some addition to the list, and still more would it be easy to add to those in which the idea of 'up' appears; but after all, the sense of 'reversing a previous act' is the one which the prefix *on* = *ava* usually carries with it. This onesidedness in the Anglo-Saxon preposition seems to admit of the following explanation. When a word has established itself in several dialectic varieties of form, it is a great convenience to distribute any varieties of meaning which may belong to the parent word between them; and thus a dissolution of partnership as it were takes place, each dialectic variety commencing business on its own account with its own separate stock. In this way the Greek *ava*, I have said, is represented in Anglo-Saxon by four particles, *on-* which we have already seen, *os-*, *at-*, and *ed-*. Rask, in his Grammar (§ 33), has noticed the peculiarity in this language by which the aspirate *s* supplants the nasal sounds *nn* and *nd*. It is probably on this principle that we must account for the appearance of the suffix *as* in the plural of the present indicative and imperative, while in the other

---

[1] See also Jamieson's Dictionary.

tenses we have the suffix *en* or *on* (Rask's Gr. Trans. p. 88). I therefore readily assent to this writer (p. 99) and to Dr. Bosworth (*sub voce*), when they tell us that *oð-*[1] represents the German *ent-* 'away, from,' as *oð-fleón = ent-fliehen* 'flee away,' *oð-gangan = ent-gehen* 'escape,' *oð-sagan = ent-sagen* 'renounce,' *oð-feallan = ent-fallen* 'fall away.' But in lieu of this *oð-* we also find *æt-* as a prefix of the same power, and probably but a dialectic variety, for the term Anglo-Saxon seems to have been applied somewhat vaguely to all the variety of Saxon dialects that were spoken in this island in early times, although the immigrants were supplied from all the coasts between Norway and the Zuyder Zee. In the present case there is the awkward fact that the language also possessed a preposition *æt =* 'to.' Dr. Bosworth indeed regards the two particles as but one, and would explain the change of meaning from the idea of 'to' to that of 'from,' on the principle that 'you approach a person or thing, when you wish to take something away.' This seems unsatisfactory. Examples of *æt-* signifying 'away,' are *æt-fleógan = ent-fliegen* 'fly away;' *æt-hleápan = ent-laufen* 'run away;' *æt-sacan = ent-sagen* 're-

---

[1] *Oð-* seems to be a corruption of some such syllable as *unð-* or *und-* (compare the Ang.-Sax. *toð* 'tooth,' and the Gothic *tunthus*, Grimm, ii. 007, *muð* 'mouth,' and Germ. *mund*); and *æt-* perhaps represents immediately the German *ent-*, the long vowel compensating for the disappearance of the liquid. But still ultimately all the four little particles are of one origin. As Grimm would distinguish between the Gothic prefixes *and-* and *und-*, so again, in p. 715, he warns his reader against confounding the Ang.-Sax. *on-* and *oð-*; yet he himself identifies the Ang.-Sax. *on-* with the Germ. *ent-*; and the examples above given are surely sufficient to identify *oð-* with *ent-*.

nounce.' On the other hand, the form *ed-* is reserved for the sense of 'again,' as *ed-niwian* 'to renew,' *ed-ledn* 'to recompense,' *ed-cenning* 'regeneration.' Here we have, as Rask has remarked, a representative of the Kymric or Welsh *ad-*. Indeed it may be assumed that the form *ad-* or *ed-* in the sense of 'again,' parted company from the other representatives of *ava* at an early stage of the Indo-European language, so that it appears with little variety of form in the Latin, Welsh, and Anglo-Saxon. In the Old German too it has its distinct representative, though with more considerable change, in *ita* or *it* (Grimm, p. 757), the vowel being such as the above-quoted *int-* for *and-* and *ent-* would have suggested, and the tenuis *t* also, as usual in that dialect, superseding a medial. It will subsequently be seen that derivatives from this *ad-* or *ed-* again hold themselves somewhat aloof from the other representatives of *ava*.

But I am strongly impressed with the belief that the Anglo-Saxon possesses yet another variety of our prefix, viz. *a-* as a corruption of *on-*, and this the more because we find in our modern language instances where our ordinary preposition *on* has been reduced to this vowel, as *a-foot, a-board*, for *on foot, on board*. The adverb *a-long*, when compared to the Germ. *ent-lang* and Ang.-Sax. *ant-lang*, is even a stronger instance of such corruption; but I would rather rely on a perusal of the following verbs, which are but a selection from many instances of a similar kind in Dr. Bosworth's Dictionary.

1. Up: *a-hebban* 'lift up,' *a-hreran* 'raise up,' *a-springan* 'spring up,' *a-timbrian* 'erect a building,' *a-weallan* 'bubble up,' *a-wacan* 'awake,' *a-lichtan* 'enlighten,' *a-tendan* 'set on fire.'

2. Back: *a-bugan* 'redeem,' *a-cerran* 'return,' *a-cwesan* 'answer,' *a-gefan* 'give back,' *a-gildan* 'repay.'

3. Again: *a-cucian* 'revive,' *a-gitan* 'know' ('recognise?').

4. Reversal of what the following word denotes, un-: *a-firan* 'emasculate,' *a-leóðian* 'dismember,' *a-scealian* 'shell' (*i.e.* 'unshell'), *a-mansumian* 'unmarry.'

5. Reversal of a previous act, un-: *a-lýsan* 'let loose' ('unloose?'), *a-slackian* 'slacken,' *a-barian* 'make bare,' *a-fúlian* 'putrefy.'

6. Beginning: *a-ginnan* 'begin.'

7. Removal, away: *a-carran* 'avert,' *a-drifan* 'drive away,' *a-faran* 'depart,' *a-ládean* 'excuse.'

Before I leave this branch of our subject, I may observe that, as Grimm led me to expect, our particle has been found to run through the whole gamut of vowels, Goth. *and-*, Old Germ. *int-*, Modern Germ. *ent-*, Dutch *ont-*, Danish *und-*. We have also seen it written with a single nasal consonant, Greek *ανα* and German *an-* (*an-fang*, &c.), Old Germ. *in-*, Mid. Germ. *en-*, Ang.-Sax. *on-*, and Eng. *un-*. Further, we have seen it reduced to a mere *a-* in Anglo-Saxon; and our language has still examples in *a-wake* and *acknowledge*, to say nothing of Shakspere's *acknow* in the same sense. Lastly, our verb *e-lope* = Germ. *ent-laufen*, or Dutch *ont-loopen* 'run off,' brings us to the extreme case of a toneless *e*.

I proceed to call a fresh batch of witnesses. It is well known that prepositions are fond of assuming a certain suffix which has in great measure the form and probably the meaning of the comparatival suffix. Thus the Latin *sub, prae, prope*, have secondary forms *super, praeter*, and *propter*. Our own *aft* and *nigh* lead to *after* and *near*, the Gothic *uf* and *nih* to *ufar* and *nidar*, the Old Germ. *ur* (= Goth. *us*) and *bit* (= our *with*) to *ûzar* and *widar*. It is on this principle that Grimm is disposed to deduce from the prefix *and-* a theoretic *andar-* (p. 716), which, though not producible in Gothic, he holds to be represented by the Old Norse *endr-* (for *endir-*). While he thus connects the prefix *endr-* with the family of the Gothic *and-*, he seems to regard the prefix *undr-* (p. 914) as one no way related to it. But I feel compelled to claim *undr-* as more nearly akin to *and-* than *endr-* itself, holding the former to be the full equivalent of Grimm's theoretic *andar-*, while *endr-* appears to me to be for the Old Norse the comparatival form of the simple prefix *ed-* 'again,' so familiar on Ang.-Sax. ground. It is not a very strange matter that languages should be capricious in their use of these particles, especially as the comparatival form differs little, if at all, in practical use from the simple particle. Thus the Romans abstain from using *ad* 'again' as an adverb, employing for this object the secondary form *iterum* (comp. the Old Germ. *it* or *ita* 'again'). A final medial in Latin was probably pronounced as a tenuis (comp. *ab*, *ob*, *sub*, with the Greek απο, ὑπο, επι; and with the derivatives from *sub* itself). Hence *ad* was probably spoken as *at*, so that *iterum* is entitled to a *t*. Again, the Ang.-Saxon has a simple prefix *ed-* 'again,' but seems to have avoided the formation of a comparative. On the other hand, the Norse *endr-*, Danish *atter*, Swedish *åter*, all signifying 'again,' have at home no positive to which they may be referred. But while the words just enumerated all agree in the limitation of their power to the one idea of 'again,' *undr-* gives to the verbs connected with it meanings of various kinds, but amid that variety only such as will flow from the idea of 'up;' indeed, one half of them are by Grimm himself regarded as equivalents of Latin compounds with *sub*.

But the prefix *undr-*, or, as Haldorson writes it, *undir-*, seems to be identical with the Ang.-Sax., Danish, and Swedish *under-*, as also with the German *unter-* and Dutch *onder-*. The forms justify the assumption that they are only comparatival extensions of the prefixes we have been considering in the preceding pages. Thus the Danish and Swedish *und-er-* stands accurately in the required relation to *und-*; and nearly so the German *unt-er-* to *ent-*, the Dutch *ond-er-* to *ont-*; and even the Ang.-Sax. *und-er-* differs in no intolerable degree from the simple prefix *on-*. But if the forms be favourable, not less so are the meanings, which the disyllabic prefixes give to verbs in composition. The arguments, if stated at length, would be for the most part a repetition of what has been said in discussing the simple prefixes; and the very variety of powers which will be found to belong to *unter-*, &c. will only strengthen the position, when it appears that this variety is in nearly every element the counterpart of what has been seen in the compounds with *ent-*, &c. In the German, *unter-halten* signifies 'to sustain, to support, to entertain, to keep up,' the last in all the varieties of its use, 'to keep up a friendship, a correspondence, a building, a fire;' comp. ἀν-έχ-. *Unternehmen* and *unter-ziehen* 'to undertake,' including the very word by which I have translated them, possess a meaning which has been already seen and considered in the Gothic *and-niman* and Old Germ. *en-nëman* (p. 30). *Unter-fangen (sich)* 'to take upon oneself, to presume,' is substantially explained in the same place. *Unter-stehen (sich)* 'to be so bold,' brings to mind what was said of the Gothic *and-standan*, to which it is immediately related in both elements; and similarly our own *under-stand* is in agreement with the Old Saxon *and-standan* and Old Germ. *ind-stantan* 'intelligere.' Further, we have *unter-stützen* 'to prop up,' *unter-wühlen* 'to grub or rummage up' (like a hog), *unter-keilen* 'to wedge up,' 'raise by wedges;' *unter-bauen, unter-mauern,* 'to support an object by building a wall, &c. up to it.' *Unter-suchen* 'to search up to the sources,' has in its prefix the same power that ανα has in ανα-κριν-, &c. *Unter-richten* and *unter-weisen*, 'to instruct,' may well be classed with the numerous verbs of 'education,' which owe their power largely to the notion of 'up,' as *bring up, educate, rear, edify, instruct, train up, instituere, innutrire, alumnus* (from *al-ere* 'to raise'). Another power of the Greek ανα and German *ent-* shows itself in *unter-lassen* 'to leave off.' The idea thus expressed by the fuller prefix is not far remote from what belongs to the German *ent-lassen* or Dutch *ont-laten* 'to let off, to release,' while it precisely agrees with what we see in the Danish *und-lade* 'to leave off.' *Unter-sagen einem etwas* 'to forbid, to interdict,' and *ent-sagen (einer sache)* 'to renounce a thing,' or its equivalent in form, the Ang.-Sax. *on-sacan* 'to refuse,' all agree in expressing a prohibitory injunction, and the prohibitory portion of the idea must reside in the prefixes. Again, such verbs as *unter-arbeiten*, *-graben*, *-höhlen*, *-minen*, *-spülen*, *-waschen*, speak of an action directed from below, i.e. upwards.

Further, I cannot but attach some little weight to the consideration that the Latin preposition *sub*, which truly represents our *up* in both form and sense, forces itself constantly upon us when we translate these German compounds into Latin: nay, it seems probable that a desire to give a literal German equivalent led to the formation of some among the following German verbs from the Latin: *unter-drücken* = 'supprimere,' *unter-werfen* = 'subjicere,' *unter-jochen* = 'subjugare,' *unter-schreiben* = 'subscribere,' *unter-siegeln* and *unter-zeichnen* = 'subsignare,' *unter-eitern* and *unter-schwären* = 'suppurare.' *Unter-bleiben* 'to remain behind,' expresses the same notion as the Greek ὑπο-λείπεσθαι and the Latin *re-manere*, and the prefixes of these two verbs are in agreement with the power of ἀνα. *Unter-mischen* and *unter-mengen* I would rather translate by the vernacular, 'to mix up,' than by 'intermix,' for here also is found the idea of upward movement, as in ἀνα-μισγ-, ἀνα-φυρ-.

But while I have been thus enumerating a long series of German compounds with *unter-*, I have probably exposed the theory to a suspicion of some weakness, by appearing to ignore that familiar preposition *unter-*, or, as we English write it, *under-*, with the sense of 'lower.' But in truth I have not lost sight of this word, nor was it my intention to claim as akin to ἀνα all the instances in which the German vocabulary presents a compound with *unter-*. In the first place, I resign all claim to those sub-

stantives which are directly formed from a simple
substantive by the addition of this prefix, as *unter-
lehrer* 'under-teacher,' *unter-kleid* 'under-garment.'
Of the other substantives, I claim only such as are
deduced from verbs in which the *unter-* has already
been claimed. It is therefore solely in the region
of the verbs that the battle between the rival prefixes
must be fought; but, to use a more pacific metaphor,
it may be asked, Where is the line of demarcation
to be drawn? Now I find a strong confirmation of
my theory in the fact, that the compounds which I
have been led to claim on the evidence of their
meaning alone, turn out to belong, every one of
them, to a natural class, and the principle of distinction on which this class is formed had wholly
escaped my attention when first making a collection
of examples. It is however a familiar fact with
German scholars, that the compounds with *unter-* are
divisible into those which have a *separable* prefix, as
unter-gehen 'to go down, sink, perish,' whence *ich
gehe unter* and *unter-zu-gehen*, and, secondly, those
with an *inseparable* prefix, as *unter-sagen* 'to interdict,' whence *ich unter-sage*, never *ich sage unter*,
zu unter-sagen, not *unter-zu-sagen*. Further, there
is an invariable distinction of accent, those with
a separable prefix accentuating the prefix itself,
únter-gehen 'to go down,' the others as uniformly
giving the accent to the verb, *unter-ságen*. Thus
we have two streams of words, which, though they
meet in a common bed, do not mix their waters, and
by this distinction seem to justify me in referring
them to different sources. Now all the verbs which
I claim possess the inseparable prefix, with the accent

on the root syllable of the verb; on the other hand, to the separable prefix and its peculiar accent is regularly attached the notion of 'down or under.' My views as to the origin of this other preposition do not belong to the present subject; and as I have enough upon my hands, I purpose to reserve them for subsequent consideration. It may be observed, however, that the compounds with my own *unter-seem* to be the older occupants of the ground. In the Old Norse, Grimm expresses his belief that *undr-* is always inseparable; and at any rate it is not until the period of the Middle German that we meet with a first attempt to import the Latin *inter* (from *in*). This was for the purpose of creating a quasi-hybrid formation, which however, in obedience to the law that holds in the physical world under like circumstances, soon died out. I allude to the use of *unter* as an equivalent to the Latin *inter* or French *entre* in the formation of reciprocal verbs, as *sich unter-küssen*, &c. in evident imitation of the French *s'entre-baiser* (see Grimm, ii. 878).

The Ang.-Saxon will also yield to my wooing. Here I find the prefixes *on-* and *under-* unmistakeably asserting their relationship to each other by the similarity of power which they bring with them to the simple verb. *On-gitan* is translated by Dr. Bosworth 'to know, perceive, understand,' *under-gitan* 'to understand, know, perceive;' 2. *on-gynnan* 'to begin, undertake,' *under-gynnan* 'to begin;' 3. *on-secan* 'to inquire,' *under-secan* 'to seek under, to inquire, to examine;' 4. *on-wendan* 'to turn upon, &c. overthrow,' *under-wendan* 'to turn under, to subvert;' 5. *on-cerran* 'to turn, to turn from, to invert,' *under-*

cerran 'to turn under, to subvert;' 6. *on-fon* 'to receive, take,' *under-fon* 'to undertake.'

Now it is plain from the translations,—'to seek under' in 3, 'to turn upon' and 'turn under' in 4, and 'turn under' in 5,—that the lexicographer was anxious to give in the first place what he deemed a literal translation, and that in his endeavour to effect this object he was biassed by the supposition that the Ang.-Sax. prefixes *on-* and *under-* had the power which belongs to the two prepositions so written at the present time. In truth the words *subvert* and *overthrow*, for *over* is but a comparatival form of *up*, give strong evidence in favour of the power here claimed for the two Ang.-Sax. prefixes; and thus *up-turn* or *up-set* would have been the simplest translation. 'Under-turn' or 'turn under' are both rejected by the idiom of our language.

In what has been said, it has been more than once assumed that the original meaning of the Latin *sub* is 'up.' But this will not obtain the ready assent of all scholars. Those whose matured intellect has been more especially devoted to the Greek language,—and this condition applies to the great bulk of classical scholars both in England and Germany,—are very apt to have what I must consider an erroneous bias as to the power of this prefix. Grimm also (iii. p. 253) puts forward views in which I cannot agree. His sections 6 and 8 in that chapter seem to me to require re-modelling; and I would put together as equivalent forms, Lat. *sub*, Greek ὑπο, Go. *uf*, Old and Mid. Germ. *uf*, Modern Germ. *auf*, Old Frisian *op* or *up*, Dutch *op*, Norse and Swedish *upp*, Eng. *up*. The Latin *sub*, as it stands superior to the rest in having preserved the initial consonant, so also exhibits the true meaning of the word with more clearness than its sister language, the Greek. Its power is well seen when it is employed as a prefix to verbs, and also in its derivatives. Thus we have *sub-veh-* 'carry up' (see Caesar, B. G. i. 16), *sum-* (= *sub-im-*) 'take up' (opposed to *dem-* 'take down'), *sub-duc-* 'draw up' (sc. naves, opposed to *deduc-*), *sub-leg-* 'gather up,' *sub-leva-* 'lift up,' *sub-sili-* 'leap up,' *sub-sist-* 'stand up,' *sub-vert-* 'up-turn,' *sub-i-* 'ascend,' *suc-ced-* 'go up,' *suc-cing-* 'gird up,' *sub-veni-*, *succurr-* 'come up or run up to a person's support,' *suc-cuti-* 'toss up,' *suf-fer-* 'bear up, sustain,' *suf-ficit* the opposite to *deficit*, *suf-fla-* 'blow up,' *suf-fulci-* 'prop up,' *sug-ger-* 'heap up,' *sup-ple-* 'fill up,' *surg-* (= *sur-rig-*) 'rise up,' with *sub-rig-* 'raise up,' *sus-cip-* 'take up,' *sus-cita-* 'rouse up,' *sus-pend-* 'hang up,' *suspic-* 'look up,' *suspira-* = 'an-hela-', *sus-tine-* 'hold up,' *sus-toll-* 'raise up,' *sursum* (= *sub-vorsum*) 'upward.'

Surely then, so far as *sub* is concerned, Grimm is not justified in the assertion "that it is merely by the addition of the suffix *er* (as seen in *super*) that this preposition obtains its full sense of upward motion."

But let us look to the derivatives from *sub* and its representatives: as, *superi*, *superior*, *summus*, all of which distinctly denote 'elevation.' So in Greek, to say nothing of ὑπέρ, we have in ὕπατος,[1] an epithet of

---

[1] Yet the following statement has been made: "ὕπατος for ὑπέρτατος, like Lat. summus for supremus." Would the supporters of such doctrines regard postumus, primus, μέσατος, πρῶτος, as contractions of postremus, priorimus, μεσώτατος, προτέρωτατος? Again, when ὑπάτη is translated 'the lowest chord or note,' it must be remembered that the names employed in the Greek musical

Jupiter on the one hand, and on the other the ordinary title in Greek writers of the Roman consul. Again, are not ὕψος 'height,' and ὕψι 'on high,' evidently connected with our preposition? But if these instances be not enough, all the Teutonic languages, with the exception of the Gothic, conspire in supporting our view; for the prepositions *uf, auf, op, up* and *upp* in the different branches of this family have a power too distinct and too invariable for any doubt. And even in the Gothic, though Grimm would assign 'under' to the preposition as its primary sense, his own short list of compounds with *uf* (ii. 902) includes *uf-haban* 'sustinere' (hold up), *uf-brinnan* 'exardescere' (blaze up), *uf-graban* 'suffodere' (dig up), *uf-brikan* 'rejicere,' *uf-kunnan* 'cognoscere' (say rather 're-cognoscere'), *uf-vôpjan* 'exclamare,' *uf-svôgjan* 'ingemiscere,' all of which contain senses such as would be suited to compounds of ἀνά, and therefore may well reside in compounds with another preposition signifying 'up.' But if we pass from the Gothic to the Old German, the evidence is of the clearest character. The following eleven verbs make up the *entire* list of Grimm (p. 897): *uf-haben* 'supportare,' *uf-hefan* 'suspendere,' *uf-kan* 'surgere,' *uf-gieno* 'exiit,' *uf-kangit* 'adolescit,' *uf-purgen* 'suscitare;' *uf-burren* 'attollere;' *uf-quëman* 'oriri, exoriri;' *uf-richten* 'erigere;' *uf-stantan* 'surgere;' *uf-stikan* 'ascendere, scandere.' Again, the comparatival forms, Lat. *super*, Gr. ὑπέρ, Goth. *ufar*, Old Germ. *upar, ubar*, Mod. Germ. *über* with *ober* as an inseparable prefix, Old Sax. *obar*, Old Fris.

---

terminology are precisely the opposite to ours. Compare ὕπατη 'the highest note,' though the word in itself means lowest.

over or contracted *ur*, Dutch *over*, Ang.-Sax. *ofer*, Eng. *over* and *upper*, Old Norse *yfir* and *ofr*, Swed. *öfver*, Dan. *over*, are not more regular in formation than consistent in sense. Grimm himself admits that they all express the idea of elevation; but if this idea did not already exist in the root, how could its introduction be effected by the comparatival suffix? how could the addition of a syllable signifying 'more' or 'of two' bring about the marvellous metamorphosis of 'down' to 'up?' To admit this would be to admit that *after* should signify *before* and *nether above*; and thus all language would be subverted.

Still there remains a difficulty not to be passed over, in the fact that *sub*, ὑπο, and the Gothic *uf* often require the translation 'under.' The explanation I would offer is this, that movement upward is the first sense of *sub*, &c.; but that when that movement reaches its limit, the body which had been moving 'up' towards a certain object, has attained the position of being 'under' it. Accordingly *sub murum ire* means 'to go up to the wall,' but *sub muro esse* 'to be under the wall.' We hang 'up' a chandelier; and the operation over, the chandelier is 'under' the ceiling. It is therefore habitual to find *sub* denoting 'under' when compounded with verbs of rest, as *subiacere, subesse*: and if it be also at times found with this sense in verbs of motion, it should be recollected that the mere verbs of 'putting,' though as verbs of motion they should require the accompanying preposition to take an accusative alone, yet often allow the case of rest (abl. in Lat., dat. in Greek) to supplant the case of motion. Thus we find *collocare in navi, in cubili, in custodia*, where the strict theory of grammar would rather demand an accusative, *in navem*, &c. In the same way the syntactical rule which justly admits a dative after verbs compounded with prepositions of rest, as *campus interiacet Tiberi ac moenibus Romanis*, is extended also to verbs of mere putting, as *anatum ova gallinis supponimus*; and this with some reason, seeing that the act of putting is momentary, and the mind prefers to dwell on the permanent state of things which follows. Hence we find that *submittere*, though strictly signifying 'to send up,' as *Terra submittit flores*, is also used of 'putting under or down,' especially in the perfect participle, where the action is over. Such a practice is well calculated to lead to equivocal results. Thus *submissus* is 'upraised' in Silius Italicus, 'lowered or low' in Cicero and Caesar. But for the most part the verb which it accompanies by its own nature prevents ambiguity, as *submergere*.

There is yet another point of view from which we are apt to attribute to *sub* the idea of 'under.' In the various processes of undermining, as by digging, the action of water, &c. the agent is of course below; but on the other hand the action is directed upward, so that *sub* is still in its proper place. A man in a cave may dig downward or upward. It is only in the latter case that the operation can with strict propriety be expressed by *suffodere*, *undermine*, *untergraben*.

In Greek the use of ὑπο as 'under' in compounded verbs was carried to the greater excess, because there lay at hand the unambiguous ανα to express the notion of 'up.' But even the Greek has distinct traces of the original power of ὑπο in compounds, as ὑποδεχομαι 'I take upon myself, undertake,' ὑπισχνεομαι the same, ὑπεχω 'I uphold,' ὑπολαμβανω 'I take up, apprehend,' (ὑπολ. ἵππον 'pull up a horse,') ὑφίστημι 'I support an attack' = *subsisto*.

Lastly, when we find two meanings as here attached to a word, one of which implies motion, the other rest, it seems generally right to give a preference to the former, seeing that verbs of the shorter form, and for that reason the older, commonly denote action. Indeed, if the mimetic origin of language be admitted, this follows as a necessary consequence.

But to leave this digression. In dealing with the German *unterhalten* there was given for one of its translations 'to entertain,' a word which in power is nearly equivalent to 'sustain.' As sustenance is connected with the one word, so we have the idea of food implied in the phrase 'good entertainment for man and horse.' Even to entertain in the sense of 'amusing' is to keep up the interest and spirits of friends. Take too the following passage from the "Life of Col. Hutchinson," by his widow (Bohn, 1846, p. 319):—
"Col. Hutchinson's cheerful and constant spirit never anticipated any evil with fear. His prudence wanted not foresight that it might come, yet his faith and courage *entertained his hope* that God would either prevent it or help him to bear it." But the word *entertain* belongs to the Norman element of our language, being the representative of the French *entretenir* and the Italian *intertenere*. We are thus brought to the Latin domain, and as *tenere* is the precise equivalent in sense of the German 'halten,' the question arises whether there can be any connexion in blood, as there is undoubtedly much external similarity, between the Latin *inter* (Fr. *entre*) and the German prefix *unter* 'up.' *Enter-prise, entre-prise, entre-prendre* compared

with *unter-nehmen* suggest the same inquiry, since the verb *prendre* is identical with the Latin *prehendere* or *prendere*. But we have also the poetical *emprise*, which conducts us in like manner to the Italian noun *impresa* and verb *imprendere* 'to undertake.' This verb is the more interesting as it also has the sense 'to learn,' thus giving a double assurance that its prefix is connected with the particle ἀνα 'up.' But besides this, I am led to assume that the Latin language also, some time or other, in some part of Italy, possessed two verbs of nearly equal import, *im-prendere* and *inter-prendere*, where we have an exact counterpart in the prefixes to the German *ent-nehmen* and *unter-nehmen*.

Invited in this decided manner to the consideration of the Latin compounds with *inter*, I find among them nearly all the varieties of power which ἀνα and its representatives possess. At the same time the Latin, like the German, has also compounds with a second *inter* of distinct origin. With this admission I lay claim to the following: *Intel-lig-* 'to pick or gather up,' and hence 'to perceive:' *inter-misce-* 'to mix up,' and *inter-turba-* (Plaut., Ter.) 'to stir up' (for the true sense of *turba-re* is simply 'to stir,' hence *turbida aqua* 'muddy water'). *Inter-iung-* (equos, boves) 'unyoke,' is a distinct example of *inter* in the to us uninteresting sense of reversing an act. As the literal meaning of *iungere* is rather 'to yoke' than 'to join,' this verb truly represents the German *ent-jochen*. *Inter-quiesc-* (Cato, Cic.) 'rest after labour' = ἀνα-παυ- (r.). *Inter-dic-* 'forbid,' *inter-mina-* (r.) (Plaut., Cic.) 'forbid by threats,' may be placed beside *ent-sagen* 'to renounce' and *unter-sagen* 'to forbid, to interdict;' and with the same we may perhaps class *inter-pella-*. As the German *ent-* often signifies 'escaping, disappearance,' so we find *inter-mor-* 'die off, die out, swoon away' (Cato, Plin., Cels.); *inter-neca-* 'kill off so that none are left' (Plaut.); *inter-fring-* 'break off' (Cato, 44,[1] but not Pliny as an independent authority, for in xvii. 18 or 30 he is only quoting Cato); *inter-aresc-* (Cic., Vitr.) 'dry up' (comp. ἀνα-ξηραίν-); *inter-bib-* 'drink up' (Plaut.); *inter-mitt-*[2] 'leave off' (comp. *unter-lassen*, Dutch *ont-leten*, &c.); *inter-rump-* 'break off' (comp. *unter-brechen*); *inter-stingu-* (Lucr.) lit. 'stamp out,' 'extinguish;' *inter-ter-*[3] 'destroy by rubbing,' a verb not itself producible, but implied in its derivatives *inter-tr-igon-*, *inter-tr-imento-*,[3] *inter-tr-itura-*; *inter-cid-* 'fall away, slip away, escape,' about which there can be less doubt, seeing it is so frequently used of 'slipping out of the memory, being forgotten,' and thus exhibits a peculiarity common to the German verb *ent-fallen*; *inter-frigesc-* (Vat. Fragm. § 155) lit. 'die of cold,' and so 'become obsolete or forgotten.' This metaphor brings to mind such passages as: 'Crimen de nummis caluit re recenti, nunc in caussa refrixit,' Cic. p. Planc. ; 'illi rumores Cumarum tenus caluerunt, Cael. ad Cic. For a time a word is warm with life, in the end it dies of

---

[1] Speaking of the boughs of the olive-tree. So Ovid has 'infringere lilia,' Cic. 'infringere florem dignitatis,' while Heinsius and Bentley would read in Horace 'teneros caules alieni infregerit horti.' All this seems to prove that *infringere* has an *in* = *ava*.
[2] Intermittere ignem 'to let the fire out,' Cato.
[3] The Bambino Scholiast, quoted by Faernus ad Ter. Haut. III. 1, 39, saw part of the truth, when he wrote: '*Inter* et *De* tantundem significant, ad augmentum ostendendum. Hinc dicitur *interfetus*.'

coldness and neglect. *Inter-im-* 'take off,' *i.e.* 'kill' (comp. *ap-aipe-* and *ab-sūm-*); *inter-fic-* 'make away with,' 'put out of the way,' *i.e.* 'kill;' *inter-i-* 'pass away,' *i.e.* 'die;' also the expressions, 'he is gone,' 'decessit.' About the Latin verb *interi-re* I had for a time much doubt, which was raised by a consideration of the German *unter-gehen*, lit. 'to go down, sink,' and hence applied to the 'setting of the sun,' &c. and by an easy metaphor to 'dying.' Had the Romans ever used *inter-ire* as they do *occidere* of the 'sun going down,' I should scarcely have doubted that it attained the sense of dying in this way; and then I must have admitted its substantial identity with the verb *untergehen*. But this German verb has a separable prefix with the accent on it, so that I could lay no claim to it.

In this enumeration I have omitted many compounds with *inter*, though fully satisfied that they belong to our preposition, as *inter-clud-* 'shut off,' *inter-nosc-* 'know one from another'= δια-γιγνωσκ-, *inter-sepi-* 'fence off,' *inter-cid-* 'cut off,' *inter-vert-* 'divert,' *inter-pung-* 'point off or separate by a point;' *inter-scind-* 'cut off.' At the same time I feel that such words admit of an interpretation by means of the ordinary *inter*, so that they should rather wait for a decision upon the words previously quoted than be adduced in proof of my doctrine. The same argument applies to many German verbs, as *unter-scheiden*. Still I am satisfied that the inseparable *unter* is always a secondary form of the German *ent* and the Greek *ava*.

The sense of 'again,' so familiar in compounds with the Greek *ava*, serves also to explain the strange verb *inter-polare*, and the adjective *inter-polus* (or *inter-*

E

polis), from which it is evidently derived. Forcellini is no doubt right when he says, 'proprium artis fullonicae,' which is fully supported by the phrase, *togam praetextam quotannis interpolare*, Cic.—and probably he is also right in connecting it with *polire*, for this word also belongs to the same business, being the equivalent in form and meaning of our own verb to *full* (cloth). Thus *inter-polus*, strictly used, should signify, 'fulled anew,' and accordingly it is so used by Cicero's friend, the lawyer Trebatius: 'Si vestimenta interpola pro novis emerit' (Dig. xviii. i. 45). Again when Cicero (in Verr. ii. 1, 61) uses the word of one who having made an erasure in his books subsequently polishes up the rough surface in order to hide the fact of erasure and substitute of new words, the verb in itself denotes only the repolishing, and not the interposition of new matter. It is only in later times that the notion of *inter* 'between,' was able to bias the interpretation. In Plautus, at any rate, the word, used metaphorically, is simply 'to vamp up anew, to furbish up old things and give them a new shape.' Pliny perhaps may have felt the wrong bias when he uses the word *miscetur* in the passage about the plant broom (spartum): 'Est quidem eius natura interpolis, rursusque quamlibeat (or quamlibet) vetustum novo miscetur.'

I next quote *inter-roga-*. This word is commonly translated 'to ask,' but this is to ignore the prefix; a neglect the less pardonable, as no family of words exhibit in their prefixes a more distinct power than the other compounds of *roga-, e-roga-, pro-roga-, in-roga-, sub-roga-, ob-roga-, ab-roga-, ar-roga-, de-roga-, prae-roga-tiva*. The present theory on the other hand secures to this *inter* a very clear meaning of its own, if we class it with such verbs as ανα-κριν-, *unter-suchen*. Nay, we find its representative in the Old German *int-phrag-en* 'requirere,' where the *int* is in immediate relation to *int-er*; and the German verb *frag-en* has probably the same root as *roga-re*. Moreover the meaning thus claimed for *interroga-* exactly accords with its use in legal language, viz. the searching examination of witnesses and suspected persons. See the Digests, Livy and Tacitus; and Forcellini, sub v. *interrogatio*. Among the Romans legal terms often passed into the language of common life, and of course with much carelessness, so that *interroga-* is often found usurping the place of the simple verb. *Inter-vis-* (Plaut.) admits of similar explanation. As *vis-* means 'go and see,' so *inter-vis-* means 'go and hunt up, go and see thoroughly into.' The idea of 'through,' which is expressed by the prefix of ανα-τιτρα-, is often found with *inter* in Lucretius, as *inter-fod-* 'dig a passage through' (iv. 716), *inter-fug-* 'fly through' (vi. 332), and *inter-datus* 'distributed through' (iv. 868). For the last compare ανα-διδωμι. So also *inter-spira-* 'breathe through' (Cato), *inter-luce-* 'shine through' (Verg.), *inter-luca-* 'let the light through' (Plin.), *inter-fulge-* 'shine through' (Liv.).

Having thus been brought back to the region of the Latin language, and endeavoured to re-establish the long-ejected *inter* 'up,' &c. in the possession of its rights, one is naturally led to cast an eye back to what has been said of Latin prefixes in the earlier part of this inquiry; and the retrospect will repay us in some measure for the trouble. If my views have been right, it follows that our prefix *inter-* is but a compara-

E 2

tive of the prefix *ad-* or *in-* 'up,' and thus their compounds may possibly exhibit instances parallel to the Anglo-Saxon *on-gitan* 'to perceive,' *under-gitan* 'to perceive;' *on-secan* 'to inquire,' *under-secan* 'to inquire;' German *ent-lassen* 'to let off,' *unter-lassen* 'to leave off;' *ent-sagen* 'to renounce,' *unter-sagen* 'to interdict;' where, as the forms differ solely in the unimportant addition of a comparatival suffix, so the meanings are nearly identical.

Such are found in Latin also. I refer not merely to the theoretic verbs *imprendere* and *interprendere*, to which our English nouns *emprise* and *enterprise* conducted me, but to pairs of words well established in the Latin vocabulary: *ad-misce-* 'mix up,' *inter-misce-* 'mix up;' *acquiesc-* 'rest after labour,' *interquiesc-* 'rest after labour;' *ad-aresc-* 'dry up,' *interaresc-* 'dry up;' *ad-bib-* 'drink up,' *inter-bib-* 'drink up;' *ad-im-* 'take away;' *inter-im-* 'take away;'[1] and perhaps also to *in-cid-* 'cut off,' *inter-cid-* 'cut off;' *in-fring-* 'break off,' *inter-fring-* 'break off.'

It will have been observed that the instances of compounds with *inter* have been drawn in a great measure from the older writers,—Cato, Plautus, and Lucretius. This is to be accounted for on the reasonable ground that the more familiar preposition *inter-* was gradually intruding itself upon the minds of the Romans to the detriment of our *inter-*. A preposition which has a separate existence, and may be used before nouns as well as in composition with verbs, has a great

---

[1] The latter verb is only used in the sense of death taking a person off, but even here compare Horace's two expressions, '*Mysten ademptum*,' and '*Asdrubale interempto*.'

advantage in such an encounter over one which occurs only as an inseparable prefix to verbs. Hence our *inter* gradually lost much of its vitality, so that it was no longer competent to form new compounds with it; and those existing, one after another, disappeared. Under these circumstances the old authors naturally contain a larger supply of such compounds than those of later date. The same state of things exists in the German language, where it is now much more practicable to establish a new compound with *unter*, signifying 'under,' than with the inseparable *unter*, which leaves the accent for the following syllable.

On reviewing what has been here written, the fear suggests itself that the mind may revolt against a theory which involves the doctrine that prepositions of different origin and power frequently assume an identity of form. For example we have—

Latin .....ad = to, Eng. another ed = ανα.
          in = in or on, Eng. ———— in = ανα.
          inter from Lat. in ———— inter akin to ανα.
Ang.-Sax .. on = our on ———— on = ανα.
          under = our under ———— under akin to ανα.
          at = our at ———— at = ανα.
Eng. ...... un = αν privative ———— un = ανα.
Germ. ..... ent in ent-zwei = in ———— ent = ανα.
          unter = our under ———— unter akin to ανα.
          an = our on ———— an = ανα.

Nay, the Greek ανα itself seems to represent two independent particles; for, besides the ordinary preposition, we have something very like the Gothic *ana* (= our *on* and *in*) in such phrases as ανα στομα εχειν 'in ore habere,' ανα θυμον εχειν 'in animo habere,' ανα τους πρωτους ειναι 'in primis esse,' examples I take from Liddell and Scott's Lexicon, but with my own translation. A similar power exists in ανα-κολλα- 'glue on or to,' &c. But if such confusion be startling, an examination of other prepositions would lead to similar results. For example, the Latin *di* or *dis*, Greek δια, German *zer*, Old Norse *tor*, appears in Anglo-Saxon and old Frisian as *to*, and thus encounters that other preposition *to*, which we still possess, corresponding to the German *zu*. Both are used in these languages as prefixes to verbs. Thus in old Frisian we have *to-delva* = 'zu-graben,' 'dig up (earth) and throw it against (an object),' and *to-delva* = 'zer-graben,' 'dig to pieces;' in Anglo-Saxon *to-dælan* 'attribuere,' with *to-dælan* 'disjungere;' *to-weorpan* 'adjicere,' with *to-weorpan* 'disjicere;' *to-clevan* 'adhaerere,' 'cleave to,' with *to-clevan* 'diffindere,' 'cleave in two.' In this last example the confusion is increased by equivocal prefixes falling in with verbs no less equivocal. Anglo-Saxon scholars may perhaps be able to say whether there was a difference of accent to distinguish such verbs. Still in written prose the only security against error was in the context. Such a state of things must have been highly inconvenient; and the struggle in Anglo-Saxon between the two prefixes appears to have ended in the utter annihilation of both sets of compounds, for we no longer possess a single verb compounded with either the one *to* or the other, at least as a prefix. Yet *to* = *dis* was still a living prefix for Chaucer, Shakspere, and the translators of the Bible.

Another marked example occurs in the Irish language. Here two prepositions originally distinct in form, and directly opposite in power, *de* 'from,' and *do* 'to,' have for the most part (Kilkenny excepted) fallen into an awkward identity of form, *do*; so that nothing but the variety of accent and the sense of the adjoining words are left to distinguish them (see Leo, Ferienschriften, 1852, p. 195).

In the Latin language the prefixes *de* 'down,' and *di* or *dis* 'in two,' are constantly interchanging their forms, so that often the sense alone is a guide to the etymology of a compound. Nay, the poor word *discribere* 'to distribute in writing,' has utterly escaped the notice of all our lexicographers, the form *describere* 'to copy,' being allowed to usurp its place. Similarly the prefix *in* ('not') of *insanus* is in form undistinguishable from the *in* of *inire*. Thus *infectus* represents two different words, as also *invocatus*, and according to our lexicons *insepultus* also, but this last assertion is the result of a mere blunder.

In the same way the Greek ανα and αν- privative become one externally when prefixed to a word with an initial vowel, so that ανισοω might à priori signify either 'I render unequal,' or 'I equalize again.'

Another fear which weighs upon me is lest it should be supposed that I would derive all the particles I have dealt with directly from the Greek ανα. The habit of treating one language as deduced from another has been carried, I think, to a most unreasonable length. Sometimes we are told that the Latin is derived from the Greek; at another, that it is made up of two elements, one Greek and one Keltic. No doubt it is easy in such cases to produce a large stock of words more or less similar in the compared languages; but this proves only a connexion between them, not that one stands in the relation of daughter to the other.

To call them 'sisters' would be a better metaphor, though even this is somewhat objectionable, for in the life of a language there is no such breach of continuity as between a parent and a child. The Greek, Latin, Sanskrit, Keltic, and Teutonic races, not to speak of others, have a large amount of common property in language, which with small exceptions they no way owe to each other, but have received from their ancestors. Were it possible to trace up each variety of language spoken by these races, we should probably see the similarity gradually increasing and at last merging in identity.

In conclusion, I would observe that a consideration of the arguments put forward in this paper will show that they ought not to be considered as a chain, where weakness in one link would endanger the continuity of the whole, and so invalidate all the results. Their nature is such that they constitute rather a close network, and the presence of a rotten thread here and there no way threatens disunion, the adjoining meshes compensating for the deficiency. Or, in plainer English, I would request any one who may have had his doubts about isolated points of the argument, to ask himself whether these doubts are not removed by other parts of the paper, for each branch of the discussion has its bearings upon the other branches.

II.

ON THE PREPOSITIONS ἐνι, in, AND RELATED WORDS.

THE inquiry into the representatives of the Greek preposition ἀνα in allied languages brought me into repeated contact with the Latin preposition *in*, and its derivative *inter* 'between.' The consideration then of this preposition *in*, and its allied forms in other languages, may next be taken up.

Grimm has more than once noticed the tendency of prepositions to appear at one time with only an initial vowel, at another with only a final vowel, an older form in his view having once possessed both. Thus, as he observes (D. G. iii. p. 252), the Gothic *ana*, whence the ordinary German preposition *an* and our *on*, takes in the Slavic languages the shape of *na*. This prefix *na* seems indeed to perform a double office, and at times to represent the Greek ἀνα in its various senses of 'up,' &c.; as from the Russian *dut'* 'to blow,' *nadut'* 'to blow up,' 'inflate;' from *ruit'* 'to dig,' *naruit'* 'to dig up.' Again in p. 254 Grimm throws out very doubtingly a suggestion that the Gothic *du*, Germ. *zu*, Eng. *to*, may be one in origin with the Gothic *at*, Old Germ. *az*, Eng. *at*, and so of course with the Latin *ad*, on the assumption that there once existed an original preposition *adu*. A close connexion in meaning, and the possession of a dental consonant in common, seem by themselves to be an insufficient foundation for such a theory; and yet I believe the theory to be true, for the evidence wanted may be supplied, I think, from the Keltic tongues. In the Gaelic Grammar of the Highland Society, p. 27, appears the following:—

'The preposition "do" loses the *o* before a vowel, and the consonant is aspirated; thus, "dh' Albainn" *to Scotland*. It is also preceded sometimes by the vowel *a* when it follows a final consonant; as, "dol a dh' Éirin" *going to Ireland*. "Do," as has been already observed, often loses the *d* altogether, and is written *a*; as, "dol a Dhunéidin" *going to Edinburgh*.'

It will be here seen that the writer treats the *a* thus alleged to be inserted as a matter too unimportant to call for explanation; but the strictness of modern philology will not allow any such assumption of intrusive letters, and we may safely assume that the *a* was fully entitled to its position in the phrase, and not a mere euphonic insertion. If we assume an old preposition *ado*, all the three varieties above seen are explained. Moreover, the assumption that *ado* is an original type which suffers more or less mutilation, according as the particle happens to come into contact with vowels or consonants in the adjoining words, is in exact agreement with the fate of the preposition *ag* in the same language. The use of this preposition in the formation of imperfect tenses in the Gaelic verb precisely corresponds with our own use of the equivalent particle *a* (= *in*) for the same purpose. Thus:—

1. Preceded by a consonant and followed by a

vowel, the preposition is entire: as 'ta iad ag éisdeachd' *they are a-listening.*

2. Between two consonants *ag* loses the *g*, and is written *a*; as, 'tha iad a dèanamh' *they are a-doing.*

3. Between two vowels the *a* is dropped and the *g* retained; as, 'ta mi 'g éisdeachd' *I am a-listening.*

4. Preceded by a vowel and followed by a consonant, it is often suppressed altogether; as, 'ta mi dèanamh' *I am a-doing.*

Indeed this very preposition *ag* of the Gaelic seems to supply another example of the same principle, for we find standing beside each other 'ag' *at* and 'gu' *to*, which I am strongly disposed to regard as deducible from a common source, *agu*. Nay, it is highly probable that this *agu* is but a variety of the Gothic *ado*, for the interchange of the guttural and dental medials is not rare in the Keltic tongues. Thus, while the Gaelic has a preposition *gu* or *gus* 'to' or 'till,' the Manx commonly writes *gys*, but at times replaces this by *dys*; and, as Leo observes, the identity of the Manx *gys* and *dys* is proved not merely by their identity of meaning, but also by the appearance of the same letter-change in *gyn* 'without,' and *dyn* 'without' (Ferienschriften, Halle, 1847). We may even go farther, for it seems not impossible that in the German *bis* 'till' we have a third variety of the initial consonant. Compare the relation which exists between the Latin *bis* and the Greek δις 'twice.'

What has been said in favour of a close connexion in form between the prepositions *at* and *to*, receives strong support in the equally close connexion as to meaning. It is true that now-a-days there are but few phrases in which an Englishman can indifferently use *at* and *to*. But that such distinctions are in origin quite arbitrary is proved by many arguments. It is considered more correct to say, 'I live at Oxford,' yet in parts of England the preposition *to* has preserved its footing in this form of words, as 'I live *to* Plymouth.' The same variety prevails in some parts of the United States, where 'I live *to* Boston' is in common use; and it may be observed, that nearly all those terms and phrases which are supposed to be corruptions, and of recent formation in that country, are genuine portions of the language which early emigrants carried out with them from the old country. I once heard ex-President Jefferson say that he had himself traced a very large number of such peculiarities to their provincial site in England. Again, where we say *at home*, the German says *to house* (*zu hause*). But perhaps the most marked example of their equivalent use is seen in the employment of the prepositions before an infinitive, where the Swedish *att taga* and Danish *at tage* correspond to our phrase *to take*. In the present day *at* is commonly preferred where rest is implied, and *to* in order to denote motion. Yet we say, 'arrive *at* a town,' 'throw a stone *at* a pig,' and, on the other hand, 'he lives close *to* the church,' 'he sat next *to* me.' Thus we may fairly conclude that *at* and *to* are substantially one in sense and probably one in origin.

If Grimm be right in identifying the Gothic *bi*, Old Germ. *pi*, *bi*, Mod. Germ. *bey*, and Eng. *by*, with the Greek ἐπι, then, as there can be no doubt that the Latin *ob* represents this Greek preposition, it will follow that our *by* and the Latin *ob* are identical. But my doubt about the truth of the first of these propositions prevents my assenting, as yet, to the conclusion.

A clearer example of two prepositions concealing their affinity by the varied position of the consonant is seen in the German *um* 'round,' and the Gaelic *mu* 'about,' two words closely akin, if not identical in sense, and the latter deduced from a fuller form, *umu*. Thus I am inclined to regard the Old German *umpi*, *umbi*, and Greek αμφι as secondary prepositions; while the old Norse *um* and Latin *am*, as well as the German *um*, Dutch, Danish, and Swedish *om*, exhibit the preposition in its simpler form. It is somewhat strange that Grimm should have failed to quote the Latin *am*, which is well seen in the compound verbs *am-icio* and *am-plector*, as well as in the adjective *an-ceps*; and though the Oscan abl. *amnud* be no longer regarded as = *anno*, the notion of a circle explains the forms *annus*, *annulus*, *ānus*, *solemnis*, *perennis*, while the interchange of *m* and *n* in these words needs no external support. Even *amare* 'to love' may first have signified 'to embrace,' and so come eventually from *am* 'round.'

Grimm has no doubt truly explained the Swedish *på* (and Danish *paa*) as an abbreviation of *uppå*, the equivalent of our *upon* (which also takes at times with us the reduced form '*pon*). Thus the Greek ὑπο on the one hand is identical with our 'up,' and on the other has its representative, so far as the consonant is concerned, in the first element of the Swedish *på*.

A similar relation probably exists between the English preposition *of* and the German *von*, Dutch *van*. To what Grimm has said on this subject (p. 262) I would add that the form with *n* is not altogether wanting, as he says, to the English language. Our vulgar, but not on that account to be neglected, *on*, as used in the forms—'six *on* us,' 'two *on* 'em,' 'I wasn't a hurting *on* 'im,' for 'six of us,' &c.—represents the derived preposition *von* or Old Germ. *fona*, itself representing, as Grimm says, a fuller form *af-ana*, from the Gothic *af* = our *off* and *of*, the Greek απο, Lat. *ab*. But in regard to this *af-ana* there is no more necessity for holding the last letters to represent the Gothic *ana* 'on,' than for assigning the same origin to the termination of the Gothic *at-ana* and *hind-ana*; so that Grimm's scruple on this head seems groundless.

The inference to be drawn from these considerations is, that whenever a preposition appears in a biliteral form, consisting of a vowel followed by a consonant, we should always look around for a second form in which the said consonant has won an initial position, and should also ask ourselves whether an earlier form of language does not present a triliteral preposition consisting of a consonant between two vowels.

Now, if I understand Grimm rightly, he has committed an error in speaking of the preposition *in*. After comparing the Gothic *ana* 'on,' with the Greek ανα and Slavic *na*, he proceeds to say that, although the preposition *in* is closely connected in signification with the Gothic *ana*, yet there is a marked external distinction, inasmuch as *ana* in its original form has always a final vowel, whereas *in* never exhibits such a vowel. Whatever be the case with the Gothic languages, he should not have passed over the Homeric ενι. In the following investigation, therefore, it will not be surprising if we find the preposition ενι and its derivatives appearing at times with, and at times without, an initial vowel; and, indeed, already in the Italian *nello, nella, nei* we have an example of this.

Again, the Greek νεροι 'those below,' and its derivatives, ενερτερο-, ενερτατο-, ενερθεν 'from below,' are with reason referred to the preposition εν as their source; but we are here brought to a variety of meaning, not so distinctly belonging to the preposition. The Latin superlative *-imo-* stands in a similar position. By form it may well claim connexion with the Latin *in*, for a more regular superlative *in-imo-*, which the analogy of *pro-imo- = primo-* and *sub-imo- = summo-* would suggest, would naturally be compressed down to *imo-*, just as the substantive *animo-* seems in the comic writers to have had a disyllabic pronunciation, something like *âmo-*; and such compression is confirmed by the shape which this word has taken in the French *âme*. Then as to meaning, although 'inmost' will suit not a few passages in which *imo-* occurs, yet the notion of 'lowest' seems more commonly implied. Nay, even the adverb *imo* or *immo* may have had perhaps for its original meaning 'at the bottom,' for the use of the particle is to correct those who give only a part of the truth, not going to the bottom of things.[1] Still the two senses of 'in' and 'down' have a natural connexion. As prepositions generally are employed to denote the relations of place, and as the earth itself is the great object to which all motions and all positions are naturally referred, the ideas of 'further in' and 'further down' have a natural coincidence. Again, the Latin *in* before an accusative, and the Greek εις for ενς, add the notion of 'into.' But where many meanings

---

[1] Mr. Parry, in his Terence, has erroneously ascribed to me an etymology of *imo* which was never mine.

belong to a word, the right course is probably (see p. 46) always to give a preference to one which implies movement. Now if we accept downward motion as the primitive idea, when such descent is checked, as for instance by the earth, we arrive at the idea denoted by *on*; but if the motion be not so checked, then we come to 'into,' and that soon followed by the result of being 'in.' What is here said is quite parallel to the case of the Latin *sub*. In the preceding paper (p. 44) I assigned to that preposition as its primitive meaning that of 'up,' or rather 'upward movement,' and contended that it was when such upward movement was terminated that the preposition acquired the sense of 'under,' with rest.

Another instance of a word in which *in* carries with it distinctly the notion of 'down' is *incurvus*, which Forcellini was contented to translate *idem quod curvus* or *valde curvus*, but which really means 'bent down.' Hence in "The Eunuch" Archidemides, whom Chaerea speaks of as of the same age with his father, *patris aequalem*, and who is therefore an old man, is subsequently described as *incurvus tremulus*, &c. Again Cicero has the phrase *Stesichori poetae statua senilis incurva*, and the same writer quotes from a poet, *Ramos baccarum ubertate incurviscere* (Or. iii. 38). So again Pacuvius (Varr. L. L. v., p. 19 of Spengel's edition) used the phrase *incurvicervicum pecus*, corresponding to Sallust's *pecora quae natura prona fecit*. The verb *inflecto* shows less distinctness in its sense; but even this we find united with *incurvus*, as *Incurvum et leviter a summo inflexum bacillum*.

Inclinare is another word which, duly examined, will lead to the same result. In many cases mere 'bending' will satisfy the uses of the word; yet still it may be presumed that the preposition at first was not added without a purpose. We may safely assume, then, that the notion of 'down' belonged to the word when used of the declining sun, as in Juvenal's 'Sed iumenta vocant et sol inclinat;' or of the heeling of a ship, 'Merso navigio inclinatione lateris unius' (Plin. viii. 208); or of a tree laden with fruit, 'Palladis arbor Inclinat varias pondere nigra comas' (Mart. i. lxxvi. 8); or metaphorically of a declining condition, as, 'Inclinata fortuna et prope iacens' (Cic. Fam. ii. 16); 'Inclinatis iam moribus' (Plin. xxv. 162); 'Is primus inclinasse eloquentiam dicitur' (Quint. x. 1). Nay, even the ordinary use of the word to denote a moral inclination to any object is in harmony with the notion of descent, for down-hill action is of course the easier; and indeed this accounts for the formation of the words *pronus, propensus, proclivis* so used. (See the subsequent paper on *pro*.)

That instances of the prefix *in* with the sense of 'down' are after all but few, is a fact which finds its explanation on two sides. When the Latin language had once established the variety of *in* for *an* or *ava* 'up,' the particle *in* = εν was liable to confusion. On the other hand, the form *de* was no way ambiguous. But even this *de* will presently be claimed as a derivative from *in* 'down.'

As regards the forms *infra, inferi, inferior, infimus,* the best course is to compare them with the opposed family of words, *supra, superi, superior, summus;* and then we are led by an irresistible necessity to the conclusion that, as the latter series have their root in the first three letters, so *inf* must contain the more radical portion of the former series. But *inf* being almost an unpronounceable combination of letters, we are further led to the assumption of an older form *enefru*, &c., following therein the analogy of many similar compressions. Thus *umbra* may be considered as a compression of *on-ub-era*, and so connected with the Latin *nube-* 'cloud,' the verb *nub-ere* 'to veil oneself;' while *nubi-la-re* and *nubil-um* bring us directly to the forms νεφελ-η and German *nebel* 'mist.' If *infula* signify really a veil, and so stand for *enef-ula*, we have a case thoroughly parallel to that of *inf-ra*. Again, ομφαλο-, if it represent, as it well may, a fuller ονυφαλ-ο, and the Latin *umbilico-*, standing for *onubil-ico-*, bring us to Germ. *nabel*, Eng. *navel;* and *ungui-* for *onugui-*, by the side of ονυχ-, to Germ. *nag-el*, Eng. *nail*.

Following these analogies then, we may conclude that *inferi* stands for *en-ef-eri*, a comparatival form which should have been preceded by a positive *enefus* or *nefus*. This has a somewhat strange appearance, but is in reality identical with the Greek νεFος and Latin *novus*, for the interchange of the sounds *f* and *w* is no way rare, and indeed our own language supplies an apposite example in two varieties for the name of the same reptile, *a newt* and *an eft*. Similarly the Greek αυτος Ευριπιδης are now by modern Greeks (and as regards the *v* were perhaps in ancient times also) pronounced *aftos Evripethes*.

I next consider the forms in which the vowel ε or ι being dropped, the liquid ν occupies the initial position. Νερθε, νερτερος are coexistent with the Greek adverb and adjective already quoted: but besides these there exists a superlative νε-ατος, which at any rate by its ordinary signification of 'lowest' seems in a very decided manner to claim kindred with the root before us; and the use of the feminine νεάτη or νήτη for the 'lowest string of a musical instrument' (lowest in position, but highest in note) confirms this view. But I have here to contend with what appears to be a rival etymology, for νέατος bears to the adjective νέος 'novus,' precisely the same relation that μέσατος does to μέσος; and this argument receives much encouragement from the fact that νέατος, like the Latin *novissimus*, also signifies the 'last or most recent.' I shall presently give reasons for the belief that this new notion is not at variance with the idea of 'lowest.'

But it will first be convenient to look in other languages for the representatives of our root. Now the Sanskrit has a particle *ni*, used as a prefix to verbs with the sense of 'down,' as from *ni + dhâ*, *ni-dhâ* 'deponere;' and from *ni + as*, *ny-as* 'dejicere.' Here again the two notions of 'in' or 'on' and 'down' belong to the preposition *ni*, so that from *ni + gam* we have *ni-gam*, 'to go into,' 'inire.' The Ossetic of the Caucasus, a language of the greater interest because it is one of the most outlying members of the Indo-European family, has also, according to Sjögren, a prefix *ny* of the same power, as *ny-fyssyn*, 'to write down,' *ny-væryn* 'to lay down.' Of the Slavonic languages it will be sufficient to take examples from the Russian, where we find *niz'* an inseparable preposition, denoting 'down,' as *niz-lozhit'* 'to lay down,' from *lozhit'* 'to lay;' *niz-padat'* 'to fall down,' from *padat'* 'to fall,' &c.; besides the verb *nizit'* 'to lower.'

Again, the Lithuanian has a prefix *nû* 'down,' of

very frequent occurrence, as *nu-degu* 'burn down,' *nu-tekù* 'flow down' (see Nesselmann's Lexicon *passim*, and especially under the word *nù*). But this *nu* is a shortened form of an older *nùg* 'down.'

But it is not merely in the humble character of a prefix or particle that this root occurs. Thus, to the Russian *niz-it'* we may add the Chinese *ni* 'to sink, descend;' while in the Greek νευ-ω and Latin *nu-o* we have verbs still carrying with them the notion of downward movement. In practice these two words are pretty well limited to the motion of the head; but in the Greek phrase νενευκως την κεφαλην 'holding the head down,' '*demisso capite*,' the very fact that κεφαλην is expressed proves that the verb itself did not imply this idea; which is as much as to say that the verbs νευειν and *nuere* meant merely 'to lower.'

The Teutonic languages also abound in examples which contain the root under discussion. Here we usually find a dental consonant attaching itself to the particle. Thus the Danish has *ned* 'down,' used commonly as a prefix to verbs, e.g. *ned-skryve* 'write down,' *ned-blæse* 'blow down,' besides an adverb *nede* 'below.' The English language possesses still, at least in poetry, the simple *neath*, whence on the one hand the preposition *be-neath*, and on the other the derived words *nether, nethermost*. But the forms with the suffix containing the letter *r* (no doubt comparatival in origin) are of most frequent occurrence in the Teutonic dialects. Thus the German has *nieder* and the Icelandic *nidr* 'down.' This latter language has also a substantive *nid*, to denote the time when there is no visible moon, although the idea of 'down' is all that the word strictly denotes. (See Holmboe's Ord-

forrand.) On the same principle no doubt the Latin
noct- Greek *νυκτ-* and *νυχ-* (as seen in *νυχα, νυχιον*, &c.),
originally meant 'sun-down.' It was natural for a
Roman to think more of the sun; but an Icelander,
less happily placed, owes a very large part of his com-
fort to the light of the moon.

Thus we have seen the simple *en* or *in* taking to
itself a suffix or suffixes with a varying consonant,
as—1. A guttural in the Lithuanian *nůg*, the Greek
νυχ of *νυχα*; 2. a dental in the Danish *ned*, Icelandic
nid, German *nied-er*, English *neath, neth-er*, Russian
niz; 3. a labial in the Latin *inf-ra*, &c. for *enef-era*;
while 4. no consonant shows itself in the Chinese and
Sanskrit *ni*, the Ossetic *ny*, the Italian *ne*, the Lithuanian *nù* or *nu*, and the Latin *nu-*, Greek *νευ-*.

I have just used the words suffix or suffixes; but I
am satisfied in my own mind that all these suffixes
are of one origin, and I believe that the Lithuanian
nůg and Greek *νυχ*, standing for *on-ůg* and *ον-υχ*, have
preserved the suffix in its purest form. But I am here
influenced by considerations which will be stated more
fully in the subsequent paper on *re* and *pro*. Our
own preposition *on* can no way be separated from the
Latin *in*, Greek *εν*; but I do not pretend to decide
between the claims of these three forms, and should
be equally pleased to find a variety *en-ek, en-eg,* or
en-ech. This suffix, *ug υχ*, &c., I believe to be of
diminutival power. Just as Dr. Johnson speaks of
the suffix *le* of our verbs *sparkle, trickle*, as diminutival in origin, yet bringing with it to these verbs the
notion of iteration, so I think that *nu-ere* and *νευ-ειν*
have in the same way obtained the power of denoting
a repetition of small acts.

But the liquid *n* habitually throws out an excrescent *t* or *d*, e.g. in *tegument-um*, from *tegumen* (*tegmen*), ἀνδρ-ὸς for ἀνερ-ὸς. Such a *d* I find in the Greek ἐνδ-ον (Dor. ἔνδοι), in the Latin *indu-perator*, and our own *und-er* (from *on*). On the other hand a *t* presents itself in the Latin *int-us*,[1] *int-er*,[1] *int-ro*, and the German *unt-er*. But here again the notion of 'down' is felt, most clearly indeed in the prepositions *under*, *unter*; but also in the phrase ἔνδον γέγραπται 'it is written below,' and the adverb ἐνδοτέρω similarly used; as also in the Latin *interula* (sc. *vestis*) 'an undergarment,' and the phrase *aqua intercus* (*i.e.* 'under the skin').

Inde is another instance of an excrescent *d*. But here caution is necessary, as scholars seem to have confounded together two independent words. *Inde* 'from this,' or 'hence,' is of course connected with the pronoun *is*, *ea*, *id*, of which, however, *in* rather than *i* is the base, as shown by the old nominative 'Is' of an Inscription (Rhein. Mus. n. f. xiv. 380, note), for the tall 'I' of this form goes far to confirm the doctrine I have contended for elsewhere (Philolog. Soc. Proc. III. 57), that all demonstrative pronouns once had a final *n*. Thus the derived *ind-e* is one with the Greek ἐνθ-εν, the *d* and θ being alike excrescent.

But the preposition *in* also formed a similar *ind-e* = Greek ἔνδον, or ἔνδοι, with the notion of down. I refer to the familiar phrases *iam inde ab initio*, &c., in which the usual practice is to ignore the *inde*; but 'down from the beginning' is so thoroughly intelligible

---

[1] In my paper on Excrescent Consonants (see below), I have given my reasons for so placing the hyphen.

that I hope it will be accepted as a more precise translation.

But this *inde* also enters into the formation of *subinde*, which must on no account be classed with *deinde, pro-inde*, &c., for in these the *inde* is the genitival *inde* 'from this,' corresponding to the Greek ενθεν. The literal translation of *subinde* is 'up and down' (i.e. 'ever and anon'). The non-appearance of a particle to denote 'and' is in agreement with the habit of the Latin language, which preferred *hinc illinc, pedibus manibus*, to *hinc et illinc, pedibus et manibus*. Then as regards meaning we have what is very similar in our own combination 'off and on.' This *subinde* has of course led to the Italian *sovente* and the French *souvent*.

I now venture to claim theoretic varieties, *ond-uk* and *end-ek*, as standing by the theoretic *on-uk, en-ec*; and then by decapitation the Greek verb δυ-, which under this view may well unite the two meanings commonly assigned to it of 'go in' and 'go down,' as used of sun-down, of diving, or in the phrase εις Αιδαο δυσασθαι. Our own 'duck,' used often like 'dive' in reference to water, but also in the sense of 'ducking' or lowering the head, as in passing under a gateway, is truer as to form than δυ- and *nu-*, both of which it represents; while our 'dive' is another variety of the same word, the guttural and labial interchanging as in *nix, nivis*. The Greek δυντω has also substituted a labial, as is usual in that language, for a guttural. On the other hand, by a similar decapitation *endek* leads to *dē*, the long vowel of the latter corresponding to that of the preposition ὲ for *ek*. That our own *down* is of the same stock can scarcely be doubted. Perhaps as our preposition *ab-ove* led to a secondary form *aboo-en* or *abow-en*, which afterwards was contracted to *aboon* (see Jamieson's Dictionary), so *down* may be for *dow-en*.

I now go back to the adjective νεος. That this word must at one time have signified 'low' follows at once from the use of the superlative νεατος as 'lowest;' and the sense of 'low' is more likely to have been original in the word than that of 'new.' A relation of place is often found to coexist in the same word with a relation of time, but few will hesitate to give to the locative idea the priority of title. Thus *ubi* and *ibi* denoted 'where' and 'there' before they were used for 'when' and 'then.' Again, in the familiar phrase *interea loci*, the latter word appears in a sense which is not primitive. Still the question remains, how we are to connect the ideas of 'low' and 'new.' The explanation I would suggest is that a considerable duration of time is commonly expressed by the simile of a river. Thus we *ascend* the stream of time to the past, and on the other hand we come *down* to recent times. But there is also another view that may be taken. Youth and lowness of stature are coincident, and every inch of growth is an evidence of increasing age. Thus νεος might pass through the meanings 'low, young, new.'

Perhaps on the same principle we may be permitted to explain the German adjective *alt*, which is represented among ourselves by *old*. This German word bears a tempting resemblance to the Latin *altus*, but a resemblance not nearer than that of the German adjective *neu* to the Greek νεF-ος. Is it possible, then, that 'high' may have been the original sense of the German *alt* ?

And if this be true, we are brought to the Latin *al-ere* 'to raise,' and the Greek αιρ-ειν of like power, the root-syllable of which I assume to be αρ, for the fuller form αειρ-ειν seems to be the result of reduplication. The Latin adjective *ard-uus* differs only in having an excrescent *d*. Possibly, too, the preposition ανα may be an offspring of the same root; and if so, both ανα and ιν will be deduced from verbs.

III.

ON THE LATIN PREPOSITIONS *re* AND *pro*.

I BEGIN this inquiry by once more quoting from the "Deutsche Grammatik" (ii. 865), the following passage:—

'The doctrine which holds true generally of particles, that they become obscure in signification and disguised in form, is specially applicable to the inseparable particles.'

The little word *re* of the Latin language belongs to this class, as it is never found doing duty as an independent preposition, but occurs only in compound verbs or adjectives, and words deduced from them. It further deserves attention, in that it is difficult in the sister languages to find its representative. But it is precisely in short forms of this kind that the destructive habit of language is found to have been most violently at work. Already the longer form *red* (*red-eo*, *red-do*, *red-igo*) exhibits a final consonant that once belonged to the particle. We must also claim *ret* as a variety, for *ret-ro* is a more trustworthy division of this adverb than *re-tro*. This appears from the corresponding adverb *por-ro*, the first syllable of which exhibits the simpler form of the Latin preposition which led to the derived preposition *pro*, i.e. *por-o*. Indeed the simple preposition *por* has been preserved in the verb *por-rig-o*, afterwards compressed to *porgo* and *pergo*; and virtually in *polliceor* and *pollingo* 'I lay out (a corpse).' But to this preposition *pro* I shall have to recur again.

But even *ret* is not the oldest form of the particle. The dental is in all probability a corruption from a guttural. Such a change is common to the last degree in language, and especially in the Latin language. In our own, for example, the diminutival suffix *et* has grown out of an older *ick*: thus, *emmet* and *gimlet* are known to have superseded *emmick* and *gemlick*. So again the Latin *abiet-* stands in place of *abiec-* (witness *abieg-no-*); and as I have elsewhere noted, the frequentative verbs, *vell-ic-are*, *fod-ic-are*, *mors-ic-are*, have the suffix in a purer form than *ag-it-are*, *quaer-it-are*, *clam-it-are*. It is true that this latter variety outnumbers the former in the proportion of about a hundred to one; but it is not by numbers that such questions should be decided. The change from a guttural to a dental is a far more familiar matter than the converse; and in the case of Latin frequentative verbs this particular change was encouraged in a large number of instances by the precedence of a guttural in the simple verb, as for instance in the three verbs just quoted. But in the instance of *ret*, we have a confirmation in the fact that *rec* has been preserved in *recu-pera-re*, 'get back,' a compound of *parare*, and in the adjective *reci-proco-*, 'backward and forward.' The verb *recu-perare* has met with much ill-treatment among philologers. It was once the practice to regard it as a derivative from *recip-ere*, and even Varro (L. L. vii. 5, p. 358) sanctions this view; but this leaves the *era* without explanation;

for *volnerare, onerare*, derive the syllable *er* from the nouns *volnus volner-is, onus oner-is*. Again for many years there was to be found in the "Gradus ad Parnassum" and similar works a statement that the *u* of *recuperare* was a long vowel, and a line ascribed to Plautus used to be quoted in support of the assertion. But the said line did not come from Plautus, whose writings on the contrary contain many passages to prove the reverse, the metres of this poet invariably demanding a short pronunciation, such as *rĕcŭperāre, rĕcŭperātor*. Of *reciproco-*, more presently.

But still further evidence in favour of the guttural presents itself in some of the allied languages. In the Greek ῥαχι-s ῥαχετρον 'back or spine,' we have evidently words of the same stock. So again in the German prefix *rück* (*rückwärts*, &c.), and the substantive *rücken* 'the back.' These again bring us to the Anglo-Saxon *hrig* 'back,' the Scotch and Old English *rig*, and the Modern English *ridge*.

On this evidence then I claim *rec* as an older form than *ret* or *red* or *re*.

But the particle has suffered more or less on the other side too. With myself the appearance of an initial *r* always raises the suspicion of a decapitation, and the Anglo-Saxon *hrig* is a witness in this particular case to the same effect; but I shall not be satisfied with claiming some initial consonant. A vowel also is missing; and in the selection of a particular vowel I am guided here, as in other similar instances, by the law of vowel-assimilation. As in the case of the Latin *pro* I was led to claim a vowel *o* as lost, the word standing for *por-o*, so for *re* I would suggest a preceding *e*, making *ere*, or rather *er-ec*. Still closer is the parallelism when for *pro* itself I find fuller forms,—first, *prod* (*prod-ire*, *prod-esse*); secondly, *prot* in the Greek προτ-ερο- (my reasons for denying the τ to the suffix have been given elsewhere); and thirdly, a still older *proc* in the very adjective already quoted, *reci-proco-*. For the letter-change it may be useful to compare the varieties *re*, *red*, *ret*, and *rec*, as well as *pro*, *prod*, *prot*, and *proc*, with the negative particle *hau*, *haud*, *haut*, representing the Greek ουκ and ου. Thus *re* and *pro* appear to me to be corruptions from disyllabic forms *er-ec* and *por-oc*. If I am asked what this guttural suffix denoted, what its power was, I answer that it is the diminutival suffix which, in my view, plays so important a part in language; and I point to a parallel case in the Teutonic family. The Old German *durah*, written also *duruh* and *duroh* (Grimm, D. G. ii. 770), corresponding to our own *through*, seems to claim connexion in its first syllable with the substantive, which we write *door*, and a German *thür*, while the second syllable has all the appearance of being the suffix of diminution. I might perhaps put forward as examples of the simple preposition the adjectives *dur-liuhtic*, *dur-nehtic*, *dur-sihtic*, quoted by Grimm from the Middle German. Of course in our tongue the word *through* is but an abbreviation of *thorough*. Thus the Anglo-Saxon *thurh-fare* becomes, in Chaucer, *thurg-fare*, and in Shakspere (Merchant of Venice, ii. 8) *through-fare*, where we write *thoroughfare*. Again Shakspere in the same play (iv. 1) has *throughly* in the sense of our *thoroughly*; and in the Midsummer Night's Dream we find: "Thorough the distemperature we see the seasons alter;" and "Over hill over dale, thorough bush thorough briar, over park over pale, thorough flood thorough fire."

But if *ec* of the theoretic *erec* be a suffix, we have for the base of the word *er*,—that is, a prefix well-known in German. In the examination of this prefix, a first duty is to consult the "Deutsche Grammatik." Accordingly I have read with some care what is contained in the article on the subject in the second volume of Grimm's work (pp. 818-832). What he says on the Gothic vocabulary I have checked with the lexicon of this language attached by Massmann to his edition of Ulphilas. But though all linguistic inquiries should include an examination of the oldest forms of language, this should not be to the exclusion of later varieties, and this for two reasons, that remains of the oldest forms of a language are for the most part very fragmentary, and not unfrequently difficult of interpretation. With a language still spoken these two evils are less to be feared. Thus I should deem it most unwise to throw out of view what lies before us in Modern German. Under this impression I have tabulated to a great extent the German verbs compounded with *er* according to the meanings assigned to them in Meissner's Wörterbuch, taking this work because it happens to be at hand. The result of my examination has been to assign to the preposition the following meanings:—

1. *Up*.—In support of this, I might quote nearly forty examples, including both physical notions, and those of a secondary or metaphorical character; but am satisfied with *erstehen* 'stand up,' *erhalten* 'sustain,' *erspriessen* 'shoot up,' *ersteigen* 'climb up,'

erheben 'heave up,' *erschwellen* 'swell up,' *erbauen* 'build up,' *erbrausen* 'surge up,' *ertragen* 'support,' *erdulden* 'suffer,' *ernähren* 'nourish,' *erziehen* 'bring up,' to which should be added the adjective, or rather participle, *erhaben* 'elevated.'

2. *Back.*—This sense naturally grows out of the preceding, inasmuch as the downward movement of substantial bodies, through the action of gravity, is more conspicuous, and thus apparently more natural, than the corresponding ascent of what is often invisible, and so the upward action is regarded as a reversal of the first. Examples are—*erlassen* 'remit,' *erkaufen* 'ransom,' *erschallen*[1] 'resound,' *erhallen* 'resound,' *ertönen* 'resound,' *erklingen* 'resound.'

3. *Again* is a meaning which flows from, or rather is scarcely separable from, the preceding. This meaning occurs in *erkennen* 'recognise,' *erneuen* 'renew,' *ersetzen* 'replace,' *erquicken* 'revive,' *erfrischen* 'refresh,' *erinnern* 'remind,' *erlösen* 'release,' *erlaben* 'refresh,' *erholen* 'respire,' and *ersinnen (sich)* 'remember.'

4. *Reversal* of the act expressed in the simple verb. —In p. 830, sub-section 8, Grimm deals with instances that fall under this head. In the Gothic indeed he finds no example, but gives not a few from the Old German: as *ur-erb-an* 'exheredare,' *ir-hals-an* 'decollare,' *ir-hirn-an* 'excerebrare,' *ir-këz-an* 'oblivisci' (where the root-syllable corresponds to our *get* in *for-get*), *ar-meinsam-on* 'excommunicare,' *ur-wir-an*

---

[1] In this verb *erschallen* and those following, the notion of loudness expressed by the idea of 'up' may perhaps be preferable. See remarks below on the Latin verb *recita-*.

'castrare.' Again for the Middle German he quotes *er-kirn-en* 'enucleare,' but for the Modern German he expressly says there is no example. We may perhaps venture to doubt the correctness of the writer both as regards the Gothic and the existing language of Germany, when we find *uslukan* 'unlock,' and *usluknan* 'open oneself,' in Massmann's Gothic Vocabulary, as also *erlösen* 'unloose,' and *erschliessen* 'unshut' (to borrow a good Old English word), in Modern German, a verb the more interesting as corresponding most precisely to the Latin *recludere*.

5. *Reaching.*—The effort to reach an object may be exercised in all directions, as downward, to get at water in a well, or horizontally, as in one of Hood's comic poems, where a child, shut in by the bar of its little chair, stretches out its arms to get at some fruit, and, unable to effect its purpose, adopts the ordinary revenge of crying, so as to justify the witticism written below the picture: 'Squall at Long Reach.' But in ordinary life the difficulty is more commonly to reach what is above us, as with the Fox and Grapes. Thus the combination 'up to' readily expresses the idea of reaching, and the *to* is virtually expressed in the accusatival form of the accompanying noun. Thus we have *ereilen* 'overtake, fetch up,' *erfahren* 'overtake by driving, come up with,' *erfassen* 'lay hold on (suddenly),' *erfinden* 'find out' (literally, let me add, by feeling), *ergehen* 'overtake, reach,' *erlangen* 'reach,' *erlaufen* 'overtake by running,' *erleben* 'live to see,' *erpacken* 'seize,' *erraffen* 'snatch,' *erreichen* 'reach,' *erreiten* 'overtake on horseback,' *errudern* 'reach by paddling or rowing,' *errufen* 'reach with calling,' *erschleudern* 'reach with a

sling-stone,' *erschnappen* 'catch with open mouth,' *erschreien* 'reach with crying,' *erschreiten* 'reach with a step,' *erschweben* 'reach by flying,' *erschwimmen* 'reach by swimming,' *erschwingen* 'soar up to,' *erspannen* 'reach by the span,' *erspringen* 'reach in leaping,' *erstrecken (sich)* 'reach,' *ertappen* 'overtake,' *ertasten* 'reach by feeling.' Note in the translations the repeated use of our two prepositions, *up* and *over* (*over-take*).

6. *Up to in daring.*—There may be added, as a sort of corollary to the preceding section, the reflective verbs, *erdreisten* 'to be bold enough,' *erfrechen, erkecken, erkühnen* 'to dare, presume.'

7. *Getting, by the act of the verb.*—A meaning closely allied to those of §§ 5, 6, but containing less of the physical action. It would be idle to enumerate instances, when in Meissner's Lexicon I find over one hundred examples. But the construction will be perhaps better understood if it be first pointed out that with compound verbs the accusative may be dependent either on the verb or on the preposition. The best proof of this is seen in such Latin sentences as *Iberum copias traiecit*, where we have *Iberum* attaching itself to the preposition, *copias* to the simple verb *iecit*. In the preceding sections (5 and 6) the accusative belongs to the preposition. Indeed in many of the examples the verb itself is clearly of an intransitive character.

8. *Making* (a) *and becoming* (b).—Where the preposition is compounded with adjectives to constitute a verb. The idea is closely akin to the preceding sections 5 and 7 and the two immediately following. Examples of this sense are tolerably numerous: (a) *er-*

bitten, erfreuen, erhitzen, erniedern, erschweren; (b) *erblassen, erbleichen, erblinden, ergrauen, erlahmen.*

9. *Opening.*—This at first may appear strange, but the close connexion of the idea is evident from the very etymology of *open*, which in its root-syllable *op* is one with the preposition *up*. The examples seem but few : *erbrechen* 'break open,' *erbeissen* 'bite open,' *eröffnen* 'open.'

10. *Beginning.*—This grows easily out of the last, or it might perhaps as easily be deduced from the sections headed 'up to,' and 'making,' for these are substantially one with the idea of commencement. For examples may be taken : *erbrausen* 'begin roaring (of the storm),' *erdonnern* 'begin to thunder,' *erdröhnen* 'begin to sound,' *ereifern (sich)* 'fall into a passion,' *erglänzen* 'begin to shine,' *erglimmen* 'begin to glow,' *ergrausen* 'shudder,' *erkälten* 'catch cold,' *erkracken* 'begin to crack,' *erkranken* 'be taken ill,' *erröthen* 'blush,' *erschaudern* 'shudder, be seized with horror,' *erschrecken* 'be struck with fear,' *erstaunen* 'be astonished,' *ertosen* 'begin to roar,' *erzittern* 'begin to tremble.'

11. *Thoroughly* or *up to* the sources (in a search), as : *erforschen* 'investigate,' *erkunden* 'explore,' *erkundigen* 'inquire after,' *erproben* 'test.'

12. *Removal, disappearance.*—This meaning may be explained in two ways. In removing a thing the first act is to lift it up. Again a thing in vanishing generally rises, *vanescit in auras*. It is especially in reference to disappearance by death that the German compounds with *er* are so used. Thus—*erbeissen* 'bite to death,' *erbleichen* 'turn pale and so die,' *erdrücken* 'press to death,' *erdrosseln* 'strangle,' *er-*

dursten (prov.) 'die with thirst,' *erfrieren* 'be frozen to death,' *erhängen (sich)* 'hang oneself,' *erlegen* 'slay,' *erlöschen* 'go out as a fire,' *ermorden* 'murder,' *ersaufen* 'be drowned,' *erchiessen* 'shoot (to death),' *erschlagen* 'slay, kill,' *erschöpfen* 'drain, exhaust,' *erspiessen* 'kill with a spear,' *erstechen* 'run through with a sword,' *ersterben* 'die (out), become extinct,' *ersticken* 'smother, suffocate,' *ertödten* 'kill,' *ertränken* 'drown,' *ertreten* 'trample to death,' *erwürgen* 'strangle.'

It has been assumed above that the Gothic prefix *us* and the German *er* are one. This is generally admitted; and in truth as the Gothic habitually has a sibilant, where an *r* appears in German, it is no matter for surprise that the Gothic form of our particle should be *us*, which then only takes the form of *ur*, when an *r* commences the simple verb.

Thus in the very limited vocabulary of the Gothic we find eight examples where Massmann translates the Gothic by the corresponding German verb with a prefix *er*, viz.: *usfullian* 'erfüllen,' *ushafjan* 'erheben,' *ushahan (sik)* 'sich erhängen,' *ushauhjan* 'erhöhen,' *usláubjan* 'erlauben,' *usláusjan* 'erlösen,' *ussteigan* 'ersteigen,' *usvakjan* 'erwecken;' while eighteen other verbs which in Gothic began with *us* or *ur*, are represented in the same book by German verbs compounded with *er, auf,* or *wieder*. Hence no one need hesitate in identifying the Gothic *us* and German *er*.

In Old German the vowel varies so that we have *ur, ar, ir,* and *er*. As regards the *u* it is perhaps safe to assume that this vowel or an *o* had precedence over the weaker vowels, because a change from a strong vowel to a weaker is more in accordance with the habit of language. Add to this that the German *ruck* 'a jolt,' and *rück* 'back,' give support to the view that the vowel before the liquid was either *u* or *o*. My reason for including the sb. *ruck* will appear presently.

If we may rely upon Grimm, yet another corruption of our particle is found in the Old-Saxon and Anglo-Saxon, where according to him it takes the simple shape *a*, as a corruption of *as* (ii. 819). But his view may be doubted, as this prefix, at any rate in Anglo-Saxon, seems better explained as a representative of the Greek *ava*. Indeed in the Greek language itself, as has been already noticed, the Æolic and Doric dialects, ordinarily employing the shorter form *av* in place of *ava*, under certain circumstances cut this down to *a*. Then as regards the Anglo-Saxon, although *on* is the ordinary representative of the Greek *ava*, there was a marked tendency in this language to exchange *on* for *a*, seeing that the ordinary preposition *on* got reduced to *a*, as still seen in our own *aboard* for *on board*, *afoot* for *on foot*, &c. I feel the more at liberty to question Grimm's theory that the prefix *a* is a corruption of *as* or *us*, because, in a few pages before (699), when he first puts forth the idea, he implies a doubt in his own mind by affixing a query.

The mention of the Greek preposition *ava* reminds me that in my paper on that little word I was led by a similar investigation to assign to it the successive meanings:—1, up; 2, back; 3, again; 4, reversal; 5, 6, loosening, opening; 7, commencing; 8, 9, removal; 10, 11, 12, thorough, thoroughly, including the special idea of searching up to the sources. And, as I have already said, the meanings so assigned by me to *ava* have since received the sanction of Pott in his recent work on Prepositions, who expressly refers to, and so far adopts, what I had written. I would beg then inquirers to contrast the meanings now assigned to the German *er* with the meanings assigned to *ava*, the parallelism being complete. Nay, I was at first led to the belief that *ava* and *ere* were but varieties of the same word, knowing, as I did, that a German, like our countrymen in Kent (a word which itself represents *Cantium*), habitually has *e* where others have *a*—as *Albis* 'Elbe,' *Amisia* 'Ems,' *Catti* 'Hesse'—and further knowing that an interchange between the liquids *n* and *r*, when not initial, is of common occurrence. But I was checked in this view by two considerations: one that the sibilant of the Gothic *us* seems entitled to precedence over the *r* of *er*, and secondly by the fact that in the 'Oberdeutsch' dialects, as Grimm informs us (p. 819, line 15), the prefix appears with an initial *d*, as *der-warp*, *der-beizte*, *der-haben*.

The loss of an initial *d* is not very rare; and in the present case the authenticity of the *d* is confirmed by the Latin *dorsum* 'back,' with which there must have been a co-existing variety *dossum*, as shown by Varro's adjective in *aselli dossuarii* and *iumenta dossuaria*, to say nothing of the Italian *dosso* and French *dos*. Moreover, the Latin *dorsum*, like our *ridge*, is often applied to a continuous mountain elevation, just as we have our 'Hog's-back' in Surrey. It may as well be observed that the combination *rs*, as seen in *dorsum*, is liable to several changes. At times an *r* in such a position vanishes altogether in the Latin language. Thus it is now a familiar fact that the Latin adverbs rursum, sursum, prorsum, deorsum, took severally the forms rusum, susum, prosum, iusum; the last of which, found in the pages of St. Augustine, accounts for the modern Italian giuso, 'down.' Another change is that of rs into rr. This is most common in Greek, as in χερσος χερρος, αρσην αρρην. But the Latin language has many half concealed instances of the same. Thus the nom. patĕr had previously passed through the changes, paters, paterr, patĕr, the last of which is justified by the use not only of Plautus and the older poets, but also of Virgil. This premised, I may safely assume as equivalent varieties, dossum, dorsum, dosum, dorrum, and dorum. Then, as regards the final letters um, I have long ago given my reasons for the belief that the neuter suffix um of the second declension has grown out of an older form ug or uc, corresponding to our own suffix ock; and this when I had not arrived at any idea of a connexion between the Latin dorsum and the German ruck, or rück. I am therefore now prepared to give my full consent to the doctrine that dorsum and ruck are substantially one, the intermediate links being dorug, doruc, and druc, or oruc.

I now return to the preposition in its Latin form, to deal with a question which naturally suggests itself. It has been seen in the examination of the German inseparable er, that it has its meanings best explained on the theory that the first meaning is 'up.' Shall I be justified in assigning this as the first meaning of the Latin re? My answer is in the affirmative; but, though in my view it is the original meaning, it must readily be confessed that the instances are few compared with the other meanings. Still this is no way fatal to the argument; nay, it is to be expected in the constant changes to which words are subjected in both form and meaning, that the older a meaning be, the fewer are the examples preserved. In the first place I find what I am looking for in the adjective *recurvo-*. Our lexicographers are satisfied to translate this word as well as *incurvo-* without much attention to the prefixes. Now it has already been pointed out that *incurvo-* is not fully translated by any phrase short of 'bent down,' as when speaking of a branch weighed down by fruit, or a man bent down by age. In like manner the full power of *recurvo-* is only given by 'turned up,'—that is, it speaks of bending where the concavity is upward. It is thus well applied to the back of the dolphin, which Arion must have found to be so far a more comfortable, or at any rate a safer seat amid the troubled waves. Ovid was right then in his choice of an epithet when he wrote, *Tergo delfina recurvo Se memorant oneri supposuisse novo* (Fast. ii. 113). Even when the crow goes off with the gilt bowl, in its flight it would carry its feet behind it, and thus there is still a propriety of language when the same poet writes: *Corvus inauratum pedibus cratera recurvis Tollit* (ii. 251); for the bird's claws, in their natural position *incurvi*, in this altered state of things would have the concavity upwards. Both Virgil and Pliny use this epithet of the bucina, where again the eye has before it a concavity with an upward presentation. *Repando-* is another available witness in my favour. Here Forcellini speaks with some accuracy when he gives as its equivalent, 'retro et sursum reflexus;' in which, however, he would have done better to drop the *retro et*. He adds, too, the expressive words, 'qualia sunt dorsa et ora delphinum.'

Indeed the word is most commonly used of the dolphin, and the compound *repandirostro-* of Pacuvius was correct in form, though laughed at as an unwieldy superfluity by Quinctilian. Again, when Cicero describes the attire of Juno Sospita in one of the Italian temples, we are at no loss to understand the phrase *cum calceolis repandis*. The verb *recuba-re*, as distinguished from the simple *cuba-re*, is intelligible, if we translate it 'lying with the head and back raised.' Such a position is well suited for Tityrus when playing on his oaten pipe; and indeed *recumbere* (like the Greek ἀνακεῖσθαι) with all accuracy denotes the attitude at meals. Accordingly, it seems to have been preferred for this sense in the later writers, as in Phædrus, the younger Pliny, and Justin, to *accumbere*; perhaps because the Romans of that day had lost the perception of the true meaning of the prefix in the latter verb, connecting it with *ad*, 'to,' rather than with *an*, 'up.' Just as *recubare* means 'to lie with the back raised,' so Celsus, speaking of a bedridden patient (ii. 4), uses the term *residere*, 'to sit up with the back raised,' or as we have it, 'to sit up in bed.' His words are: 'Contra gravia morbi periculum est, ubi supinus iacet porrectis manibus et cruribus, ubi residere vult in ipso acuti morbi impetu praecipueque pulmonibus laborantibus.' The Latin verb *recitare*, 'to read aloud,' finds no satisfactory explanation in the meanings commonly assigned to *re*. Now in discussing the powers of the Greek ἀνα, I had occasion to refer to some thirty or forty examples in Liddell and Scott's Lexicon, where verbs of more or less noise, when compounded with this preposition, denote a loud noise: for example, ἀνα-βοά-ω and ἀνα-κράζ-ω; and I quoted three phrases of our own where the idea of 'up' is expressive of loudness: *speak up, raise your voice, you speak too low to be heard.* An application of the same principle accounts for the peculiar meaning of *recita-*. In Horace's *Dissolve frigus ligna super foco large reponens*, the best way, it seems to me, of giving due force to the *re* is by translating the participle 'piling up.'

Another word which invites consideration is the so-called adjective *recenti-*, which has at least the external appearance of a participle, and contains in what is clearly its first syllable precisely the form which I have been led to assign to the prefix *re* as once belonging to it. Nor am I startled at finding the syllable performing the office of a verb. I have long thought that prepositions are many of them verbs in origin; and some years ago, when one of the most valued members of the Philological Society of London, Mr. Garnet, opposed to the doctrine that all words are in origin verbs, the argument that not a few verbs themselves were deduced from prepositions, as to *utter* from *out*, to *intimate* from *in*, I was led to think that he had not gone to the bottom of the matter. Again it is under the feeling that so-called prepositions originally were expressive of change of place or motion, that I have claimed for the Latin *in* (and Greek ἐν) the active idea of 'down,' as preceding the resulting position of *on*, and of *into*, as preceding that of *in*. So again with *sub*, I placed first among its meanings 'up,' and regarded the resulting position 'under' as secondary. That prepositions are actually used with the power of verbs is clearly seen in the well-known phrase, '*Up*, Guards, and *at* them.' I find then no difficulty in connecting a participial form *recenti-* with our so-called preposition *rec* as to form. But how as to meaning? Here also a fairly satisfactory solution presents itself when we look at such phrases as *recens a lecto, a somno, a cena,* 'only just risen from bed,' &c. I say, 'only just risen,' rather than 'rising,' on the authority of such a construction as : *Romam veniens comitia edixit* (Liv. xxiv. 7), 'immediately on his arrival he,' &c. A still stronger argument is found in the phrase of Persius, *sub sole recenti,* to represent Eastern climes, for 'under the rising sun' is exactly what we want, and is in accordance with most, if not all, the terms employed to designate the East, as *Orient* of the French, and the familiar geographical names of *Anatolia* and *Levant.*

But there stands in the way of my argument the adjective *reciproco-*,[1] which I have already translated as 'backward and forward;' yet even this word will turn out to be not altogether refractory, for it cannot be separated from the compound *rig and fur* of the Scotch or from the *ridge and furrow* of our own Southern dialect. *Rig* and *ridge* I have already claimed as representatives of *rec*, and it is no less certain that the Latin *porca* (= *poroca*) is one in meaning and substantially in form with our *furrow*. Thus Festus interprets *porcae* by the phrase "rari sulci." It is true that Varro (R. R. i. 29, and L. L.

---

[1] My origin of this adjective, if indeed it need any support, receives it in an unmistakable manner from the line in Ennius :—

"—— rusus prosus reciprocat fluctus forum."

iv. 4) makes *porca* the 'elevation' in a ploughed field, damaging his authority however by a foolish etymology. In the nature of things ridges and depressions go together, and so have a tendency to confound the words that denote them. Not unlike this change of meaning is that which has befallen the Latin *versu-*, for here also the ploughed field is the origin, but the word originally meant the 'turning' of the oxen between the end of one furrow and the commencement of another, yet after a time it came to denote the line of ploughing, for every new turn marked one line finished and another to begin. A far more pertinent example occurs in the Latin noun *lira*, which by one writer is used in the sense of 'ridge,' by another in that of 'furrow'. (see Forcellini). Again, in our own language the words *dyke* and *ditch*, which in origin are the same word, are used at one time to denote the hollow made by the removal of earth, and at another the bank made by the earth removed. Thus an Irishman talks of hiding behind a ditch, which to the English ear sounds somewhat strange. Nay, the German *furche* itself has suffered from this confusion. Thus Campe, in his Lexicon, says: "*Die von der Pflugschar aufgeworfene Erde die eine eben so lange Erhöhung ausmacht, als die Furche einer Vertiefung ist, wird von Einigen auch die Furche genannt.*"

Again, when we look at the idea expressed by 'back,' we come across what confirms the view. It is true that the human back generally presents only a vertical direction, but in nearly all other animals we see what is elevated, and more or less horizontal. A *ridge* of hills has the same character, and so also a hay-rick. In the German noun *ruck*, 'a jolt,' we also find a short upward movement. Similarly in the roof of the Crystal Palace with its 'ridge and furrow' of glass we clearly denote the elevation by 'ridge,' the depression by 'furrow.'

Still the ground is not clear unless I can establish in favour of the Latin preposition *pro* the notion of 'down.' Here again I cannot dispute the ordinary doctrine that forward movement very generally belongs to this word; but, as I have already said, first meanings are apt to disappear; and I shall think it enough to produce some clear examples in support of my views. Now the adjective *prono-* is the precise opposite in power of the adjective *supino-*, the two meaning respectively 'looking downward' and 'looking upward.' Thus Cicero (Div. i. 53) speaks of the three directions of motion, under the terms *prono-*, *obliquo-*, *supino-*, that is, straight down, oblique, and straight up; and with this authority in our favour we need not be stopped by the fact that for Cæsar the word had already attained in part to the notion of forward, so as to be used in the sense of 'obliquity' or 'slanting,' as is clearly the case in the passage (B. G. iv. 17); *Tigna non derecta ad perpendiculum, sed prona ac fastigiata.* The idea of 'downward' is also seen in Sallust (Jug. 98), *Ilex paulum modo prona, dein flexa atque aucta in altitudinem.* The adjective *proclivi-* is habitually translated 'downhill.' The adverbs *prorsum* and *prorsus* seem not to obtain their full sense until represented by our English 'downright.' It has been long taught that in treating prepositions we should start from the relations to the earth. Now what is thrown perpendicularly downward strikes the horizontal plane with all its momentum, whereas in an oblique blow a portion is of course wasted. But the first idea being so fixed by reference to the earth, the word is afterwards applied to a movement perpendicular on any plane, and there results what we may express by 'completely,' 'absolutely.' Among verbs I find no inconsiderable number where the motion of 'down' predominates, as *procellere, procidere, procumbere, proclinare, proculcare, profligare, proicere, prolabi, proruere, prosternere* (*prostrato-*), *proterere*; nor is it unknown to *promittere*, witness the phrases *p. capillum, barbam, comas, sues ventre promisso, palearibus ad genua promissis*. In the common phrase *promere vinum*, and Horace's *depromere Caecubum*, the idea is seen to prevail when we call to mind the Roman habit of storing wine in the uppermost part of a house. To explain the substantive *propagon-*, and verb *propagare*, Forcellini employs the phrase 'depresso ramo.' *Propendere* is a word more than once used by Cicero for the descent of the heavier scale in a balance. The verbs *proscindere, provolvi, proturbare*, and the participle *propexo-*, seem often to require the translation 'down;' and lastly *prodere* in two of its uses involves the same idea: first, in *prodere memoria* or *memoriae*, 'to hand down a tradition;' and secondly, when it denotes 'betrayal or abandonment.' This will be seen when we compare it with the verbs *deserere, destituere*, used in a similar sense. He who is about to abandon what has been entrusted to his care (say an infant) sets it down in some exposed place and then goes away. Where language has to speak of a series of acts, it often expresses the first and leaves the others to be inferred, as, for example, in the military phrase *colligere vasa*, the first of many acts in abandoning a camp.

But it will no doubt be objected to much that I have here said that the notion of 'down' is so closely allied to the notion of 'forward' that it is readily derived from it. When a person throws a stone, for instance, the forward motion is soon followed by descent. This is quite true, but the argument is applicable in both directions. When I want to throw a thing down, I naturally give it something of a forward impetus, rather than drop it on my own toes.

But I pass to another pair of words in which what we find in our dictionaries is not altogether satisfactory, *profano-* and *profundo-*. As *fa-num* seems to be the neuter of an adjective, and to signify 'consecrated' (ground), so we have a negative notion in the prefix of *profano-*. Again, *profundo-* should, I think, be translated 'without bottom,' so that Cicero's *mare profundum et immensum* contains something of exaggeration in both epitheta. Now if the original meaning of *pro* be 'down,' we have a use of the prefix parallel to what is felt in *demens, dedecorus, decolor.*

There remains for me to say a few words on the verbs which I would connect with the particles *re* and *pro*. Calling to mind that *re* according to the theory is a corruption of a disyllabic form *er-ec* or *or-uc*, I am disposed to connect with it the verb *ori-*, which stands for *or-ig-*, as shown I think by the noun *orig-on-*. The meaning of course suits. I am also disposed to claim as of the same kin the Greek ορεγ-εσθαι, 'to reach,' when I call to mind the German verbs, which obtained this idea through the prefix *er*. But from the Greek ὀρέγ-εσθαι I think it impossible to separate the Latin verb *regere*, to which the sense of 'rule' is generally without reason ascribed, in the belief no doubt that it is connected with the noun *rĕg-*, 'a king,' whereas this word is probably of a distinct origin and represents the Eastern *raj* or *rajah*, while *rĕg-* means simply 'stretch,' and so 'make straight;' nor indeed would I object to the translation 'rule,' if the idea were limited to ruling straight lines. The Latin noun *regio* (*regionis*), which of course comes from it, is correctly translated 'direction.' A Latin *g*, by Rask's law, is commonly represented in English by a *k* sound; but the law needs so far modification that in the south of England at least the *k* is supplanted by the palatal *ch*. Thus *frang-* of the Latin corresponds to our words *break* and *breach*, *broke* or *broken* and *broach*. We must therefore include in our family both the English verb *reach* and the English noun *reach* used in speaking of so much of a river as retains the same direction. But I would also claim the verbs *arise* and *arouse*, if it be true, as is thought by some of our best English philologers, that these do not contain any preposition, but have passed into *rise* and *rouse* by decapitation. To these I add the Greek ὀρ-ω, ὀρ-νυμι, and ὀρθ-ος, with an excrescent θ.

I next take the particle *pro*, and with it the substantive *porca*. The latter seems to point to the idea of digging; but this in its primary form is no more than scratching, which as applied to the earth is rather a horizontal than a vertical movement. This however is of no moment, as downward action soon becomes the prominent idea. The verbs of digging accordingly seem to have been originally imitations of the sound that accompanies scratching. Hence χαρ-ασσ-ω, γραφ-ω, i.e. γαρ-αφ-ω, σ-καρ-ιφα-ω, g(a)r-aben of the German, s-c(a)r-atch and s-c(a)r-ape of our own language, and then with the loss of the initial guttural αρ-ο-ω, and ar(-a)-o of the Latin, together with the Greek ορ-υσσ-ω. But the rough liquid r is often superseded by the soft l. Thus we have γ(ο)λ-υφ-ω, and s-cal-p-o, and in a simpler form col-o, in which the title of 'digging' to the first place in meanings is established, not only by Latin usage, but by the fact that its Scotch analogue, holl, had no other meaning. But let us ask what shape would col- of Rome take in the mouth of rustics. The answer is that por might well be the prevalent form, it being the provincial habit of the country outside of Rome to present a p where the polished dialect had a c. Thus pitpit is the Oscan form of quicquid; palumbe-, 'the wild pigeon,' corresponds to columba-, 'the tame dove,' and the country people coming to Rome gave the cookshop which they frequented the name popina, when the city dialect would have preferred coquina. The doctrine that digging was the first idea represented by the Latin particles por and pro accounts for the power of the preposition per, 'through,' and at the same time for the fact that the Roman ear cared little for the distinction between per and por, writing at one time porgere, at another pergere, perinde as well as proinde. The Greek language too, in its verb πειρ-ω, 'I pierce,' and πορο-ς, 'a passage,' presents us with words of the digging family, which have the precise form we should desire. I conclude then that reci-

proco- may well be translated by 'up and down,' and so correspond precisely to the Scotch phrase 'rig and fur.'

In this paper I have not dwelt at any great length on the various secondary meanings of the Latin *re;* but there is little difficulty here. Besides the primary notion of *up*, and the ordinary meanings of *back* and *again*, there is of course the not unfrequent meaning of *reversing* an act, which, strange to say, Professor Ritschl seems to deny in the Prolegomena to his Trinummus (p. lxxv.), where, in reference to the line

"Proin tu te, itidem ut Charmidatus es, rursum recharmida,"

he ventures, in defiance of the MSS., to substitute *decharmida* on the ground that such a compound with *re* can only mean 'rursus indue Charmidis personam.' As his authority is deservedly high, I deem it right to place the matter beyond dispute by a liberal quotation of examples to the contrary, viz. *red-argu-* 'disprove, refute,' *re-calcea-=excalcea-*, *re-can-* (Plin. xxviii. 19), and *re-cin-* (App.) 'reverse a charm, disenchant,' *re-canta-* (Ov.) the same, *re-cid-*, implied in the adjective *recidiuo-* 'getting up again after a fall,' *re-cing-* 'ungird,' *re-clud-* 'unshut' (so to say), *re-cuti-* implied in *recutito-*, *re-fell-* 'undeceive, refute,' *re-feru-* (Cic. Brut. 91) 'become cool again,' *re-fibula-* 'unbuckle,' *re-fig-* 'unfix,' *re-fod-* 'dig up again what has been buried,' *re-frena-* 'unbridle,' *re-gela-* 'thaw again what has been frozen,' *re-glutina-* 'unglue,' *re-laxa-* 'unloose,' *re-liga-* (Catul. Lucan.) 'unbind,' *re-lin-* 'unwax' (so to say), *re-ne-* 'unspin,' *re-nuda-* 'unbare,' *red-ordi-(r.)* 'unweave,' *re-pect-* 'uncomb (so to say), dishevel,' *re-pignera-* 'take out of pawn,' *re-plumba-* 'unsolder,' *re-secra-* 'undo what is

H

expressed by *obsecra-*,' *re-sera-* 'unbolt,' *re-signa-* 'unseal,' *re-solu-* 'unloose,' *re-string-* (Plaut.) 'open,' *re-su-* 'unsew,' *re-teg-* 'uncover,' *re-tend-* (arcum) 'unstring,' *re-tex-* 'unweave,' *re-torque-* as in '*mentem laetata retorsit*' (Juno in Verg.) 'smoothed again a soul so long by passion wrung,' *re-tura-* (compared with *obtura-*) 'uncork,' *re-uela-* 'unveil,' *re-uinci-* (Colum.) 'unbind,' *re-uolu-* 'unroll,' *re-uorr-* 'unsweep (so to say) what has been swept.' Here are already over forty examples; and I have yet to add another, which cannot be dealt with in so summary a manner, for both editors and dictionary-compilers have done their best either to destroy it altogether or to falsify its meaning. I refer to the substantive *recubitu-*. This appears to be an ἅπαξ λεγόμενον. It is found in Pliny (xxiv. 13, 7), and to make the matter clear I must quote part of the passage:—'Baculum ex ea' (he is speaking of the *aquifolia* or holly) '*factum, in quoduis animal emissum, etiamsi citra ceciderit defectu mittentis, ipsum per se recubitu propius adlabi.*' Unhappily Sillig, abandoning the Paris MS. *a*, which he assigns to the eighth or ninth century, for a reading of the Paris MS. *d* of the thirteenth, gives, what is altogether senseless, *per sese cubitu* in place of *per se recubitu*. He probably did not know that *recubitu* would signify 'by ricochet.' On the other hand our current dictionaries are utterly false guides. Thus we find the word translated by Freund '*das Niederfallen*' and by his copyists of course 'falling down.' One of these indeed assures us that while he took Dr. Andrews' (American) Dictionary as 'the basis' of his labours, 'each article was compared with the corresponding word in Forcellini;' but it is difficult to reconcile this statement with what is to be seen under *recubitus* in the great Italian work, for here the true translation is distinctly given. After the general remark that *recubitus* means 'actus recumbendi' Forcellini adds the definite interpretation, '*subsultus ille quem faciunt corpora in solum durum incidentia*,' that is, what in shorter language we call 'ricochet.' This word has of course come to us from the French; but that it was previously imported into France from Italy may perhaps be inferred from the form of the prefix, *ri* in place of *re*. A genuine French noun would probably have been *recouchet*. But over and above identity of meaning, there is a close connexion in form between the Latin *recubitu-* and the modern *ricochet*. But a friend suggests that I must here assume a secondary verb *recubica-re* from which a substantive *recubicatu-* would readily flow, and then from a contracted *recub'catu-* we should be led to a French *re-couch-et;* and this view is confirmed by a similar series *cubare, cubicare, coucher*. Thus, while the obsolete *cumb-ere* meant 'to fall,' the compound *recumbere*, reversing the meaning of the simple verb, must have come to signify 'to get up again,' 'rise again,' before the derived substantive *recubitu-* could bear the interpretation 'ricochet;' much as from *cadere*, 'to fall,' we obtain first *recidere*, 'to rebound,' and then the adjective *recidiuo-*, 'rising again.' Of course after what I have said above (p. 75) on Latin frequentatives, I am very ready to give admission to such theoretic forms as *cubicare*, and the very idea of ricochet is thoroughly consistent with repeated action, whether we have in view the movement of an oyster-shell on the surface of a pond, or of a cannon-ball on the surface of the sea.

One word more in apology for the wide space I have given to the consideration of the German *er*. I have long thought that insufficient attention is paid both in grammars and dictionaries to the power which such little words bring with them to the composition of verbs; and the want is nowhere more felt than in dealing with the German prefixes *ent* and *er*. I discussed the former in my paper on *ava*. I have now spent not a few lines on the corresponding problem for *er*.

IV.

ON THE GERMAN PREFIX *ver* AND ALLIED FORMS.

IN the paper on *ava* and its analogues I had to dwell upon the fact that inseparable prefixes are apt, as Grimm says, to undergo violent changes both as to form and power; and upon the further fact, that in consequence of this liability, particles of totally different origin not unfrequently pass into an identity of form, thus bringing about a confusion, which ends in the disuse of both prefixes, and the employment of fresh forms of speech to make up the consequent deficiency. It is probably in this way that our own language has pretty well ceased to employ prefixes in the formation of compound verbs, finding it more convenient to take the simple verb and place after it an independent preposition; as, 'he put *upon* me, he put me quite *out*, he put me *up* to something, he put this bad practice *down*, he put *off* the meeting, he put the door *to*, he put his hat *on*, he would not put *in* more than sixpence.' Similarly we have *take up, take off, take in, take to*, with peculiar meanings, which give much trouble to the foreigner, as they are often left unexplained in our dictionaries. We have now no verbs compounded with a prefix *to*, although the Anglo-Saxon had many such, including both those in which *to* was an equivalent for the Latin *ad*, and others with *to* = Greek διά, *dis* of the Latin, *tor* of Old Norse, and *zer* of German, as *to-brek*, *to-brest*, *to-hew*, *to-race*, *to-rend*, *to-shred*, *to-skatir*, *to-swink*, of Chaucer; *to-cleve*, *to-dele*, *to-drag*, *to-part*, of the 'Ayenbite of Inwyt' (A.D. 1340). Even the Bible (Judges ix. 53) has the words, 'A certain woman cast a piece of millstone upon Abimelech's head, and all *tobrake* his scull;'—and so also in Shakspere we find :—

"Where (*i.e.* whereas) these two Christian armies might combine
The blood of malice in a vein of league,
And not *tospend* it so unmannerly."
King John, v. 2.

"Then let them all encircle him about,
And, fairy-like, *topinch* the unclean knight."
Merry Wives of Windsor, iv. 4.

A similar case of the accidental confluence of prefixes originally distinct, and a consequent disappearance, is to be seen in the particle *of*. Here three independent words have fallen into an identity of shape. Thus in the older forms of our language, whether called Anglo-Saxon or Old English, we have this little word representing in turn what appears in Latin and Greek as *ab* ἀπό, *ob* ἐπί, *sub* ὑπό. Examples of the first abound in Gothic in the form *af*, and also in Anglo-Saxon, both in the form *ofa*, as *ofa-drifan*, 'to drive off,' *ofa-heawan*, 'to cut off,' and *of-ferian*, 'to carry off,' *of-irnan*, 'to run off.' The Danish and Swedish also have numberless instances; but here, as in Gothic, the original vowel was preserved, *af*, not *of*.

With the word ἐπί, I have already claimed to connect our own *aft*, the *t* being excrescent; as it is also in *aft-ana* of the same language, compared with *ut-ana*, our own *aft-er*, and the old superlative *aft-uma*. But ἐπι has yet another representative in the prefix of the Anglo-Saxon *of-axian* 'ask after,' *of-ridan*, 'ride after,' *of-spyran* 'search after,' and *of-sitan*, 'besiege' (obsidere); as also of the Old English *of-seche* 'seek for,' *of-sende* 'send for' ('Ayenbite of Inwyt,' Mr. Morris's Preface, p. lxvi.), and perhaps of the Anglo-Saxon *of-licgan* 'to lie upon.'

Taking *sub* and ὑπο next, I quote from the paper on *ava*, p. 41, the forms in our northern dialects which I hold to represent these; viz. Goth. *uf*, Old and Mid. Germ. *uf*, Mod. Germ. *auf*, Old Fris. *op* or *up*, Dutch *op*, Norse and Swed. *upp*, Dan. *up*, Eng. *up*, but Old Eng. also *of*. Now in the examination of the German *auf*, I find much that reminds me of what I came across in the study both of *ava* and its representatives and of the Latin *re*. Thus for German, leaving out of view the numberless instances where the idea of *up* is distinctly retained, I find (1) above sixty where the idea of 'opening' appears; (2) some eight of 'beginning,' *auf-blühen*, *auf-brausen*, *auf-jammern*, *auf-krähen*, *auf-kreischen*, *auf-lachen*, *auf-seufzen*, *auf-toben*; (3) of 'loud noise,' six: *auf-lachen*, *auf-röcheln*, *auf-sagen* = recitare, *auf-snarchen*, *auf-schnauben*, *auf-stöhen*; (4) full fifty where 'completion' is denoted; (5) with the notion of 'back:' *auf-behalten*, or *auf-bewahren* 'reserve,' *auf-halten* 'hinder' (= inhibere), *auf-krämpeln*, *auf-streifeln*; (6) not less than fifty meaning 'again;' and (7), what is of much interest, nearly fifty in which the idea expressed by our English prefix *un*, i.e. the reversal of a former act, shows itself, viz.:—auf-binden, auf-decken, auf-drehen, auf-driesoln, auf-eisen, auf-fädeln, auf-falten, auf-fasen, auf-fitzen, auf-flechten, auf-gürten, auf-häkeln, auf-haken, auf-heftelu, auf-heften, auf-hüllen, auf-klinken, auf-knebeln, auf-knöpfen, auf-knüpfen, auf-koppeln, auf-künden, auf-lassen, auf-leimen, auf-lösen, auf-löthen, auf-nesteln, auf-packen, auf-rebbeln, auf-riegeln, auf-ringeln, auf-rollen, auf-sagen, auf-schliessen, auf-schnallen, auf-schnüren, auf-schnurren, auf-schrauben, auf-schürzen, auf-spunden, auf-thauen, auf-weben, auf-weichen, auf-wickeln, auf-winden, auf-wirken, auf-wirren, auf-zaubern.

To these I add two corresponding Swedish verbs, *upp-täcka* = *auf-decken* and *upp-lösa* = *auf-lösen*.

The Anglo-Saxon, besides its many verbs compounded with *of* = 'off' (Latin *ab*), retained a few, as we have seen, where *of* = *ob* or *επι*; and again it has a small group in which *of* = the Germ. *auf*, as *of-standan* = *auf-stehen*, *of-gifan* = *auf-geben*, *of-delfan* 'dig-up,' *of-frettan* = *auf-fressen*, *of-hæbban*, 'retain,' like *auf-halten*; with which we should no doubt include *of-blindan* 'make blind,' *of-munan* 'remember,' *of-lician* 'dislike,' *of-thincan* 'repent,' *of-unnan* 'refuse,' from *unnan* 'give.' And I further quote again from Mr. Morris's Preface to his edition of the 'Ayenbite of Inwyt,' or from the body of the work: *of-thincke* = '*forthink*,' 'repent,' *of-guo* 'forgo,' *of-healde* 'withhold,' *of-take* 'overtake,' *of-serve* 'deserve.' The last two verbs seem to call for a little explanation. If *of-take* and *over-take* mean, as by etymology they should mean, 'catch *up*,' we have what is still a familiar phrase for the same idea. Then *of-serve* may well mean, like the Latin *emeritus*, 'serve out one's full time.' The same old English work which supplied these examples has also *of-acksed* for 'thoroughly questioned,' *of-dret* for 'thoroughly frightened,' and *of-tyened* for 'thoroughly enraged.' *Of-guo* and *of-guoinge* also occur in the index of the same book, with the translation 'meriting or deserving,' but how this meaning is to be assigned to them I do not see. 'Overgoing,' like the Latin 'transgredi,' might mean transgression, passing the border of what is right, and so correspond to the German *vergehen*; but we cannot assign to the simple *of* ' up,' the notion of the comparative *over*.

But as the words *with*, *hind*, as has been just noticed, lead to secondary forms, *wid-er*, *hint-er* (*hinder*), and the simple preposition *in* to *int-er* in Latin, *und-er* Eng., *unt-er* Germ., so two at least of our prepositions also assume a comparatival suffix. Thus, to take first the forms allied to ἐπί, we have, as has been already said, *aft* and *after* in English, together with the Gothic *afar* without the excrescent *t*; and in the Ang.-Sax. *overnoon* (I take it from Bosworth's Dictionary) we have probably a variety of our *afternoon* and no compound from the more familiar preposition *over*.

Whether *far* and *farther* stand in the relation of comparatives to ἀπό *ab* and the Ang-Sax. *af* 'off' I will leave for future consideration. But on the other hand, as the Latin has alongside of *sub* both *super* and *subt-er* with an excrescent *t* (pronounced *supt-er* and frequently so spelt in good MSS.), and as the Greek too has ὑπέρ from ὑπ of ὑπο, so we find both *upper* and *over* in English and *über* in German.

But when a preposition has given birth to derived forms, it is very common for the initial vowel in such derivatives to disappear. This is a matter which has been considered at some length in the second paper on ἐπί; and in accordance with what was there said I now venture to claim the familiar Germ. prefix *ver* as a corrupted comparative of *auf*, in other words, as a decapitated variety of *über* 'over.' The corresponding Ang.-Sax. prefix *of-er* has in its *f* the very sound which is heard in the initial consonant of *ver*. But the best proof of the substantial identity of the two forms will be found in the meanings, as seen, first in the following individual words: *ver-brücken* 'to bridge over,' Ang.-Sax. *ofer-brycgean*; *ver-jähren* and *ver-alten* 'to become superannuated,' compared with Ang.-Sax. *ofer-geare* 'antiquated,' and *ofer-eald* the same; *ver-kehren* 'overturn,' *ver-fahren* and *ver-führen* 'transport;' *ver-schlafen* (*sich*) 'oversleep' oneself, *ver-schiessen* 'overshoot,' *ver-schlagen* 'strike (a ball) out of bounds,' *ver-sprengen* 'strike a billiard ball off the table;' *ver-walten* 'administer,' and *ver-weser* 'manager,' i.e. 'one set over others;' *ver-lesen* 'call (names) over :' *ver-hehlen* 'cover over' (conceal) = Ang.-Sax. *ofer-helan*; *ver-sehen* 'over-look,' i.e. 'neglect,' *ver-achten* 'overlook,' i.e. treat with contempt, *ver-dunkeln* 'darken over.' *Ver-nehmen* I would place alongside of the Lat. *intellegere*, and as I assign to this for its literal translation 'pick up (knowledge),' so *ver-nehmen* may well mean 'to take up,' like the Scotch *uptake*. (See paper on *ava*, p. 28.)

Secondly, I set down a whole class of words in which the notion of 'over' ('covering') in its physical sense is undeniable: verblechen, verbleien, verdachen, verdielen, vereisen, vergittern, verglasen, vergolden, verkleiden, verlacken, verlarven, verlatten, verledern, vermanteln, vermoosen, vermörteln, verpanzern, verpichen, verquecken, verrasen, verreisern, verrinden, versanden, verschalen, verschalmen, verschienen, verschilfen, verschindeln, verschlämmen, verschleiern, verschmutzen, verschneien, versilbern (Comp. Ang.-Sax. *ofer-sylfrian*), versteinen, verstobern, verteufeln, verzäunen, verzinken, verzinnen, verzuckern, together with verdecken, verhüllen, vermalen.

Thirdly, a class of words with the meaning of 'overmuch, excess:' *verbluten* 'bleed to exhaustion,' *verfliegen* 'fly too far,' *verhitzen* 'overheat,' *verklettern* 'climb too high,' *verkochen* 'overboil,' *verpfeffern* 'pepper too much,' *verrennen* (*sich*) 'run too far,' *versalzen* 'oversalt,' *versauern* 'make too sour,' *verschneidern* 'cut too short,' *verschwärmen* 'swarm too much,' *verspäten* (*sich*) 'come too late,' *versteigen* (*sich*) 'climb too high,' *versüssen* 'oversweeten,' *verwirren* 'spice too much,' *verzärteln* 'spoil (a child) by too much tenderness' (with *auf-zärteln* the same), *verzuckern* 'sugar too much.'

Fourthly, with the notion of transferring, and so changing, bartering, selling, paying: verändern, verdeutschen (comp. the general term übersetzen), vergriechen, verfahren; vertauschen, verkaufen, verwechseln.

Fifthly, the notion of 'passing over,' 'getting to the end of,' and so 'consuming all,' of which the examples are too numerous to quote.

Sixthly, the notion of excess is akin to that of misdoing, as *verdeuten* 'misinterpret,' *verdrehen* 'distort,' *verdrucken* 'misprint,' *verheben* 'lift in the wrong way,' *verkalben* and *verlammen* (cf. our *miscarry*), *verkennen* 'mistake,' *verleiten* 'mislead,' *verrathen* 'betray,' *verrechnen* 'misreckon,' *verrücken* 'derange,' *verchieben* 'misplace,' *verschleppen* 'misplace,' *verwiegen* (*sich*) 'make a mistake in weighing,' *verwöhnen* 'spoil (a child),' *verzählen* 'misreckon,' *verziehen* 'draw wrong,' *verzielen* (*sich*) 'miss one's aim.' And with these may be included the notion of destruction or negation in the words *verbieten* 'forbid,' *vergessen* 'forget' = Ang.-Sax. *ofer-gitan*), *verhören* (= *überhören* 'not to hear,' and Ang.-Sax. *ofer-herran* or *ofer-hyran*); *verlernen* 'unlearn,' *verthun* (Ang.-Sax. *ofer-don*, our *fordo*); *verschwören* 'forswear,' with which compare the Ang.-Sax. *ofer-cysan*.

So far only the fuller forms (in *ofer*) of the Ang.-Sax. have been quoted; but of course this language has *for* as the ordinary form of the prefix, like the Danish *for* and the Swedish *för*. And the fact that Ang.-Sax. possessed both forms adds greatly to the argument which treats the German *ver* as the result of decapitation.

It must no doubt be admitted that it is difficult at times to find in the prefix an explanation of the meaning which it conveys to a verb. But the verb *verdienen* may well mean 'serve all one's time,' and so correspond to the old English *of-serve* above-mentioned, as having the meaning of 'deserve.' But the best proof that the prefix *ver* is but a decapitated *über* is found in the German vocabulary itself, as will at once be seen by prefixing first *ver* and then *über* to the following, and so testing their substantial identity; -blechen, -bleien, -brücken, -dachen, -decken, -dunkeln, -fahren, -gattern, -glasen, -golden, -heben (sich), -hören, -kochen, -lassen, -ledern, -moosen, -ölen, -pfeffern, -pichen, -salzen, -schiessen, -schleien, -schneien, -schnüren, -sehen, -springen, -tafeln, -zinnen.

In Latin it has been for a long time the habit of scholars to identify with our own *for* of *forswear*, *fordo*, *forlorn*, *forget*, *forgive*, the *per* of *periurus*, *perdo, pereo, perimo, perfidus;* and no doubt with reason: and to these may be added *peruideo,* as found in Horace's

> "Quum tua peruideas oculis male lippus inunctis,
> Cur in amicorum uitiis tam cernis acutum ?"

for it seems to have been an unnecessary proceeding on the part of Bentley to give up the reading of all the other MSS. in favour of one. It is scarcely a grave difficulty that the Latin language also used *peruidere* in another sense, seeing that we give two different meanings to our *overlook,* and the Germans to their *versehen* and *übersehen.* But the Latin seems to have examples where the prefix *per* has the original meaning of *über, over*—viz. *percell-* 'knock over,' 'upset,' as seen in the use of this word in the very oldest writers, *e.g.* with *plaustrum* in Cato, *quercus* in Ennius, to say nothing of Plautus and Terence, both of whom have the word in its true physical sense. *Peruert-* again means 'overturn,' 'upset,' as with *pinus proceras* (Enn.), *aulas* and *turrim* (Plaut.), and especially in 'si réx obstabit óbviam, regem ípsum prius peruórtito' (Stic. ii. 1, 14). The meaning 'over' gives the best interpretation to the compounds *perfund-, perlin-,* and *perung-.* A further claim must be put in for the intensive *per* of adjectives, like *permagnus, permultus,* especially when we compare this with ὑπερ as a prefix to the adjectives -ασθενης, -ατοπος, -ελαφρος, -καλος, -λαμπρος, -πικρος, -πολυς, -σοφος. The assumption here made is that *super* was cut down to *per*, and the loss of two letters may offend; but such loss may well have been gradual, first one letter disappearing, and then the other. Thus the Lat. *sub* (pronounced *sup*) seems to have lost its sibilant in one derivative, viz.: *aperio apertus*, the root syllable of which is the same as *op* of our *op-en* and our preposition *up*. This will be more readily accepted if contrasted with *op-erio op-ertus*. That *ap-eri-* and *op-eri-* (with their participles *ap-er-to- op-er-to-*) have their origin in prepositions is a matter on which I have little doubt, the *eri* of these words corresponding to the *eli* of *sep-eli* (*sep-ul-to-*), the root of which is one with θαρ of θαρρ-ω; and indeed a suffix *er* or *el* is well known in our own language as in *quiver*, *shiver* from *quake*, *shake*, *gambol* and *gamble* from *game*. But as to the root-syllables *ap* and *op*, my first thought was directed towards *ab* 'from' and *ob* 'to,' for 'opening' is separation and 'shutting' is re-union, and indeed we ourselves have the phrase 'put to,' in the sense of 'shut.' The other alternative was to look out for prepositions signifying 'up' and 'down,' which would correspond to our phrases 'put the window up' and 'put it down.' Now our own verbs *ope* and *open*, the Germ. *offen* and *öffnen*, the Dutch *open* and *openen* connect themselves beyond a doubt with the several prepositions *up*, *auf*, and *op*, to say nothing of such a word as the German *aufmachen* 'to open.' But where am I to find *op* 'down' for '*op-eri-*'? I answer, in the *ob* of *occid-* 'fall down,' 'die,' 'set as the sun,' *occid-* 'cut down,' *oppet-* and *obi-* 'go down,' *i.e.* 'die,' *occuba-* 'lie dead,' *obter-* 'tread down,' *opprim-* 'press down.' The Sanskrit gives this prefix in the shape *ava* 'down,' and the Latin also has it in the *ab* 'down' of *abici-* (*abiecto-*) 'throw down,' *ab-sorbe-* 'suck down,' *afflig-* 'dash down,' *appos-* (*appon-*)

'set down.' The German too has this very form with the sense of down in several words, especially in *her-ab*, *hin-ab*, and *ab-wärts* 'downward.' I am not blind to the fact that on this theory *op-eri* might as well have signified 'to open,' and *aperi-* 'to shut.' But language is somewhat arbitrary and uncertain in such matters.

The adverb *perendie* is sometimes spoken of as a hybrid word, made up of the Latin *die* and the Greek πέραν, or Sansk. *param*; but here again, without denying the identity of the three words, πέραν, *param*, and *peren*, I would claim the last as a native and a corruption of *superen*, whence the adverb *supern-ē* 'from above' (with a suffix like *ind-e*, *und-e*, and the Greek ὀπισθ-ε, &c.) so that *perendie* shall correspond in its first element to the *über* in *über-morgen* of precisely the same meaning. This theoretic *peren* or *peran* exists, though a little disguised, in the contracted form *tran*. Before an *r* the Latin language was much given to a change of consonant. Thus *trem-ere*, as has been often noticed, is a corruption of *cremere* (Fr. *craindre* and Old Fr. *cremir*). A thoroughly parallel example to our theory about *trans* is seen in the adjective *tranquillus* for *planquillus*, a double dim. of *plancus*, as that again is a dim. of *planus*. The verbs *trādo*, *trāduco*, *trāicio* seem formed from *tran* rather than *trans*; and the co-existence of two forms, one with, one without an *s*, is seen in many of the prepositions, as *ab*, *sub*, *ob*, *ec*, *di*. It may be noticed too that this theory brings the French particle *très* 'very,' so commonly used with adjectives, into immediate connexion with the Latin *per* and Greek ὑπέρ of the same habit. Even within the limits of the Latin language we have what is really identity in the two forms *trans-fuga* and *per-fuga* 'deserter,' or more literally in German, *überläufer*.

In the Greek language I would first observe that certain compounds with the full form ὑπερ present peculiar meanings which go far to support the doctrine that *ver* is a shorter form of *über*, viz. ὑπεροραω ὑπεριδειν 'overlook,' and ὑπεροπτος 'slighted' compared with *versehen, overlook,* and *verachten*. Indeed, the simple verb *achten* 'to look' is probably the analogue of the Greek οπτ-ομαι, for the π of this word appears as a c in the Latin *oc-ulus*, while *ac* itself is seen in the Lith. *ak-i-s*, as also in *ac-tutu-m* 'in the twinkling of an eye,' '*in einem augenblicke*,' to adopt Dr. Ebel's explanation of the word (Kuhn's Zeitschrift, iv. 320); and then a c in Latin should be represented by *ch* in German, while the o again should give place to an a. In both *acht* and οπτ the t I regard as excrescent. Again, in ὑπεραγωνιζομαι, ὑπερμαχομαι, ὑπεραλγεω, ὑπεραγρυπνεω 'fight, &c. *for*' —, we have an explanation of the *ver* in *verfechten* and *vertheidigen;* and above all ὑπερ-αποκριν-ομαι 'answer for' corresponds with all accuracy to *ver-antworten*. Then again, the negative power of *ver,* though in itself it means '*über*,' is in agreement with the use of ὑπερκαιρος 'over or beyond the time,' hence 'at wrong times,' like ακαιρος —to quote the words of the Lexicon.

But the Greek also seems to have a decapitated variety: παρ for ὑπερ, or παρα for ὑπαρα; for I cannot but think that language was in possession of two distinct words παρα, which have accidentally taken the same form. From the words in which παρα means 'presence,' or 'by the side of,' I would separate those in which is to be found the idea of 'over,' or 'what is wrong,' or 'negation.' No doubt there are cases where 'passing by' and 'passing over' afford equally good explanations of the excessive. But to παραπηδα- 'leap over' and so 'transgress,' and παρ-οριζ-, alike in the sense of 'outstepping one's own boundaries,' or 'driving another over them into banishment,' the notion of *over* seems alone applicable. So with παραιρε- when used either of 'transferring a curse,' or 'drawing over to one's own side.' The verb παραφημι may well mean 'persuade,' if it have for its literal translation 'to talk over,' '*über-reden*.' The same applies to παραπειθω. In παραδιδωμι and παραλαμβανω, παρα 'over' is suited to denote a transference of property, like *trans* in the Latin *trado*. Then in not a few words the notion of covering is added by παρα, which suits well, if this be a variety of ὑπερ, as παρακαλυπτ-, and, what is probably the same word at bottom, παρακρυπτ-, παραλειφ-, παραμπεχ-, παραπεταλο- 'covered with plates (of silver, &c.),' παραπεταννυ-, παραπηλωτο- 'besmeared with mud,' παραπωμαζ- 'cover with a lid,' παρασκηνο- παρασπιζ-, παραχρι-. So, too, παριδυλασσ- will bear the translation 'watch over,' παρουρο- that of 'one who watches over.' Again I cannot but give the preference to παρα = *über* over παρα 'by the side of,' in such cases as παρανθ-= '*verblühen*,' παργηρα-, παρακμαζ-, παρηβα-, παρηλικ-, compared with *verjähren*, *veralten*, the Ang.-Sax. *ofer-geare*, *ofer-eald*, and our own *superannuated*. So also παραβλεπ- παροπα- must go with Horace's *perride-*, with the German *übersehen* and *versehen* of like meaning, Ang.-Sax. *for-seon* 'despise' and our own *overlook*. Here indeed something is to be said for those who find the explanation in 'looking by the side of;' but when we come to the sense of hearing the explanation fails. Still there can be no doubt that we must class παρακον- and παρακροα- (r.) 'hear wrong,' or 'fail to listen to,' with the German verbs *über-hören, verhören (sich)*, and the Ang.-Sax. *ofer-heoran* or *ofer-hyran*, all of like meaning. Then the adjectives παραθερμο- 'overhot,' παρατολμο- 'foolhardy,' παραυστηρο- 'exceedingly austere' (I take the translations from L. and S.), are at one with the German *überlang* and Greek ὑπερλαμπρο- &c. while παραπρο- corresponds to ὑπερκαιρο-. To these I add two rare words, which alike seem to show that παρα is a corruption of ὑπαρα, viz. 'παραπαγος (or παρπαγος) the *upper* bolt of a door (Hesych),' and παρασειον 'a *topsail*' = Lat. *supparum*. As to σειον of παρασειον, I would suggest the possibility of its having supplanted a fuller σεχ-ιον, which as a dimin. of a form σεχ, would correspond to the German *seg-el*, our *sail*; and, on the other hand, the word *supparum* (there is also a reading *siparum* with a single *p*) seems to confirm the argument that παρα of παρασειον is, as elsewhere, a corruption of a fuller ὑπαρα.

A form σεχ is commonly assumed as the base of ἐχ-ω; and, again, the Latin *ueh-o* must be one with ἐχ-ω, as shown by the meaning of the derivatives ὀχ-εσ- (cf. the Homeric ὀχεσ-φιν), and ὀχο- 'a vehicle.' But a sail is the chief instrument in the movement of a ship. Hence *uēlum*, i.e. *uek-el-um* (cf. for the guttural *uexillum*, and *pauci, paulum, pauxillum*), the German *seg-el* and the theoretic σεχ-ιον will be all diminutives from a common root. The appearance of a σ by the side of a *u* is not to be explained by any interchange between two sounds so utterly unlike. We should rather start from a base σοχ, which, when followed by a weak vowel (*i* or *e*), would give way to the 'umgelautet' *swech*, and so to *wech* or *uch*.

With this evidence before me of the close connexion between παρα and the prepositions ὑπερ, *über*, and *ver*, I am strongly of opinion that we should in all the cases where the notion of wrong or negation lies in the prefix παρα, claim it as a totally different word from παρα ' by the side of.'

But I must return for a short time to the Teutonic family of languages, to say a few words on a Norse prefix which seems to be allied to those which we have been discussing, viz. *of*, in the sense of too much, as given in Rask's Grammar (§ 302), viz. in *of-mikill* 'too much,' *of-gamall* 'too old,' *of-snemma* 'too soon,' *of-seint* 'too late,' *of-át* 'gluttony,' *of-dryckja* 'drunkenness.' Here all would have been intelligible, if instead of the simple *of* we had had some comparative as *ofer*, for then we should have had forms corresponding to the Ang.-Sax. *ofer-eatan* 'to overeat' and *ofer-etol* 'a glutton,' &c. Possibly the explanation may be that, in accordance with the law that irregular comparatives, just because of that irregularity, are permitted to drop the final suffix, for example *bet*, *mo*, *leng*, *less*, of our own language, in place of *better*, *more*, *longer*, *lesser*; *ma* (*mālo*), *sat*, *aut*, in Latin, in place of *magis*, *satis*, *alterum*, so this Norse *of* may be a curtailed variety of *ofer*. This would serve to justify the use of *of-tyened* 'very angry,' and *of-guoing* 'transgression' (The 'Ayenbite of Inwyt,' pp. 66 and 215). But for the case of *of-take* (p. 104), I have already provided in another way.

ON THE GERMAN PREFIX ver AND ALLIED FORMS.

In dealing with a German particle, I have the feeling that I am an intruder, and the more so as my knowledge of the language is a very loose one. At the same time an outsider is often alive to difficulties which never present themselves to a native, for the simple reason that a mother tongue is acquired without much exercise of the reasoning powers. It is probably due to this cause that there are so few good grammars of any modern language. At any rate in my own case it was the inability to find satisfactory explanations of the inseparable prefixes of German that induced me at different times to look with some care into the facts as presented by dictionaries, and then to connect such words with the equivalent forms of the kindred languages. It is in this way that I have dealt with the inseparable prefixes *ent*, *unter*, *er*, *zer*, and *ver*, and their representatives. I do not expect my views to be blindly accepted. It will be enough if I stir up an intelligent inquiry into the subject on the part of those who are better qualified to deal with it.

V.

Post AND *after* THE SAME WORD.

My first sketch of this paper, as it was drawn to be read before the Philological Society, I wrote without any knowledge of what Ritschl (Rhein. Mus. n. f. vii. 573) and G. Curtius (Kuhn's Zeitschrift, i. 268) had said before me. Where our views agree I find much in their testimony to strengthen my argument; and where we differ I will give my reasons for the difference.

I begin with the assertion that in both these words, *post* and *after*, the letter *t* is excrescent (see my paper on this subject below); in other words, that the more genuine, or, as the Germans say, the more organic forms are *pos* and *afer*.

As regards the assumed *pos*, I first pointed to the old dactylic inscription (Mommsen's OIL. 1454): 'Qúr petis *postémpus*[1] consílium; quód rogas nón est;' to another inscription (Orelli-Henzen, 6561) '... lib. libertabus *posrisq*. (= posterisque) eorum;' to the Umbrian *pustertiu* of the Iguvian Table (1 b. 40, Huschke); and to the phrase *pus-ueres* of the same

---

[1] In the instances *postempus, pustertiu, præterganeus, postu, postemplum*, the *t* might have been supposed to be performing double duty but for the abundant examples where the word following *pos* begins with other letters.

(1a. lines 7, 14, and 24), opposed to *pre-ueres* (lines 11 and 20), which are respectively translated 'post portas or muros' and 'ante p. or m.;' to the adjective *posterganeus* of late writers; to what Velius Longus (2237, 13 P.) quotes from Cicero's Orator (43): '*posmeridianas* quoque quadrigas libentius dixerim quam *postmeridianas*' (for which last word Ritschl, I now find, suggests the substitution of *pomeridianas*); to *pomerium* and *pomeridianus*, as naturally growing out of *posmerium* and *posmeridianus*, just as *remus* stands for *resmus*, and *Camena* for *Casmena*; to *posquam*, as given by one of the most trustworthy MSS. of Catullus (xi. 23), and adopted by Bergk; to *pos legem* and *pos te*, said by Diez (Gr. iii. 215) to occur in the Agrimensores; and lastly, to *pōne*, as standing for *pos-ne*, and so receiving its best explanation. Cf. *pōno* for *posno*, the root *pos* alone appearing in *posui*, *positus*, while the *n* of the imperfect tenses performs the same office as in *sterno*, *cerno*, *sperno*; for I unhesitatingly reject the theory which would make *pono* a compound of *sino*. The old form *posiui* seems at first to support this view; but compare *quaero quaesiui*, *peto petiui*. In fact it is common for consonant-verbs and i-verbs to coexist, and then interchange their tenses, as in *uenio ueni*, *farcio farsi*.

To this evidence I now add from the MSS. of Plautus, as pointed out by Ritschl (*l. c.*), 1, *posquam*, Glor. 124, CDa; 2, *posquam*, Bac. 277, Ba; 3, *pesquam* (for *posquam*), Poen. Pr. 104, BCD; 4, *poshac*, Poen. i. 2, 66; 5, *postu* (= *post tu*), Trin. 975, BC; and then in abbreviated form with the symbol *p*', which he with reason interprets as = *pos* (or perhaps *pus*?); 6, *p'quam*, Glor. 121, B; 7, *p'id* (for *pos id*),

Trin. 529, D; 8, *p'hunc*, Men. i. 2, 3, C; 9, *p'qui* (where other MSS. have *postquam*), Glor. 1331, Da; 10, *Pquam* (with the mark ' accidentally omitted, he thinks), Pseud. 1,269, C; 11, *p. . illa* (with two letters erased), Men. v. 9, 58, Ba (*p'illa°* Bb); and then from other sources, for which also I am indebted to Ritschl, 12, *postemplum*, and 13, *poscolu[mnam]*, Iscr. Marini Atti, &c., 182 and 258; 14, *pusmeridianae*, Cic. Att. xii. 53, Med. MS.; 15, *posquam* res Asiae, ap. Marium Victorinum, 2,467, Putsch.

That *pos* rather than *post* is the older form is further confirmed by the Sanskrit *paç-cat* 'post,' and the S. adj. *paç-cha* 'after-coming,' with its superl. *paç-ch-ima*; as also by the Lith. *pas-kuy* 'postea,' and Old Prus. *pans-dau* of like meaning (Pott E. F. i. 88, and Bopp's Gl.). Part of this I take from Curtius (*l. c.*).

Hence I confidently assume that the *t* of *post* is excrescent, as in the Germ. *morast*, our *morass*, Fr. *marais*, Germ. *palast*, Fr. *palais*; or, to draw examples from the classical languages, *ost-ium* by the side of *os oris*, and *oar-eor* by the side of *os ossis*.

Our preposition *after*, and the Gothic *aftra*, Bopp (V. G. § 295, vol. ii. p. 28 of the second edition) would divide so as to attach the *t* to the suffix, as *af-ter*; and on the same principle he places the hyphen before the dental in the Old Germ. prepositions or adverbs, *wi-dar*, *ni-dar*, *hin-tar*, *sun-dar*, *for-dar*. But that such a proceeding is erroneous is proved by the form of our simpler words *aft* (*ab-aft*), *with*, *neath* (*be-neath*), *hind* (*be-hind*), and *forth*. Had our adjective *yonder* fallen under his view, he would no doubt in all consistency have divided it *yon-der*; but here again we once had a simple *yond* as well as *yon*, and still have *be-yond*.

Of course he is thus driven to erroneous results. For example, his division of the Gothic *wi-dar*, Germ. *wi-der*, calls for some explanation of the first syllable; and accordingly he finds this in the Sanskrit particle *vi*, which denotes, he says, 'separation' ('trennung'). Had he thought of the identity of the English verb *with-stand*, and the German *wider-stehen*, *widerstand*, he would probably have admitted that *wid*, Eng. *with*, is the root-syllable, with the meaning of 'union' instead of 'separation;' for though union often includes the idea of peace and friendship, a meeting may also be preparatory to hostile proceedings. *Tecum coniungi* generally implies an amicable union, but then we have also *tecum pugnare* as well as *congredi*, and *conferre signa*. A thoroughly parallel case is seen in the Latin *contra* and its primitive *con* or *cum*, two words which render it impossible to doubt the connexion of *wider* with our *with*; and though *contra* very often carries with it the idea of hostility, yet such is certainly not the case with the Fr. *contre-danse*, and our English equivalent but misspelt *country-dance*, where the parties are brought indeed face to face, but not for war.

The Gothic *aft-ana*, too, compared with *ut-ana*, &c. goes far to prove that the *t* belongs to the first syllable. Accordingly, as Bopp himself remarks, Grimm gave a preference to the division *aft-uma* for the Gothic superlative. In a subsequent paper I hope to show that generally *er* rather than *ter* or *ther* is the suffix of comparatives, thus giving a preference to what is seen in ἐν-εροι, sup-eri, inf-eri, and making the division σοφωτ-εροι, βελτ-εροι; ἑτ-εροι, *alt-er, oth-er;* ποτ-εροι, *ut-er, wheth-er*.

For the present purpose I have still more valuable evidence: first, in the Gothic forms *afar* and *afara*; secondly, in the Sanskrit *apara* 'posterior,' and the Vedic *apama* 'postremus.'

But I am also called upon to justify the assumption that an *f* in our Teutonic family has a tendency to throw out a *t*; and I give as examples, *left* by the side of the Latin *laevus*, the Germ. *saft* compared with our *sap*, the English *sift* in connexion with the noun *sieve*, and our adverbial *aloft* and the Germ. noun *luft*, so closely allied to the nautical verb *luff* or *loof*. The adverb *often* also is so commonly pronounced without any regard to the *t*, that one is tempted to conclude that an earlier form was *of-en*. As *s* of the Latin *sub* is lost in our *up*, so *subinde* (see p. 71), or rather *supinde*, may be one with our *often*, as it is one with the Fr. *souvent*.

It was from a belief in the excrescent character of the *t* in *aft* that I was led to identify the root-syllable *af* with the Latin *ob*, and the Greek ἐπί. The *b* of *ob*, as of *sub* and *ab*, is proved to have supplanted a *p* by the Greek equivalents, and also by such derived forms as *superi*, *supra*. Thus the *f* in *aft* obeys Rask's law, while the vowel change between *ob* and *af* corresponds with what is seen in *domare* and our *tame*, Germ. *zähm-en*; in *rogare* and Germ. *fragen*; *collum* and *hals*; *rota* and *rad*; *folles* and *balgen*.

I next revert to the doctrine so often put forward already (p. 57, &c.), that prepositions which begin with a consonant have often attained this form by the loss of a preceding vowel, and that such lost vowel is either one with or akin to that which follows the said consonant. On this principle *pos* suggests the form opos; and we have a parallel case in the noun *pomum* as having grown out of an older *opomum*. (See paper on 'α privative.') This assumption of an initial *o* seems fully justified by the form οπισω (οπισσω) with the very meaning one would desire; the more so that the opposed word προσω (προσσω), i.e. προ-οσ-ω, tells us that οπ alone belongs to the root, while ισ-ω and ιατ-ω also compel us to mark off the ω of οπισ-ω and προσ-ω, as in itself a suffix.

Now the form *op-os* thus placed beyond doubt bears so strong a likeness to our English theoretic *af-er*, allowing for the usual letter-changes, that it may well raise the suspicion that they are virtually the same word. The ordinary suffix of the Latin comparative is of course *ior*, but this we know grew out of an older *ios*, the neuter, as *melius*, and the diminutive, as *meliusculus*, still retaining the original *s*. But of this suffix *ios* one or other vowel is apt to disappear (cf. Bopp's V. G. § 303). In *minor*, *minus* (for *minior*, &c.), and *secus* (for *secius* 'other'), the weak vowel is lost, but the *o* in *magis* and μεγιστος (for μεγιοστος), in *nimis* and *satis*, and in *pris* of *pristinus*. In this last word we have again an excrescent *t*, just as we have in *crastinus* from *cras*; and the *pris* stands for *prius*, being one with the Greek πριν (of Homer) for πριον. Looking then from this point of view, we find a comparative which has lost the weak vowel in our theoretic *op-os* of the Latin, and one which has lost the strong vowel in οπ-ισ- of the Greek. Nay, the preposition προς itself, i.e. προ-ος, must also be of comparatival form.

The doctrine that the *os* of *pos* (*op-os*) is of comparatival character seems confirmed by the old Prussian *pans-dau*, for *ans* is so far nearer to the Sanskrit suffix *yans* of comparatives. It is also to be observed that the *o* of the form *pos* is long, as in a comparatival form it is entitled to be. This appears from two of the passages to which Ritschl refers, viz.—

'Ilíco equidem Venerém uenerabor, mó [ut] amet pótiliac própitia.'—Poen. L 2, 66.

And the line of Cretics :—

? Práeterhac at mihi tále pós hûno diem.'—Men. i. 2, 3.

And I venture to add yet a third from among those he brings forward, viz. :—

'Néque patrem umquam pósilla (usquam ?) titti. M. Quid nos tüm patri,' &c.

Here the first four words (*posilla* or *postilla*) are given in the order of all the MSS., and hence we may safely infer that the metrical accent fell on *pos*. I have inserted *usquam* on conjecture, as the lost word must have begun with a vowel. Ritschl's correction is more violent when he transfers *umquam* to the fourth place, and changes *postilla* into *postillac*.

The appearance of a short vowel in the Greek form Ποστούμιος for *Postumius*, which seems to have influenced Ritschl in his view that *pos* has a short *o*, deserves, I think, to have no more weight than Plutarch's transliteration of the Latin *deciēs* (*deciens*) by δέκιες.

But the appearance sometimes of *is*, sometimes of *os*, in the Latin comparative, has its counterpart in the Teutonic family. Thus the Gothic has comparatives *ald-iz-a* 'older,' *minn-iz-a* 'less,' &c., and also *frum-ōz-a* 'former,' *frod-ōz-a* 'prudentior,' &c. So again in Old German we find in abundance such forms as *alt-ir-o* or *alt-er-o*, *menn-ir-o* or *menn-er-o*; and on the other hand *jung-ôr-o* 'younger,' and *frot-ôr-o* corresponding to the Gothic *frod-ōz-a*, &c. And, to complete the resemblance to the Latin forms, the comparatives in *i* (*e*) have a short vowel, while the *o* is always long. Of course the *er* of the Modern German, as *ält-er*, must be of the same origin of the corresponding syllable in *alt-ir-o* or *alt-er-o*. Hence if we apply to the Teutonic family what has been said of Latin, the *iz* and *oz* of *ald-iz-a frum-oz-a* have in all probability grown out of an older *ioz*; but the form *iz* is substantially the same as the *ir* or *er* of Old German and the *er* of Modern German. Consequently the *er* of *after* is not merely of the same power, but also one in origin with the *ōs* of *pōs* (*op-ōs*).

Thus the proposition with which I started, I venture to say has been established. But a few more last words may be permitted.

It may be as well to note once more the habit of prepositions to take a comparatival suffix, in which case the secondary form not unfrequently supplants the original simpler word. Thus with ourselves *near* (for *nigh-er*) is in more frequent use than *nigh*. In this way I would account for the fact that *ob* lost the signification of 'after,' which its Greek representative επι long retained, as for example in επιγονος.

I gather from G. Curtius (*l. c.*) that Aufrecht considers the Sanskrit *pas* 'post' as decapitated from *apas*, to which I so far of course assent; but when they connect this assumed *apas* with the Sanskrit *apa* and Greek απο I cannot but differ from them; and I am no way surprised that Curtius, holding this view, hesitates to connect with this family of words the Lithuanian *pas* 'propa.' But all difficulty on this head disappears when επι and *ob* are substituted for απο and *ab*.

It may be observed as not improbable that the Fr. *puis*, It. *poi*, Span. *pues*, together with the compounds *depuis*, *dopo*, *despues*, owe the non-appearance of the *t*, not to any aphaeresis of that letter, but to the fact that they came directly from the true form *pos*. The Italian has also the compound forms *posdomani*, *posporre*, *postergare*, *posvedere*.

I would further remark that Ritschl's theory which treats *post* as a curtailment of *poste*, and which regards the *d* of *postidea* and *antidea* as inserted for the purpose of avoiding *hiatus* (*hiatus-tilgende*) as in both respects questionable. I should rather be disposed to look upon *post-id* and *ant-id* as derivatives from simpler prepositions, which passed ultimately into the forms *poste* and *ante*. This suffix *id* may perhaps be one with the *ed* of *red* (for *er-ed*), of which I spoke in the paper on *re* and *pro*. Thus *post-id* would correspond to *r-ed*, *post-e* to *re* (*er-e*). Of course in this view *post* is no longer a curtailed *poste*.

In speaking above of the law of letter-change which holds between the mute consonants of the classical and Teutonic languages, I have thought it right to use the name of Rask rather than that of Grimm, having before me Bopp's note (§ 87, or vol. i. p. 119 of the ed. 1857), which it will be well to translate at length, as the whole credit of the discovery is still for the most part unduly assigned to Grimm. Bopp's words run thus:—

'In my former treatment of this matter (1st ed. p. 78, fol.) it had escaped my notice that Rask, in his prize essay, "Undersögelse om det gamle Nordiske eller Islandske Sprogs Oprindelse" (Kopenhagen, 1818), had clearly and conclusively put forward the law here given, which indeed it would have been difficult to overlook. A translation of the most interesting portion of Rask's paper was also given by Vater in his "Comparative Tables of the European Family of Languages." Rask's discovery, however, must be so far qualified that he deals only with the relation between the northern and classical languages, so as to take no notice of the second law of interchange as exhibited in German, which was first demonstrated by Grimm. Rask's law (p. 12 of Vater's work) is that among the mute consonants the following changes are especially common:—

'π to f, as: πατήρ, fadir.

'τ to th, as: τρεῖς, thrir; tego, eg thek; τύ, tu, thil.

'κ to h, as: κρέας, hræ (a corpse); cornu, horn; cutis, hud.

'β is often retained: βλαστάνω (sprout), blad; βρύω (well), brunnr (a spring of water); bullare, at bulla.

'δ to t: δαμάω, tamr (tame).

'γ to k: γυνή, kona; γίνος, kyn or kin; gena, kinn; ἀγρός, akr.

'φ to b: φηγός, bōg (beech), fiber bifr; φέρω, fero, eg ber.

'θ to d: θύρη, dyr.

'χ to g: χύω, gyder (gush); ἔχειν, ega; χύτρα, gryta; χολή, gali.'

VI.

ON THE SO-CALLED α PRIVATIVE.

THE old doctrine which treats a mere vowel *a* as the original form of this prefix, the *ν* being an epenthetic consonant, still maintains itself in some quarters. Thus in a Sanskrit Grammar published at Oxford not long ago, the form *a* is assigned to the prefix with the qualifying remark that 'when a word begins with a vowel, *an* is usually substituted.' Perhaps it is to such words as ἀεικής 'unseemly,' ἄυπνος 'sleepless,' ἄωρος 'untimely,' that the false explanation owes its vitality; but the lost initial digamma or σ, or asperate, accounts for these anomalies, the older forms having been ἀϝεικής, ἀσυπνος, ἀ-ὡρος (see Proc. Philolog. Soc. iii. 52, &c.). Again, the original *αν* accounts satisfactorily for the long vowel of ἀ-θάνατος, and for the μ of ἀμ-βροτος. But the strongest argument in favour of *αν*, as against the claim of a mere *a*, is seen in the prevalence for the most part of a nasal in the corresponding prefixes of allied languages; as—

Lat.	Sansk.	Goth.	Welsh.	Gothic, &c.	Dutch.	Old Norse.	Swed.	Dan.
in	an	ana, an, am	an		un	on	o	o	u

It may be as well to add that the '&c.' attached to the heading 'Gothic' must be interpreted as including

German of all ages, Old Saxon, Anglo-Saxon, and of course our own language.

So much for the final letter of the prefix. The question whether the word once possessed a still fuller form will be considered presently. The next question is as to the meaning of the little particle. Our Greek lexicons assign to it not a few meanings. But no one probably will claim as of one origin the prefix with negative power, and that which signifies unity, or something like it. Αλοχος, ακοιτις, ασκελης = ισοσκελης, &c. have in all probability a common prefix with απλους; in other words, have lost an initial asperate. Those, then, may be thrown aside. Then again, it is perhaps nearer the truth to regard the forms αστεροπη, ασταφις, ασταχυς, as more genuine than the familiar στεροπη, σταφις, σταχυς, instead of giving precedence to the shorter form, and calling the α a euphonic addition. But in either case, the α of such words has no connexion with the prefix which is under consideration.

I have next before me the claim of the so-called α επιτατικον, or *intensive alpha*. It has often been said that the Greek grammarians gave an undue extension to this particle, and indeed it has been objected to them that some of the examples which they quote are but inventions of their own. That they were guilty of such a deliberate offence is altogether unlikely. I hope presently to show that a prefix with the sense of intensity, one in form with the negative particle, and, as I believe, one in origin with it, was in extensive use in some members of the Indo-European family of languages; and if this be admitted, then it will be rather matter of surprise that the Greek language has so few claimants for the meaning. No doubt it was found to be a serious inconvenience that a language should have compounds with the same prefix bearing two meanings at first sight so inconsistent as negation and intensity. An ambiguity of this kind is pretty certain to be got rid of by the disappearance of one or both meanings. Still I must contend that in the Homeric forms ασκελες and ασπερχες the *a* may well have added to the words the notion of intensity. Not so however with the adjective ατενης, which maintains its position down to a late period in Grecian literature. This word seems to me to be only a variety of εντενης, and so immediately connected with the familiar verb εντεινω; and I would justify the change of form by the tendency of the Greek tongue to drop an ν, especially before a dental, at the same time changing a preceding ε to α. Thus the very verb τεινω (τεν) exhibits the change in its tenses εταθην, τεταϰα, τεταμαι, so βενθος, πενθος coexist with βαθος, παθος; and generally *men*, the termination of Latin substantives, is represented in the Greek vocabulary by μετ or μα.

As it was in the Gaelic language that I was first led to the conclusions which will appear in this paper, and as that language still furnishes, I believe, the most abundant as well as the most decisive evidence in the matter, I propose to give in some detail what is there found bearing on the subject. But before doing so, it will be convenient that I should state the theory by which the two apparently irreconcilable ideas of negation and intensity are brought into harmony. I would assign then *male* as the primitive idea of the prefix, the influence of which is most opposite, according as it is attached to an idea desirable or not desirable.

K

While *male sanus* can only mean 'unsound,' *male turpis* is an equivalent to *turpissimus*. This latter use of *male* has been well noted by Orelli (Hor. Carm. i. 17, 25), in the phrase, *Ne male dispari incontinentes iniciat manus*, where he quotes the parallel cases, *male laxus calceus*, Hor. Ep. i. 3, 31; *oculis male lippus inunctis*, Sat. i. 3, 25; *insulsa male et molesta*, Catul. x. 33; *male inepta*, Tibul. iv. 10, 2; adding the just qualification, *Homonymum est vv. 'valde, admodum' cum vocabulo ingratae qualitatis*. There are of course words which in themselves are neither eulogistic nor dyslogistic. These however take their colour from the context. Thus, as Orelli again writes, *male pertinax* has the negative power in the *digito male pertinaci* of Horace (Carm. i. 9, 24), because firmness was then to have been desired, but not so in Prudentius (Cathem. Praef. 14), *Male pertinax Vincendi studium subiacuit casibus asperis*.

The fact that the so-called privative particle sometimes implied blame has of course attracted notice; but the explanation commonly given, though in itself thoroughly intelligible, seems to me to be ill founded; 'Ἀβουλία = δυσβουλία, ill-counsel, and ἀπρόσωπος, ill-faced, ugly,' say Liddell and Scott, are 'strictly a hyperbole, *counsel that is no counsel*, i.e. bad, *a face no better than none*, i.e. ugly.' The issue, I think, will be that this explanation is untenable.

I now proceed to the quotation of examples from the Gaelic Dictionary of the Highland Society of Scotland, omitting for brevity those words where the negative notion prevails. It should be noticed, however, that in the words now to be given the editor sometimes gives to the prefix the epithet 'intensive;'

sometimes, pursuing a course which he finds more convenient, omits all epithets, and confines himself to the safe phrase, 'a prefix.' The compound words then, in the order in which the dictionary presents them, are—

* *aimfheoil* 'proud flesh' (*feòil* 'flesh').
  aimhreit 'discord' (*réit* 'harmony').
  aimhriochd 'disguise' (*riochd* 'form'); also *dinriochd* 'pitiful, or unseemly appearance.'
* *ainbheus* 'immorality' (*beus* 'habit').
† *ainbhfheirg* 'rage' (*fearg* 'anger').
  aincheist 'doubt' (*ceist* 'anxiety').
  aindeallbh 'unseemly figure' (*deallbh* 'form').
  aindlighe 'unjust law, trespass' (*dlighe* 'law').
* *aineachd* 'misapplied prowess' (*euchd* 'feat').
10 † *aineogail* 'astonishment' (*eagal* 'fear').
† *ainghean* 'excessive love' (*gean* 'love').
  ainghearrahd 'a short cut' (*gearradh* 'a cut').
† *ainiarmartach* 'most furious' (*iarmartach* 'furious').
† *ainiomad* 'too much' (*iomad* 'much').
  ainlean 'to persecute' (*lean* 'to follow').
  ainmheas 'ostentation' (*meas* 'valuation').
† *ainneart* 'violence' (*neart* 'strength').
  ainnis 'poverty' (*èis* 'want').
* *ainsgean* 'bad temper' (*gean* 'mood').
20 *ainteann* 'constrictus' (*teann* 'tense, stiff').
* *ainteist* 'false witness, bad character' (*teist* 'testimony, character').
† *ainteas* 'excessive heat' (*teas* 'heat').
* *aintighearn* 'tyrant' (*tighearn* 'lord').
† *aintreun* 'ungovernable' (*treun* 'brave').
* *amhfhortan* 'misfortune' (*fortan* 'fortune').

amhsgaoileadh 'diarrhoea' (*sgaoileadh* 'scattering').
amlubach 'curling' (*lùb* 'curve').
anabarr 'excess' (*bàrr* 'excess').
anabeachdail 'haughty' (*beachdail* 'observant').
* *anablas* 'bad taste' (*blas* 'taste').
anabraise 'immoderate keenness' (*brais* 'keenness').
anabuirt 'madness' (*burt* 'ridicule').
* *anacainnt* 'ill language' (*cainnt* 'speech').
* *anacaith* 'misspend' (*caith* 'spend').
anaceist 'difficulty' (*ceist* 'anxiety'). Another variety of this word occurs below.
* *anacleachdadh* 'bad custom' (*cleachdadh* 'custom').
* *anacleas* 'a bad deed' (*cleas* 'a deed').
* *anacradh* 'object of pity' (*cràdh* 'pity').
* *anacriosd* 'antichrist' (*Criosd* 'Christ').
† *anacruas* 'avarice' (*cruas* 'hardness').
anacuibheas 'immensity' (*cuibheas* 'enough').
anacuimse 'immensity' (*cuimse* 'measure').
† *anacùram* 'excessive care' (*cùram* 'care').
anaghlas 'milk and water' (*glas* 'grey').
† *anaghlaodh* 'loud shout' (*glaodh* 'call').
anaghleus 'disorder' (*gleus* 'order').
* *anaghlòir* 'ill language' (*glòir* 'speech').
anaghlonnach 'renowned for valour' (*glonn* 'deed of valour').
* *anaghnàth* 'an ill habit' (*gnàth* 'custom').
* *anagrach* 'litigious' (*agarrach* 'claiming').
† *anagràdh* 'doating love' (*gràdh* 'love').
anaimsir 'unmeet time' (*aimsir* 'time').
anaire 'necessity' (*aire* 'want').

ON THE SO-CALLED α PRIVATIVE. 133

anám 'unseasonable time' (ám 'time').
* anamharus 'wrong suspicion' (amharus 'doubt').
* anamhiann 'lust' (miann 'desire').
anárd 'very high' (árd 'high').
anbhas 'a sudden death' (bàs 'death').
anbháthadh 'a deluge' (báthadh 'drowning').
60 † anbhorb 'furious' (borb 'fierce').
anbhroid 'tyranny' (bruid 'a thorn').
* andán 'foolhardy' (dàn 'bold').
andéistinn 'squeamishness' (déistinn 'disgust').
† andóchasach 'presumptuous' (dóchasach 'hopeful').
* andòigh 'bad state' (dòigh 'condition').
† andòlas 'excessive sadness' (dòlas 'woo').
anduine 'wicked man' (duine 'man').
aneanraisd 'a storm' (aonrais 'tempest').
† anfhad 'too long' (fada 'long').
70 anfhann 'weak, feeble' (fann 'weak').
* anfhlath 'tyrant' (flath 'prince').
* anfhocal 'reproach' (focal 'word').
anfhosgladh 'chasm' (fosgladh 'opening').
† anfhuachd 'excessive cold' (fuachd 'cold').
* aniarrtus 'wrong desire' (iarrtus 'petition').
aniùl 'bad guidance' (iùl 'guidance').
anlaoch 'exasperated warrior' (laoch 'hero').
† anluchdaich 'overload' (luchd 'load').
anmhurrach 'valiant' (murrach 'able').
80 * annspioradh 'a devil' (spiorad 'spirit').
anobair 'idle work' (obair 'work').
† anrachd 'violent weeping' (rachd 'tears').
* anriadh 'usury' (riadh 'interest').
* anriar 'a wrong gratification' (riar 'pleasure').
* ansannt 'avarice' (sannt 'desire').

ansaoghalta 'worldly' (*saoghalta* 'worldly').
ansgdineadh 'chasm' (*sgdineadh* 'bursting').
ansgairt 'loud cry' (*sgairt* 'loud cry').
antarruing 'strife' (*tarruing* 'drawing').
90 * *antogradh* 'criminal propensity' (*togradh* 'desire').
antoil 'self-will' (*toil* 'will').
antráth 'wrong season' (*tráth* 'season')
† *antrom* 'grievous' (*trom* 'heavy').
* *anuair* 'evil hour, bad weather' (*uair* 'hour').

If we look to the meaning of these words, it readily appears that in those which are marked with an asterisk, neither negation nor mere intensity supplies what is required. It is true, that *anaghleus* 'disorder,' may be considered as the negation of *gleus* 'order,' and *aimhreit* 'discord,' as the negation of *réit* 'harmony.' But no such interpretation will account for *ainbheus* 'immorality,' beside *beus* 'habit,' or for *anddigh* 'bad state,' beside *doigh* 'condition,' or *anfhocal* 'reproach,' beside *focal* 'word.' On the other hand, intensity seems rarely if ever to characterise the compounds, except where that intensity is in fact excess, in other words an evil, as in *anfhad* 'too long,' from *fada* 'long,' *anfhuachd* 'excessive cold,' from *fuachd* 'cold,' and generally in those examples to which † has been prefixed. There are indeed among the quoted examples some in which the assigned translation does not bring out the notion of badness, but these exceptions are probably to be referred to the inaccuracy of the translator, as *aincheist* 'doubt,' from *ceist* 'anxiety,' *ainnis* 'poverty,' from *eis* 'want,' *anaghlonnach* 'renowned for valour,' from *glonn* 'deed of valour.' As regards the last, a reputation for valorous deeds, though acceptable enough to those in whose behalf those deeds are exhibited, excites a very different feeling in the sufferers. Thus, the Hindoo and Mahratta had more fear than love for one whom in the last century they designated the 'Daring in war.' Again, *andrd* 'very high,' from *drd* 'high,' is not easy of interpretation to a member of the Alpine Club. But the Highlander was not of so romantic a disposition. He thought rather of the labour of ascent, and so to him every addition to the height of a place was an evil. In the same way, a mere fissure in the ground was of little moment, so long as an easy leap would clear it; but when it was both wide and deep, it was either dangerous to cross directly, or required a somewhat laborious circuit to turn it. Hence probably the suffix seen in *anfhosgladh* and *ansgdineadh*, both translated 'a chasm.' On the whole, then, it may perhaps be safely affirmed that few will read through the list of ninety-four words without coming to the conclusion that the notion of badness is distinctly marked in a large proportion, and that the same notion gives a thoroughly satisfactory solution of the cases where intensity is the favoured explanation; and thirdly, that even in the few cases where the idea of negation would also supply a reasonable explanation, the idea of badness is, to say the least, no less applicable. This being so, the only sound conclusion is, that the one idea which will explain all the cases is to be preferred; in other words, that the prefix *an* carries with it the notion of *malus*.

Hence we must invert the order of the meanings which, under the heading 'AN, *prefix*,' the Gaelic Dictionary above mentioned puts forward, viz.: '1. Privative.... 2. Intensive.... 3. It is frequently found' (says the lexicographer) 'having the same acceptation as the adjective "olc" or "droch," placed before its adjunct: pravitatem nonnunquam designat.' We have here indeed an error, not uncommon in lexicons, and in one view pardonable. No doubt ultimately the privative notion was the prevalent one; and what is most common seems at first sight to have the best claim to precedence. It is in this way that our Latin Grammars place the secondary verbs in *are* at the head of the series of conjugations, in disregard of the claims of the simpler conjugation called the third. The spirit of modern philology however requires that the order of time should be observed here as much as in geology.

On the varying forms of the prefix in the Gaelic tongue some notice will be taken below. It may be observed however that among them is *amh*, which also occurs as an adjective in the same language, and one of the meanings assigned to it is 'bad, naughty, pravus.' This meaning is given on the authority of the well known Gaelic scholar, Shaw. Now the Latin *malus* is at present, I believe, an isolated word. It begins too with a letter which always incurs my suspicion, as occupying an initial place to which a liquid is not entitled. Thus, if I also assume the law of similar vowels for this adjective, an older form would be *am-alus*, of which *am* alone would be radical, *alus* being a suffix just as in the Greek μεγαλη, ὀμ-αλος, χθαμ-αλος, ἀπ-αλος. This view I first threw out as a loose conjecture; but it seemed even then to receive some confirmation from our own adjective *evil*, Germ. *übel*, which may well represent a Latin *amal*.

But what was so far doubtful I regard as transferred to the region of certainty, when it appears that an adjective *avol*, in the sense of 'bad,' was once known to the Provençal, Catalonian, Spanish, and Portuguese languages. It is to Diez's Dictionary of the Romance languages that I owe the knowledge of this. But, as my explanation of the word differs wholly from his, I think it due to him to state in English what he says :

'*Avol*, Prov. (adj. of one termination) "bad, wretched," sb. *avoleza*. The word also occurs in Old Catal. Span. and Port.; but is so rare that the statements as to its meaning fluctuate. Sanchez translates *avol ome*, in Berceo, by 'ladron,' but this with hesitation; Moraes translates the Port. word in Nobiliario (where moreover he exhibits a various reading *avil*) by "máo," *i.e.* "bad." In Prov. it is of very common occurrence, though now, as in the other languages, obsolete, and signifies the opposite of *pros*, Fr. *preux*. That the first syllable has the accent is shown by the contracted form *ául*, which stands to *ávol* just as *fréul* to *frévol:* Seckendorf therefore is wrong when he writes *avól*. As regards derivation, a guess has been made at the Gr. ἀβουλής, "disagreeable," but this does not satisfy the meaning. Ducange, on the authority of a document of the year 1411, notices a form *advolus* = *advena*, which is literally the Romance word. As the Span. *cuerdo* is abbreviated from *cordatus*, and the Prov. *clin* from *clinatus*, so *advolus*, *avol* might be abbreviated from *advolatus*, *avolé*. The fundamental notion was "hergeflogen," *i.e.* "homeless, foreign," and the complete word was often so used : *Ceux qui estoient ainsi bannis . . . les appelloit-on avolez* (Ducange, v. *advoli*); *garce avolée*, Théâtr. Fr. p.p. Michel

449. From this notion that above mentioned might easily proceed, just as in our *elend* 1, "peregrinus," 2, "miser." It is true that in this way an adj. of two terminations was to have been expected; but the word met with the same fate as *frêvol* = *frivolus, frivola*.'

This far-fetched etymology I think Diez himself would have been the first to reject, had it occurred to him that *malus* was a decapitated variety of an obsolete *amalus*, especially as the change from *amol* to *avol* agrees with the law which he himself lays down (Gr. i. p. 200), that a Prov. *v* corresponds to a Latin *m*. The same change is seen in *evil*, which in this respect stands to *amal* just as *amn-is* to *Avon*, as *Damn-onii* to *Devon*. Even the difference in the two vowels of *evil* is accounted for as soon as we call to mind that, as ελ of μεγαλη is a suffix of diminution, so the same office is performed in English by syllables which have a weak vowel attached to the *l*, viz. *le*, as in *mick-le, litt-le;* and of course a weak vowel in a suffix generally produces an 'umlaut' in a strong vowel of a root-syllable, *evil* rather than *avil* or *avle*. A further argument for connecting the two words is that, as in Prov. *dvol* is reduced to *dul*, so our *evil* takes the form *ill*.

It may be objected to this view, as to the connexion of the prefix *av* or *amh* with the theoretic *amalus*, that the more common form of the prefix is *an*, rather than *am*. This is true, but it is a special characteristic of the Latin language that it prefers the labial to the dental nasal. Still, in many roots which exhibit an interchange of *m* and *n*, it is difficult to say which form has the better claim to originality, as when we find χθον- of the Greek standing beside χαμαι and χθαμαλος, and the Latin *humus, humilis*, and again the Greek Fαν-ερ- (ανηρ) with Latin *hom-on-*, and Italian *uomo*. *Mem-or* indeed of the Latin has in its first or root syllable what seems to have been originally *men*, as in the Greek μεν-ος, με-μν-ημαι. So again an *n* seems to have the better claim as between *om* of *om-it-* (*omitto*) and *αν* of ανιημι.

The examples so abundantly quoted from the Gaelic might be supported by no little evidence from the other members of the Keltic stock; but I will confine myself to a few instances drawn from the Welsh, *anngwres* 'full of heat,' from *gwres* 'heat,' *anngwyth* 'wrathful,' from *gwyth* 'wrath,' where the intensive power seems to predominate; and *anhap* 'mischance, mishap,' from *hap* 'chance,' *anlliw* 'a stain,' from *lliw* 'colour,' *anfod* 'ailment,' from *bod* 'being.' Here the notion of badness is beyond doubt, and in the first of the three, the English representative by the prefix *mis* confirms the theory. From the Cornish I take one example, for which I am indebted to Pott (E. F. i. 382), *ananhel* 'procella,' from *anhel* 'aura.'

In the Teutonic family, to take first the German, as the most familiar member of it, I find *unart* 'bad behaviour,' *unbild* (provincial) 'disgusting figure,' *unbot* (prov.) 'improper bidding,' *undienst* 'bad service,' *unding* 'monster,' *unfall* 'mischance,' *unfug* 'misdemeanor,' *ungeld* (prov.) 'a tax,' *ungemach* 'trouble,' *ungethier* 'monster, hobgoblin,' *ungewitter* 'thunderstorm,' *ungezogen* 'ill-bred,' *unglück* 'mischance,' *ungott* (obsol.) 'idol,' *unkraut* 'a weed' (Lat. *mala herba*), *unmensch* 'inhuman being, monster,' *unmuth* 'bad spirits,' *unrath* 'dirt,' *unsitte* 'bad habit,' *unthat* 'misdeed,' *unthier* 'wild beast,' *unweg* 'bad road,' *unwetter* 'stormy weather,' *unzeug* 'nuisance.'

The German *untiefe* I must deal with apart from the rest, as I find the most opposite translations assigned to it. In dictionaries, among which I include those of Sanders, Adelung, and Campe, as well as Meissner, the only meaning is that of shallow water, and this in Sanders on the authority of passages quoted from Humboldt and Niebuhr. On the other hand, I am assured by two German friends, who are enabled to speak with the highest authority on such matters, that in society they only know the word as signifying very great depth of water. But Pott (E. F. i. 387) speaks of the twofold meaning of the word, and to myself this ambiguity is most acceptable, for the doctrine that the German *un* = *male* in power explains alike the negative and intensive meaning of the word. To the mariner shoal water is the gravest of dangers; and I may observe that it is in connexion with the sea that this notion is found to prevail, as for example in the passage from Niebuhr, to which reference has been made. On the other hand, with the landsman, or at any rate with the bad swimmer, it is deep water that is to be avoided. In the same page of his book, Pott quotes from Swiss dialects, the forms *ungross* (= *sehr gross*), *Unkuh*, *Unmaul*, as 'positive Steigerungen des Begriffes.'

In the Norse our prefix drops the nasal, and takes *o* in place of the German *u*. Here we find the following examples bearing testimony in favour of the power *male*:—

óár 'annonae difficultates' (*ár* 'annus').'
óbæn 'exsecratio' (*bæn* 'precatio).'
óáád 'nefas' (*áád* 'virtus;' or perhaps 'factum').
óáámr 'foetor' (*áámr* 'sapor').
ódaun 'odor foedus' (*daun* 'odor').
óhapp 'infortunium' (*happ* 'bona sors v. fortuna inopinata')
ókynd 'monstrum' (*kynd* 'genus').
óкӧr (n. pl.) 'sors adversa' (*kӧr* 'sors').
óland 'terra infelix' (*land* 'terra continens').
ólestr 'mala fama' (*lestr* 'calumnia').
ólund 'indoles prava' (*lund* 'indoles').
ómadr 'nequam, nebulo' (*madr* 'homo').
óráά 'imprudens consilium' (*ráά* 'consilium').
óρefr 'foetor, odor ingratus' (*ρefr* 'odor').

Lastly, Haldorson, from whose work the above are selected, has a general article: 'O, litem praefixa plurimis dictionibus, vim habet negandi et sensum invertendi, item interdum in malam partem trahendi,' where, as usual, the primary meaning is made to give place to that which is more common.

I turn next to the Dutch, not so much to find parallel examples in *ondaad, ondier, onding, onkruid*, corresponding to the German *unthat, unthier, unding, unkraut*, as to point to another variety of the prefix, viz. the form *wan* so often found in the Dutch vocabulary with a power the same as that we claim for the German *un* and Greek *αν*. It will be convenient to give the meanings in German, as the power of the prefix will be then self-evident.

wandaad 'missethat, un-   *wandank* 'undank.'
    that.'   *wangebruick* 'missbrauch.'

142   ON THE SO-CALLED *a* PRIVATIVE.

wangedrocht 'missgeburt.'
wangelaat 'üble mine.'
wangeloof 'missglaube.'
wangeluid 'misslaut.'
wangeschikt 'ungeschickt.'
wangevoelen 'falsche meinung.'
wangevolg 'irrschluss.'
wangunnen 'missgönnen.'
wangunst 'missgunst.'
wanhebbelijk 'unreinlich.'
wanhoop 'verzweiflung.'
wanhout 'verdorbenes holz.'
wankleurig 'missfärbig.'
wanlust 'verkehrte lust.'
wanorde 'unordnung.'
wanraad 'schlechte wirthschaft, unrath.'
wanschapen 'missgestaltig.'
wanschepsel 'missgeschöpf.'
wanshik 'unschicklichkeit.'
wansmaak 'übelgeschmack.'
wanspraak 'falsche sprache.'
wanstal 'misstand.'
wansijdig 'ungleichseitig.'
wantaal 'sprachfebler.'
wantroostig 'untröstlich.'
wantrouw 'misstrauen.'
wanvrucht 'missgeburt.'

The Scandinavian branch, too, is familiar with a prefix *van* of the same power. The High German also employs *wahn* in much the same way. So also in Old English we have not merely *unlust*, *untyme*, *unthank*, *untrust*, *unrest*, *unfaith*; but also *wanhope*, *wantrust*, and *wanton*, i.e. *wan-towen* = *un-gezogen*.

But in spite of the oneness of meaning in the two prefixes *un* (*on*, &c.) and *wan* (*van*, &c.), the question of their identity involves matter for controversy. It is true that words beginning with *u* and *o* are precisely those in which the loss of a digamma is to be suspected, as in the Danish *uld*, *ulv*, *under*, *urt*, and *ol*, *ord*, *orm*, compared with our own *wool*, *wolf*, *wonder*, *wort*, and *wall*, *word*, *worm*. On the other hand, the prefix *van* (*wan*, *wahn*) has been referred with mucl reason to the family of words which denote emptiness or defect, as the Norse adj. *van-r* 'empty;' and the Gothic *van-s* 'wanting,'—to say nothing of our own verb *wane*, and the sb. *want*. These again claim kin with the Latin *uanus*; but if so, the nasal is no longer radical, seeing that *uac* of *uac-are*, *uac-iuus*, or rather *uoc* of *uocare*, *uoc-iuus*, exhibits the root from which *uanus* is deduced, much as *plenus* from the obsolete *ple-re* (*explere*, &c.).

Leaving this point open, I would next draw attention to the prefix *ue*, *uae* or perhaps rather *ueh*, which presents itself in a small number of Latin adjectives. Here we have the very same difficulty which we had with the prefix *an*. In *uepallidus* the *ue* is said to have an intensive power, whereas it seems to represent a negative in *uesanus*, *uegrandis*, *uehemens*. I propose then the same solution, viz. that the word really meant *male*, so that *uepallidus* might well be equivalent to *misere pallidus* and *uegrandis* to *male grandis*; and I put this forward with the more confidence when I call to mind the Ovidian—

'uegrandia farra colonae
Quas male creuerunt,' &c.

That *grandis* in the best writers is especially used of growth will be admitted; and indeed it is probably of the same stock with our word *grow*, so that *quae male creuerunt* seems to be an absolutely literal translation of *uegrandis*; and such probably was Ovid's meaning when he added these words.

That *male* is the more precise power of this prefix seems confirmed by the use of the so-called interjection *uae* in *uae tibi* 'ill betide you;' and then we have the same word in the German substantive *weh*, and in our own *woe*. In the Latin *uehemens* we find the asperate preserved; and indeed in the passage just quoted from Ovid (Fast. iii. 445), many good MSS. give *uehegrandin*.

One of my colleagues at University College, when I communicated to him in words the substance of this paper, pointed out to me that the theory gave a satisfactory explanation of the name of the god *Veiouis* as 'the *bad* Jupiter.' Aulus Gellius (v. 12) includes this god among the *laeua numina*, as one *in laedendo magis quam in iuuando potentem*. In the same chapter he tells us that he had a temple at Rome between the Arx and the Capitolium, and further that the statue in that temple was armed with arrows, *Sagittas tenet quae sunt uidelicet paratae ad nocendum*. The old form of the name appears to have been *Vediouis*. So *Vediouei patrei*, Mommsen's CIL 1. 807; but the MSS. of Ovid, in the Fasti iii. 430 and 447, have *Veiouis*. Still in either case *Ve* is the prefixed syllable, not *Ved*, for *Iouis* is connected with *dies*, and had at first an initial *d*. Hence also the *d* in the Greek oblique cases Διος, &c.

It will be no violent assumption that this *ue* is but a curtailed variety of *uan*. A parallel case is to be seen in the root *uan* 'blow,' whence the Latin nouns *uannus*, *uent-us*, &c. In Sanskrit we find this root taking the two forms *va* 'blow,' and *an* 'blow;' and the Greek αημι exhibits the root, first as Fα and then as a mere vowel α or η, thus again coinciding with the short form of α privative.

In the preceding investigation I have passed over the Latin language. Let me now briefly supply the omission. The Latin *informis*, which corresponds precisely to the Germ. *ungestaltet*, I claim to be an equivalent of *male formata*, and this on the direct authority of Priscian (1, iii. 10, Krehl): *Informis dicitur mulier, non quae caret forma, sed quae male est formata;* and this he says without any theory to bias him, for he is not dealing with etymology. *Infamis* again agrees with the notion 'having a bad character;' and *intemperies* corresponds with the German *unwetter*. *Ignominia* also implies an adj. *ignomin-i-s* corresponding to the adj. *cognomin-i-s*; and the prefix (*in*) of *i-gnomin-i-s* must have carried with it the notion of 'bad.' The word *impotens* is usually interpreted by scholars as an abbreviation of *impotens sui* 'unable to restrain oneself, ungovernable'—a theory somewhat too violent. But a scholiast on the phrase *Aquilo impotens* in Horace makes the adjective an equivalent of *ualde potens*. This view leads me to suggest that the full meaning of the word is brought out by the phrase *male potens* 'using power badly;' so that 'furious' is a tolerably satisfactory translation of the adjective.

But a still more decisive instance is seen in the adjective *inuidus*, which is very unduly considered to be a derivative from *inuideo*. The stream runs the other way, for it is contrary to the habit of the language to deduce adjectives in *o-* (*inuido-*) from compound verbs. Rather then let us treat *inuidus* as an equivalent to a theoretic *maliuidus* 'having the evil eye;' and from *inuidus* let us deduce *inuide-re*. This verb cannot have been formed from the ordinary preposition *in*, as it means far more than 'to look at.' I should have been prepared to regard it as a compound with *in* = *male*, if the Latin language had so compounded verbs. We ourselves indeed have no difficulty in creating compounds, such as *mistake, misspend, misunderstand*; and the Gaelic, as seen above, gives us *ain-lean* 'to persecute,' from *lean* 'to follow,' and *ana-caith* 'misspend,' from *caith* 'spend.' Hence it is very possible that the Latin *insequi* 'to pursue as an enemy,' may have the *in* = *male*. The adjective *insignis* stands apart from the other adjectives commencing with *in*. We have here probably the ordinary preposition, so that the word corresponds to the Greek ἐπίσημος.

There is a question of form which has been passed over. It was probably noticed that some twenty of the Gaelic compounds had *ana* as the prefix rather than *an*. Here we have a parallelism with the Greek ἀνάελπτος. I might also have quoted ἀνάεδνος, but that the better form seems to be ἀνέϝεδνος (cf. ἐϝέδνα of the Odyssey).

I go back to the forms *van* and *amalus*, to point out that these suggest a fuller *uam-alus* 'bad' of which *vam* alone belongs to the root, and this in English should take the form *wav*, the comparative of which should be *wav-er*,[1] which is all but one with our provincial *waur* 'worse.' It is here assumed that the suffix *al* of the positive has no right to enter into the formation of the comparatives and superlatives, and this is a point which has long been established (see Bopp's V. G. § 298 A). Thus in Sanskrit *kship-ra* 'quick,' leads to *kshép-tyas* 'quicker,' *kshep-ishtha* 'quickest;' αἰσχ-ρο- to αἰσχ-ιον-, αἰσχ-ιστο-; μεγ-αλ-η to μειζον- (for μεγ-ιον-), μεγ-ιστο-; *mag-no-* to *maior* (i.e.

---

[1] So *Wavertree* near Liverpool is called *Wa'rtree*.

mag-ior); *litt-le* to *less-er* (for *lett-er*, cf. Germ. *besser*, Eng. *better*), and *least* (for *let-est*, cf. *best* for *bet-est*, *last* for *lat-est*).

In order to strengthen the argument that *malus* is a corruption of *amalus*, let me point to the fact that *mālus* ' an apple tree,' seems also to have supplanted a fuller *amālus*, seeing that the Welsh write the word as *afal*, which is of course one with the German *apfel*, and our *apple*. In some parts of England (Mr. Morris, in the 'Ayenbite of Inwyt,' Introd. p. 4, says Wiltshire, Gloucestershire, and Somersetshire) the form *opple* prevails, and this opens a new vista. A German friend to whom I had communicated these ideas writes to me as follows: ' That before the *a* of (*a*)*mālus* " an apple tree," an original consonant, not unlikely a digamma, has been lost, I should venture to conclude, on the evidence of the Russian word *jabloko* and the Bohemian *gablko*. Grimm recognises in *apf-el* the same root as in *ob-st*, and indeed evidence might be given that the *a* in this word is by no means original. Even in the modern dialects we hear sometimes the plural *öpfel*, comp. Lith. *obolys*. *Obst* again, or as the original form is *opaz, obez*, seems to be the same as Ang.-Sax. *ofät*. May we compare the Greek ὀπ-ώρα *i.e.* the season when "obst" is ripe ?'

In giving an affirmative answer to this query, I may notice that the Latin *opes* 'wealth, power,' may well have had for its primitive meaning the fruits of the earth, and that Ops, as the Goddess of Fertility, contains the same idea. Then again as *mālum* in this view stands for *amālum*, so *pomum* is probably a shortened form of *op-omum*. Lastly, this interchange of *p* and *m* seems also to explain the appearance of the *p* in *peior* and *pessimus* by the side of *malus*. Possibly *malus* first exchanged its *l* for a *d* (cf. our *bad*), and then *pedior pedsimus* would easily have passed into *peior pessimus*.

I ought perhaps to add that Pott (E. F. of 1859, i. 174) gives a very different origin both to the *av* privative and to the *ue* of *uesanus*. His words are: 'Insanus (in-, Gr. ἀν-, Sskr. an- eig. das. Pron. ana, jener) und vêsanus (Sskr. vi-vom Zahlw. dvi; jedoch nach Anderen aus vahis, aus).' From the same work (p. 386) I borrow also a passage of Simplicius, in which he speaks of the view which Chrysippus took of the prefix *αν*. After showing that the use of the particle exhibits much confusion, he says: συμβαίνει ποτὲ μὲν ταῖς ἀποφάσεσι (*negationibus*), ποτὲ δὲ τοῖς ἐναντίοις συμφύρεσθαι; and soon after, καὶ τὸ κακὸν δὲ δηλοῦται πολλάκις, ὡς ἄφωνον ἐλέγομεν τραγῳδὸν τὸν κακόφωνον. Thus we have a direct confirmation of the chief points contended for in the present paper.

P.S. A friend draws my attention to the following note of Davis on Cic. Tusc. ii. 8: 'Vecors Oenei partu edita] quae Ciceroni *uecors*, ea Sophocli Trach. 1061 est δολῶπις. Apposite Festus: "uecors est turbati et mali cordis." Vide et eundem in *uegrande*. Non priuationem, sed malitiam seu prauitatem particula (ue) denotat, quemadmodum etiam in Vcioue; licet eam uocem aliter interpretetur A. Gell. N. A. v. 12.'

VII.

THE LATIN *et, que, atque (ac)*, AND THE GREEK και, τε, ALL OF ONE ORIGIN.

It has probably struck many philologers as somewhat strange, that the Latin language possesses three particles to express the idea of 'and.' Such a superabundance is at any rate an unusual phenomenon; but it has conferred on Latin writers an advantage of which they have not been slow to avail themselves. I refer to the power it gives of grouping the parts of a complicated sentence, so as to enable the mind to take in all the subordinate clauses without confusing them. This is a point to which I drew attention many years ago in a review of Mr. Henry E. Allen's valuable treatise entitled 'Doctrina copularum linguae Latinae,' in the 'Quarterly Journal of Education,' of the Useful Knowledge Society (vol. iv. p. 135). Thus in the passage (Cic. in Cat. iii. 8, 19),—'Caedes atque incendia, et legum interitum, et bellum civile ac domesticum, et totius urbis atque imperi occasum—appropinquare dixerunt'—it will at once be perceived that *et* is employed to unite the longer clauses, while *atque* (*ac*), filling a more subordinate office, connects words within each clause. But if we translate both *et* and *atque* alike by our ordinary conjunction 'and,' the repetition at once offends the ear and confuses the mind. A better course is simply to leave the *et* untranslated and to supply the loss by a pause. Thus:—

'Massacres and conflagrations, the annihilation of law, civil and domestic war, the downfall of the city and the empire—all these were approaching, they said.'

The insertion of the words 'all these' serves in fact as a compensation for the several omissions of *et*.

We see a similar fitness in the use of the conjunctions in such a phrase as (Liv. xxvii. 18): 'Equites Numidas, leviumque armorum Baliares et Afros demisit,' where troops of the same class are united by *et*, those of different classes by *que*.

So far but two conjunctions are called upon to serve. In the following, all three are turned to account (Caes. B. G. vii. 79):—'Itaque productis copiis ante oppidum considunt; et proximam fossam cratibus integunt atque aggere explent, seque ad eruptionem atque omnis casus comparant.'

In this sentence we have first the taking a position, and secondly the active measures that ensued. These general ideas are connected by the particle *et*. But the active measures are again subdivided. On the one side we have a step towards action on the offensive in the dealings with the ditch; on the other, what is for the purpose of defence, in the precautions against a surprise of any kind. To mark this distinction *que* is employed. But these two ideas also admit of bifurcation. The obstruction of the ditch to an advance may be got over in two ways, by bridging it with hurdles, or by filling it up. So too of the threatened dangers, the most prominent, that of a sally, may well be selected for special notice. In these subordinate divisions *atque* is available. Thus in Latin the particles *et, que,* and *atque* are employed to mark those distinctions, which in English we can often only denote for the eye by a variety of stops.

No doubt at times *et* alone is employed throughout a long period to connect all the single words and phrases and clauses; especially when the object is rather to deluge a hearer's mind with a torrent of ideas than to place them in due subordination before him, confusion for once being preferable to distinctness.

But if the Romans, having the three conjunctions at their disposal, made an intelligent use of their wealth, it still remains to account for the existence of that wealth. Now of the three particles, the one most open to suspicion is *atque*, and that on account of its greater length; for it is the habit of language to use for such an inferior office only short words. Some years ago I had placed before me an interpretation of a Lycian inscription, in which the interpreter had assumed that a certain repeated word of not less than four syllables meant 'and,' a suggestion against which my mind revolted. But even a disyllabic word has in it what is slightly suspicious; and this feeling is encouraged by the very form of the word, which may well be looked upon as made up of the ordinary preposition *ad* and *que*. Such at any rate was the view of Scaliger; and if this view be right, then the translation ought to be, not 'and,' but 'and what is more.' With this idea before me, I have been led of late, while reading any Latin author, to feel my way whether such a translation accords with the use of the word; and I am strongly inclined to answer the query in the affirmative, so far as a very large proportion of

the examples is concerned, at the same time readily
admitting that there are instances where the word
seems to have been used with the power of a simple
et or *que*. Of course the non-translation of the *ad* of
atque will still leave an intelligible sentence in which
but little is lost through the omission. Thus a reader
is apt to be satisfied with the ordinary translation of
atque as a mere 'and.' But my own conviction has
been strengthened by what recently occurred to me.
Having made known my feeling on this subject to an
accomplished scholar, who happened at the moment
to have the 'De Amicitia' in his hand, I found that
he entertained a strong doubt on the subject, and, in
support of this, pointed to two passages in the last
chapter of that treatise; viz.: 'Nemo unquam animo
aut spe maiora suscipiet, qui non sibi illius (Scipionis)
memoriam atque imaginem proponendam putet;' and
soon after: 'Num quid ego de studiis dicam cognoscendi semper aliquid atque discendi?' In these cases
he was disposed to regard *memoriam* and *imaginem*,
cognoscendi and *discendi*, as practically synonyms.
But I could not help feeling that in the first passage
the more complete translation would tell us that the
aspirant after glorious thoughts and deeds would think
it a duty to place before himself the memory of the
great Scipio, ay, and if possible, to have his bodily
form in his mental view, for his statue or bust must
have been familiar to the citizens of Rome. Again, in
the second passage *cognoscere*, at any rate in the imperfect tenses, means strictly only 'to look thoroughly
into,' 'to study with all care;' but after all such study
may be profitless; *discere*, however, is 'to learn,'
denoting successful study. It is true that the Latin

Nosce teipsum, and the Greek γνωθι σεαυτον are usually translated 'know thyself,' yet a more exact rendering would be, 'study thyself.' I hope then still to win over my friend to my opinion. At any rate, I have to thank him for drawing my attention to the use of προς δε in Homer and Herodotus, and of και προς in many Greek writers, where προς like *ad* of *atque* is used without a substantive, or, as the phrase is, 'absolutely,' so that we have a precise equivalent to *atque* as understood by me.

Let me notice, too, that in such constructions as *Est id quidem magnum atque hau scio an maximum* (Cic. Fam. ix. 15, 1) the *atque* fully supports the part I would assign to it, and to substitute *et* or *que* would be wholly inadmissible. Again, in Horace's *Vocatus atque non uocatus audit*, how incomparably more forcible is the *atque* than a mere *et*?

I am not sorry to find some confirmation of my view in what Wagner has written in his 'Quaestiones Vergilianae,' as first (q. xxxv. p. 563): 'Haec quoque exempla confirmant, id quod supra indicavi, *ac* gravius esse copula *et*;' and again (567): 'Singularem huic particulae (*atque*) esse gravitatem, quum alia mihi indicare videntur, tum haec,' &c. where he goes on to quote a number of passages in proof, to which I can only refer.

In the case of the familiar phrase *atque adeo*, 'and what is more,' we have what may be used alike for and against the present theory. On the one hand, the use of *atque* rather than *et* is consistent with the power here claimed for *atque*; but it may be urged, that, as the second particle already contains the preposition *ad*, we have a tautology that has no justification. It may perhaps be enough to reply that in the Latin as in other languages such tautologies are of frequent occurrence. Thus phrases like *ad Caesarem accedere, incurrere in columnas*, with a repeated preposition, are met with everywhere ; and, what is more to the point, tautology is one of the means employed in language to mark emphasis. Thus a verb of the first person ending in *o* has already in that final letter a compression of *ego*, and yet whenever the idea is to be made specially prominent, another uncompressed *ego* is attached : *ego scribo* in preference to *scribo*. In Spanish again, although *tigo*, *migo* are already full representatives of *tecum*, *mecum*, it is found more intelligible to say *contigo*, *commigo*; no doubt because the *go* had ceased to carry with it its proper meaning.

In the two formulae *atque utinam* and *ac veluti* there seems to be some reason for suspecting that the *atque* (*ac*) is but a deceitful imitation of our conjunction. To some extent this view receives support from two of the most distinguished scholars of Germany. Thus Lachmann, speaking of *atque utinam* in a line of Propertius (iii. 15, 51), says that in this construction ' delitescere copulativam *ac* particulae significationem.' So Haupt again tells us: ' In optandi formula *atque utinam* prior particula nonnunquam non connectit orationem, sed cum altera artissime cohaeret.' (See Haupt's 'Observationes Criticae,' of the year 1841, p. 38.) In the same pamphlet (pp. 46, 47), four passages are quoted where *atque utinam* occurs in a position which seems at variance with the usual habit and meaning of the conjunction *atque*. First from Caesar, in the verses where he addresses Terence :—

'Lenibus atque utinam scriptis adiuncta foret uis,
Comica ut aequato uirtus polleret honore
Cum Graecis, neque in hac despectus parte iaceres.'

Then from Valerius Cato:

'Istius atque utinam facti mea culpa magistra Prima foret.'

Thirdly, from Valerius Flaccus (vi. 599):

'Est atque utinam superetque labores.'

And lastly, a passage from Appuleius (lib. vii. p. 199, Elm.), where *atque* commences a sentence in such a manner that the idea of connexion, commonly belonging to the particle, seems out of place, viz.:—

'Atque utinam ipse asinus, inquit, quem nusquam profecto uidissem, uocem quiret humanam dare meaeque testimonium innocentiae perhibere posset.'

I have quoted the passages at length because the treatise of Haupt, like most of those occasional addresses which are published in Germany, is not very accessible to English scholars.

In the case of *atque utinam*, what appears to me to be a satisfactory explanation may be given. That *utinam* stands to *quisnam* in the same relation as *uti* to *quis*, will I think, be readily admitted; but in our own language the particle 'that' needs a preceding 'oh,' before the idea of a wish or prayer is fully expressed. Now, the interjection *ah* is well suited for introducing a wish, as in the Fasti (iv. 240):
'Ah pereant partes quae nocuere mihi.' But this interjection on the best authority should be written as a simple vowel *a*. Thus Wagner in his 'Orthographia Vergiliana' has: '*a* interjectio ubique in Mediceo Romano aliisque optimis libris sine aspiratione scribitur .'. . . Idem volunt veteres gram-

matici.' In the second place, as *ubi, unde, uter* are now admitted to have had originally an initial *c*, as *cubi, cunde, cuter*, so for *ut* we may claim an older variety *cut*, making it in fact a mere neuter of the relative,—that is, an equivalent to *quod*; and so for *utinam* we are bound to insist on an older variety, *cutinam*. Now it is precisely where a combination with a previous vowel-ending word occurs that the guttural might be expected to maintain its ground. It is thus that in an inscription of the Augustan age, we find *ne-cuter*, which afterwards gave way to *neuter*. So again in *si-cut* and *hu-cusque* the *c* may well belong to the second element, for *si* 'so' is older than the compound *si-c* (for *si-ce*): witness the phrase *si dis placet* 'such is the pleasure of heaven.' Thus Mommsen in his interpretation of his Inscription 1447 unnecessarily assumes the loss of a *c*, where the recorded letters run *sei si fecerit*, which may well represent *si sic fecerit* of the later language. So again, *hō* 'hither,' as seen in *horsum* (for *hō-vorsum*), is older than *hōc* or *huc*, which arose from a compound *ho-ce*. This theoretic *hō* would correspond to *isto* (= *istuc*), *illo* (= *illuc*), for the forms *isto illo* are of far more frequent occurrence than our editions of Latin writers would lead us to believe.

Putting then the two points together, that *a* is more correct than *ah*, and that *cutinam* must have been an older form of *utinam*, we have in *a cutinam* a good phrase for the expression of the idea 'oh that;' and, as the words are closely combined in pronunciation, they readily pass first into *ac utinam*, and then, under the ordinary doctrine that *atque* rather than *ac* should be preferred before a vowel, into *atque utinam*, which in sound would still be identical with *ac utinam*.

As regards *ac ueluti* it is not easy to find so satisfactory a solution; but still as the adverb *sem-el* is admitted to have for its first syllable what denotes 'one,' as also *sim-plici-*, *sim-plo-*, *sing-ulo-*, &c., we can scarcely refuse to treat the second syllable of *semel* as that suffix of diminution which is so familiar in the Latin language, but is commonly converted into *ul*. Thus we have *oc-ul-o-* and *ocello-*, the latter standing for *oc-el-el-o-*. Similarly, *semel*, *semol*, and *simul* are now regarded as equivalents in form. Again, *proc-ul* may well be formed from *proc* as an older form of *pro* (see p. 77), by addition of the same suffix. Following these clues, I would suggest as a possible adverb from the same stock as the adjective *aequo-* a form *aequel*; and then the combined formula *aequel uti* 'just as,' would readily slip into *ac ueluti*. Be this as it may, I venture to deny that in the phrase *ac ueluti* we have any representative of the ordinary conjunction *atque*.

I next proceed to the main purpose of the paper, the identification of the particles *et*, *que*, καὶ, and τε. That τε is really one with *que* has, I believe, been long an admitted truth. The use and power of the two little words are in all respects identical; just as the pronouns τις of Greek and *quis* of Latin are the same. But of the two forms we cannot hesitate to regard the guttural as the earlier occupant of the ground, for the passage of a guttural to a dental is of familiar occurrence. But if τε has supplanted an earlier κε, we have in the two forms καὶ and κε no great difference. Indeed in some alphabets the combination αι is the only mode of designating an ε. Still there remains, or seems to remain, a difference of quantity. I say 'seems,' because the Homeric hexameter abounds in examples of a lengthened τε, as (Il. ii. 495),

Αρκεσιλαος τε Προθοηνωρ τε Κλονιος τε.

It is true that the Homeric examples generally have two initial consonants or the suspicion of two initial consonants in the word which follows τε; for not a few words commencing with a liquid have lost a preceding consonant, and such derived forms as εσσευα, εσσυμενος, imply that σευω itself has undergone some such change. Thus we cannot altogether rely on such a case as

Εγχἴι τ' αορι τε μιγαλοισι τε χερμαδιοισιν,

although Mr. Brandreth's form Fμεγαλοισι seems unsatisfactory, if only because it is unpronounceable.

Nay, even the tenth line of Il. xi. affords no sure ground—

Ενθα στας' ηυσε θεα μεγα τε δεινον τε—

for several of the secondary forms of δειδω (with which, of course, δεινος is closely connected), as εδδεισα, υποδδεισαν, raise a suspicion that this family of words commenced with something more than a simple mute consonant. In confirmation of this view, one of my colleagues observes that the perfects βεδοικα and δειδοικα cannot justify their possession of the diphthong οι by such a form as λελοιπα, for this belongs to the class of so-called second perfects, the π forming part of the root, whereas the syllable κα of δεδοικα, as of πεφιληκα, belongs to the tense-ending. Thus the best explanation in his view of δεδοικα is on the supposition that the ο is part of the base of the verb, so that δο sounds as the *dw* of our *dwell*.

Further, it may be observed that the adjective δεινος has the power of giving length to other final vowels than that of τε, for example, in

Αιδοιος τε μοι εσσι φιλε εκυρε δεινος τε—

where εκυρε, as the same scholar points out, must have supplanted a fuller form σFεκυρε, corresponding to the Sanskrit *svasru*, the Gothic *svaihra*, and the German *Schwager* and *Schwieger*. Thus the final of φιλε becomes for the time long before the combination σF of the following word.

In the Latin language, however, the examples of a lengthened *que* before a single initial consonant are more indisputable, for already Attius (Fest. p. 146) has

'Calones famulique metalliqué caculsoque.'

In Virgil indeed, as in Homer, the examples have for the most part two consonants, as

'Aestusque pluuiasque et agentis frigora uentos.
Terrasque tractasque maris caelumque profundum;'

or else a liquid, as

'Liminaque laurusque dei totusque moneri.'

But as the *l* of *laurus* is but a substitute for a *d*, as shown by its analogue the Greek δαφνη, we have no ground for suspecting the loss of a consonant before the *l*. Yet even Virgil has (xii. 363)

'Chloreaque Sybarimque Daretaque Therailochumque.'

Ovid again, who is generally more strict in metrical matters than Virgil, was not afraid to write:

'Faunique Satyrique et monticolae Silaani' (Met. l. 193).

'Telasque calathosque infectaque penas reponunt' (iv. 10).
'Sideraque nantiqus nocent anidasque uolucres' (v. 484).
'Othryaque Pinduaque et Pindo maior Olympus' (vii. 225).
'Liliaque pictasque pilas et ab arbore lapsas' (x. 263).
'Pelenaque comitesque rogant; quibus illa profatur' (xi. 200).

While later writers, who were much more scrupulous in these respects than is commonly thought, have occasional instances of a similar liberty, as:—

'Taxique pinusque Altinatesque genestas' (Grat. 130).
'Electra Alcinoeque Calaenoque Meropeque' (German. 262).
'Laeuaque dextraque acies astare uideres' (Corip. Laud. Just. iii. 177).[1]

On the whole then we must not reject the theory that τε and *que* had once a long vowel, though of course the short vowel in the end thoroughly established its position, and this was to be expected when we consider the enclitic character of the words.

I have not stopped to discuss the favourite and convenient doctrine that the quantity of τε and *que* in such lines is to be ascribed to the influence of what is called caesura or arsis, because I believe this doctrine to be merely a screen for the concealment of ignorance. I hold it to be a more just explanation that the two little words have lost a final consonant, a former possession of which would remove all the difficulties. For this theory I find a parallel in the case of *uel* 'or,' which as an enclitic takes the shorter form of *ue*, as *uel mater*, or else *materue*.

This *uel* is in origin probably an abbreviation of *uele*, i.e. an old imperative of the verb *uol-* 'wish,'

---

[1] These three examples, together with that quoted from Attius, were suggested to me by Lucian Müller's elaborate work on Latin metres.

where the root vowel has passed from *ŏ* to *ĕ*, under the influence of the final *e*, in accordance with the law of 'umlaut.' Another example of such a modified vowel is to be seen in *heus* 'harkee,' an abridgment of an imperative *heuse*, from a theoretic verb *haus-* 'hear,' a verb which would stand to the Latin sb. *ausi-* or *auri-* much as our own vb. *hear* to our sb. *ear*. Again, the assumed loss of an *e* in *uele* would be in accordance with the formation of the imperatives *es, fer, dic, duc,* and indeed *ama, doce, audi* also. Again, from an obsolete verb *gon-*, or *con-* 'look' (the parent of the secondary *gn-osc-*, i.e. *gon-osc-* 'learn'), I assume an imperative *gene*, or *cene* (*kene* in sound), which first cut down to *cen* prepares us for two other varieties, viz. by decapitation, *en* 'look,' 'behold,' and, by loss of the final, *ce*, the familiar suffix of demonstratives, and demonstratives alone, as *hic, istic, illic, sic, nunc*. Here, too, let it be noted that it is only when doing duty as an enclitic that it discards the final *n*. Nay, *con* and *cen* themselves are perhaps truncated words, for σττ-ομαι and οκκο- of the Greek, and *oc-ulo-* of the Latin point to a stem *ok* (*οκ*) or *οκκ*, whence *ecce* would be a good imperative; so that the verb *con* would be a truncated derivative for *oc-on*. It may be noted, too, that the original symbol for the vowel *o* was a picture of an eye, and the Hebrew name for the letter meant 'an eye.' This view accounts also for the *ε* of εκεινο-. Another instance of a word losing a final consonant when employed enclitically is seen in the family of words και, κε, Dor. κᾱ, and the more familiar αν. Why the degraded form κε should be selected as that under which Lexicons deal with these particles, it is difficult to say. The more legitimate course would be to start from καν, for few will now defend the doctrine of a paragogic ν. Still the error is a common one. Our English grammars, for example, still speak of an indefinite article *a*, which assumes, they say, an *n* before vowels; and in the same way Greek grammars persist in the folly of talking of *a privativum*, when the more genuine form is αν. What however is important for our present purpose is admitted, that the form κε is only used as an enclitic. But I may also call attention to the Doric κᾱ as showing that here too a long vowel was once known, and secondly to the disappearance of the initial guttural in αν, for this also is a matter which will throw light upon what is about to be said. It will be well however to note that, as the several forms of καν, κε, κᾱ, and αν may be well deduced from a form καν, it is highly probable that our own language still possesses the verb from which all may have been deduced, I mean the verb *can*, which by its meaning is thoroughly fitted to supply the root of a 'potential' word; and further, the verb was known to the Latin language in the form *que-o*, for here also a final *n* once existed, as is proved by the archaic *ne-quin-ont*.

But the connexion between καί and *que* may next receive illustration. First of all the *u* in Latin words, which divides a preceding *q* from a vowel, must, as still in French, have been silent. This is shown by the shortness of the preceding vowel in such words as *alĭquis, nĕque, ăqua, lŏquor*.

It still remains to consider the passage of the diphthong *ai* first into *ē* and then into *ĕ*. Now a parallel case presents itself, as it seems to me, in a comparison of a certain class of Greek infinitives and the ordinary

Latin infinitive. In Greek, as in Welsh, we find a great variety of forms for the infinitive, as τύπτειν, τύπτεμεν, whence with the loss of the μ, τύπτειν for τύπτεεν; also τύπτεναι and τύπτεμεναι, to take these as types, rather than as all representing actual forms. With the disyllabic suffix of τύπτ-εναι I compare the suffix of the Latin *scrib-ere*. That a Greek ν should be represented in the first place by a Latin *s*, and then by a Latin *r*,[1] is always to be expected. Thus the plural τύπτομεν 'we strike,' goes with a Doric τύπτομες and a Latin *tundimus*. Again the comparatival suffix ιον of the Greek has for its Latin analogue an archaic *ios, melios*, and a later *ior, melior*; and even the change in the quantity of the vowel of the Latin comparative follows the law, which gives us *scriptōres* in Latin by the side of the Greek ῥήτορες. In the Latin infinitive *esse*, and the archaic passive *dasi*, for *dari*, we have the earlier sibilant retained. There remain then for comparison the final diphthong αι of τύπτεναι and the final *e* of *scribere*. Now a final αι in Greek soon lost much of its diphthongal power. Even Buttmann, a most zealous advocate of the prevalent accentual theory, lays it down, with others, that a final αι or οι, though long for metrical purposes, must for the most part be considered as short in the rules of accentuation (Ausführl. Gr. Gr. Spr. § 11, 7). 'Thus,' says he, 'the plural nominatives τρίαιναι, &c., the passives in αι, as τύπτομαι, &c., and the infinitives ποιῆσαι, &c., are all accentuated in a manner that is inconsistent with the usual law for words with a long final;' and he adds the remark, 'It is therefore clear that in these very

---

[1] We have already an example in the Greek ἑαφνη, Latin *lauru-*.

common suffixes these diphthongs had been so far worn away that in the ordinary language they sounded to the ear as short, and that it was only in the sustained language of poetry that the long quantity was maintained.' So much for the Greek αι. Much the same occurred in the final *e* of the Latin infinitive, for this also was once long in the old language. Some instances of this occur in Plautus, as:

'Átque argento cómparando fíngerē falláciam.' (Asin. ii. 1, 2.)
'Quid brácciam ? Illut dícerē noluī femur.' (Glor. i. 1, 27.)
'Nunquam édepol nidi prómerē. Verum hóc erat.' (Glor. iii. 2, 34.)
'Tē salutem mē iussarunt dícerē. Salutē sient.' (Glor. iv. 8, 6.)

And also in Terence, as:

'Potin de mihi verum dícerē ? Nil fácilius.' (Andr. ii. 6, 6.)
'Auscdita. Pergin crédere ? Quid ego óbsecro.' (Phorm. v. 9, 7.)

In the 'Rheinisches Museum' (xxii. 118) Dr. W. Wagner has added to this list, from Plautus:

'Egó scelestus nūnc argentum prómerē possim domo.' (Pseud. 855.)
'Nam cértumst sine dote hán darē. Quin tu í modo.' (Trin. 584.)
'Eum opórtet amnem quáerere comitém sibī.' (Poen. iii. 3, 15.)
'Non índes aliquod[1] mihi darē munusculum.' (Truc. ii. 4, 74.)

And from Terence:

'Male dícerē, male fácta ne nosсánt sua.' (Andr. Prol. 23.)

To say nothing of the cases where the *e* in question closes the first dimeter, as in Plautus:

'Abscede ac sine me pérderē qui sémper me ira incéndit.' (As. 420.)
'Quid rálicuom ? nisi réddere quom extémplo redditum sunt.'[2] (As. 442.)

---

[1] Or 'aliquid . . munusculi.'   [2] Add fore (Most. i. 3, 67.)

'Vix hóc uidemur crédere: magis qui credatis dícam.' (Poen. v. 4, 94.)

'At éccum e fano récipere uideó se Suncerástum.' (Poen. iv. 1, 6.)

These from septenarii, or comic metre. Instances from complete tetrameters are:

'Studeo hūnc leonem pérdere qui méum erum misere mácerat.' (Poen. 4, 1, 2.)

'Peril, ánimam nequeo uórtere: nimis nīli tibicen siem.' (Merc. 135.)

'Qui adm pollicitus dúcere? qua audácia id facere áudeam.' (Ter. Andr. 613.)

The passage quoted from the Gloriosus (i. 1, 27), though it has the full sanction of the MSS., Ritschl already condemned in his Prolegomena (p. ccxxix.), and again in his text of the play. In the Rh. Mus. (vii. 312) he discusses the question at some length, arguing, on the authority of what he deems parallel cases, that the order of words, *illut dicere uolui femur*, is against the habit of Plautus. But in fact the cases he quotes are not parallel; and I venture to assert that when *illut* is used, as here, to draw attention to a coming word or words, in opposition to what precedes, it is a law of the language that the word or words so referred to should lie at a distance from the pronoun, as seen in the examples which I have quoted in my Grammar (§ 1106).

All this, then, tends to justify the doctrine that a Greek καὶ may well have for its analogue in Latin both *quĕ* and *quē*.

But if καὶ, τε, and *que* be admitted to be one in origin, there still remains the Latin *et*. This some have thought to explain as only a metathesis of τε. Such a doctrine I of course put aside as untenable.

My view is that as the Latin particles *en* 'behold,' and *ce* 'look,' are corrupted varieties of a fuller *ken*, so *και*, *τε*, and *que* have all lost a final consonant, while *et* has lost an initial, viz. a guttural, or *k*-sound. This theory, that *et* and *que* grew out of a fuller *quet*, is confirmed by the fact that *que* of the Latin *quandoque uterque* is *pid* in Oscan and *pe* or *pei* in Umbrian (Corssen's Aussprache, i. 337). But I am not wedded to a *t* as the original final. I think it not unlikely that the earlier letter was an *n*. Indeed a Greek particle could not have ended in a *t*. I am led to a preference of an *n* over a *t* by the form of our own *and* and the German *und*, for these virtually end with an *n*, a final *d* after an *n* being a common outgrowth in these two languages; and indeed in not a few combinations we ourselves practically drop the *d*, as for example in the phrase, 'four an twenty blackbirds,' &c.; and this not merely when a consonant follows, for we also habitually say, 'five an eight make thirteen,' dropping the *d* of *and*. I am the more tempted to identify the Latin *et* and English *and*, when I find the Greek. ἕτερος taking in German the form *ander*; and it may also be observed that the syllable ἐτ of ἕτερος represents the ἑν of the numeral ἕις, thus furnishing an instructive example of the interchange of *ν* and *τ*. But if *et* belongs to the same stock with *και* and *que*, it must have lost an initial guttural. Of the loss of an initial consonant numerous examples have already been noticed in this paper, and the loss of a final *ν* in Greek is the great characteristic of forms in that language, a fact which has commonly been concealed under the theory of the ν ἐφελκυστικόν or παραγωγικόν. The Latin, too, shares the habit: thus while the Greek wrote indifferently προσθεν or προσθε, κεν or κε, &c. the Latin has *inde* in place of ενθεν, though it is not unlikely that *indus*, or *indis*, rather than *inden*, prevailed in the older Latin, for we have here virtually a genitive with the power of 'from.' Exactly in the same way in our own island there co-existed forms *henn-en*, *heth-en*, *henn-es*, as well as our still current *hence*. Nay, over and above these Chaucer in the Knightes Tale (2,368) has the abbreviated *hen*—

> 'The fyrée which that on mine auter bren
> Sholn the declaré or that thou go hen.'

Thus we have a form scarcely distinguishable from the French *en*, which is the representative of the Latin *inde*, to say nothing of *hin* as it appears in *hin-c*.

But, to return to the little family of copulative particles, let me ask whether they may have grown out of the demonstrative family. The adverb *item*, signifying 'likewise,' has what is very near the meaning of our little word, but it is itself a compression of *itidem*, which stands to the adjective *idem* much as *ita* 'so' to *is* (*ea*, *id*). If this be admitted, a form *ken*, which as before stated I have long regarded as the primitive form of the family of third-person pronouns, is in its exterior well suited to have been the origin whence came the particles και, τε, *et*, and *que*, as well as τε and *que*, with long finals.

I was first led to the train of thoughts out of which this paper has grown by the consideration that και and τε, on the one hand, could not well have been correlative particles unless they had been one in origin. But *que* and *et* also serve together; at any rate in short phrases. Thus, Livy has *seque et cohortem* (xxv. 14), *et singulis universisque* (iv. 2); and Sallust, *seque et oppidum* (Jug. 26), *seque et exercitum* (ib. 55).

It was of course reasonable that the Greek language should use in correlation a repeated τε, and the Latin in like manner both a repeated *et* and a repeated *que*. Thus in exactly the same way the latter language has *aut* .. *aut* .. , *vel* .. *vel* .. , *sive* .. *sive* .. , *simul* .. *simul* .. , *qua* .. *qua* .. , *tum* .. *tum* .. , *nunc* .. *nunc* .. , *modo* .. *modo* .. So in English we at times use *or* .. *or* .. , *nor* .. *nor* .. But here the more prevalent forms are *neither* .. *nor* .. , *either* .. *or* .. , in which the principle seems to be violated. The explanation however is not far to seek. Our *either*, so used, of course corresponds to the Germ. *entweder*, Old Germ. *ein-weder* (Grimm, D. G. iii. 38), where the *ein* is the mere numeral and *weder* a comparative of the relative. Hence it is virtually the same with the Latin *alter-uter* 'one of the two (no matter which)'; and this has for its positive *ali-quis* 'any one of any number.' In the same way *neither* seems to have grown out of a form *ne-whether*, corresponding to the old Latin *ne-cuter*, aft. *neuter*. Hence the just explanation of the combinations above quoted, is that originally a pause occurred after the words *either* and *neither*, as : 'either (of them), A. or B.,' 'neither (of them), A. nor B.' In the second of these cases the omission of the negative before A. has its parallel in the old construction, still admissible for poetry, which is seen in Shakespere, as (Antony and Cleopatra) : 'For Antony, I have no ears to his request. The queen of audience nor desire shall fail ;' and again in Gray : 'Helm nor hauberk's twisted mail, nor e'en thy virtues, tyrant, shall avail.' Indeed we find the same in Greek poetry also, as (Aesch. Agam. 532): Πάρις γάρ οὔτε συντελὴς πόλις Ἐξεύχεται τὸ δρᾶμα τοῦ πάθους πλέον. Nor is there any real difficulty or ambiguity in such phrases. The negative which precedes the second member makes its appearance in time to affect the following verb, and through this to influence the first of the two members. The same principle is at work in those Latin sentences where *non modo* was once said to stand for *non modo non*. Thus in such a sentence as: 'Assentatio non modo amico sed ne libero quidem dignast,' the *ne* of *ne libero quidem* converts *digna* into *indigna*, and so acts upon the preceding *amico*. I may add that this explanation of *neither* and *either* is also applicable in such constructions as: 'both (of them), A. and B.,' 'whether (of them), A. or B.' A strong confirmation of this argument is seen in the occasional use of two interrogative particles after the Latin *utrum*, as in Ter. (Ad. iii. 3, 28), '*Utrum*, studione id sibi habet *an* laudi putat fore, si,' &c. 'Which of the two is the just explanation—does he look upon it as an amusement, or does he think it will be a credit to him, if' &c.? Thus the particles which really correlate with each other are *ne* and *an*; and these may well be of the same origin, the two being connected by the disyllabic *anne*, which instead of being a compound I believe to be the original word whence both *an* and *ne* proceed.[1] Thus, as already noticed, *αν* of Greek, and *ni* of Sanskrit, find themselves co-existing in the Greek *ἐν*; *αν* of Greek, and the Sclavonic *na* in the Greek *ανα*; to say nothing of the other cases quoted above.

---

[1] See the following paper.

VIII.

ON THE LATIN PARTICLES *aut, an, ně.*

As I have been led to connect these little words with the adjectives *alio-* and *altero-*, Sanskrit *anya-* and *antara-*, I must commence by considering the origin of the latter; and in doing so my first duty is to put aside some derivations to which others have lent their sanction. Thus Bopp (V. G. § 19, vol. i. p. 33), and Pott (E. F. of 1859, pp. 301, 381, 393), are disposed to treat *alius* as a derivative of the Sanskrit *ana*, Latin *ille;* and the former connects *ullus* with *ille* and *ultra*. Dr. Donaldson in his Latin Grammar is so enamoured with the first of these two views, that he puts it forward three times, as p. 45, '*alius* (like *ille* "that other," of which it is a by-form),' &c.; p. 74, '*alius* "another," is in constant use as a by-form of *ille;*' p. 386, '*alius*, which is merely another form of *ille* = *ollus*.' That *ille* and *ultra* are of one stock is past doubt; but *ullus* is of course the diminutive of *unus*, as *uillum* is of *uinum*, as *bellus* of *bonus* (cf. *bene*).

Again, the doctrine of the Indian grammarians that the Sanskrit *antara-* (*altero-*) is formed from *anta* 'end,' and a verb *ra* 'reach or attain,' may be accepted as an example of the way in which native Sanskritists, satisfied with external similarity, deem it superfluous to consider the meaning of words; and the same one-sided examination of etymological problems is not unknown among European Sanskritists.

That *n* of the Sanskrit *anya-*, *antara-* is more genuine than the *l* of *alio-*, *altero-* is rendered probable by the prevalence of the *n* in the Teutonic family, as Germ. *and-er*, Norse *ann-ar*; as also by the fact that the Latin language had a special love for the soft liquid, which often led it to substitute an *l* for other consonants. But besides *alio-* the Latin also possessed a short form *ali-* (whence *alis*, *alid* of Lucretius, and *aliter*). The ratio then of *alio-* to *ali-* suggests for the Sanskrit an equal ratio, *anya-* to *any-*; and this theoretic *any* is for Englishmen an actual word. But our *any* is one with the German *einig*, two words which are in fact diminutives of the numeral *an* Eng., *ein* German; just as *ullo-* 'any' is a diminutive of *uno-*. Hence, reserving for the moment all question as to the connexion of ideas, the *an* of the Sanskrit *an-ya-*, *ant-ara-* seems to be identical with our numeral *an*, and consequently with our *one* and the Latin *uno-*. But the *g* of *einig* also claims attention, and this suggests the idea that *alio-* is only a variety of *unico-*, the guttural having disappeared. This explanation seems preferable to Bopp's explanation (§ 292) that the *ya* of *anya-* is the stem of the relative, for the two Latin forms *ali-* (*alis*) and *alio-* (*alius*) bear evidence that the *y* and *a* of *anya-* are two independent suffixes.

Some support to the doctrine that *al* of *alius*, &c. originally carried with it the notion of 'one,' is to be found in the identity as to meaning of the Greek ἀλλήλοι (evidently consisting of a repeated ἀλλο-) and the German *ein-ander* and our own *one another*.

In *alio-* and *altero-* it is commonly held that 'difference' is the primary meaning of the first element; but this in no way suits the compound forms *aliqui-*, *aliquot*, *aliquanto-*, *aliquando*; nor indeed all the uses of *alio-* and *altero-* themselves. The doubled *alter* and the doubled *alius* render it necessary to give to the adjective on its first occurrence the translation 'one' (pl. 'some'); and even the following clause makes no objection to the same translation, though the word 'other' is then admissible. Thus *aliud est maledicere, aliud accusare*, 'it is one thing to abuse, one to accuse.' So again *alter exercitum perdidit, alter vendidit*, 'one of the two lost, one sold an army.'

Although it seems at first a strange result that a word formed from *one*, itself so often employed to denote identity, should eventually attain to the sense of difference, cases nearly parallel may be adduced. Thus when Ovid, describing the half-military character of the farmer in his place of exile, says, 'Hac arat infelix, hac tenet arma manu,' the repeated pronoun evidently refers to different objects; and so we may, in place of the literal translation 'this,' substitute the words 'the one,' 'the other.' This repetition of *hic* has its counterpart in a similar repetition of *ille*, as (Ter. Ph. iii. 2, 16):

'G. Qui istuc? Ph. Quia non réto accipitri ténditur, neque milno,
Qui male faciunt nóbis: Illis qui nihil faciunt ténditur;
Quia enim in *illis* frúctus est, in *illis* opora ldditur.'

We may quote, too, as an illustration what Bopp says

in his V. G. (§ 371) : 'That which in Sanskrit signifies "this" means also for the most part "that," the mind' (he should have said the finger) 'supplying the place whether near or remote.' Hence there is nothing very strange when we find in our oldest writers such a line as that which occurs in the Life of St. Edmund the King (Trans. Philolog. Soc. 1858), v. 9:

'Hubba was poper ibote : & poper het Hyngar.'

Just as the finger serves to distinguish 'this' and 'this' when they are to be referred to different objects, so no real confusion occurs when Davus in the Andria (ii. 2, 12) addresses first Pamphilus and then Charinus as a *tu*—

'Id paves ne ducas tu illam ; tū autem ut ducas.'

Again in Ovid's Fasti (ii. 676) a consideration of this simple kind would have led to the correction in the easiest way of what in the received texts, even that of Merkel, is mere nonsense.

The passage is one in which the poet addresses the god Terminus ; and, as both Merkel and Paley give it, runs—

'Et seu vomeribus, seu tu pulsabere rastris,
Clamato, suns est hic ager, ille tuus.'

while others have, '*Meus est hic ager, ille suus.*'

Now *meus* and *suus* are clearly wrong, because with *meus* Terminus would be claiming the land as his own ; while *suus* would mean that the land belongs to itself, that is, if the phrase has any meaning at all, that the land is without an owner. Common sense requires '*tuus est hic ager, ille tuus,*' the god addressing first one person, and then another. Strangely enough, '*tuus est hic ager*' is the reading of nearly all the MSS.; and thus the substitute of *meus* or *suus* in place of *tuus* is, on the score of authority and on the score of meaning alike, utterly indefensible.

In the compounds *aliqui- aliquot* &c. the notion of 'some' or 'any' prevails; but this is a meaning that constantly connects itself with words of numerical origin, as for instance in our own *an-y*, Germ. *ein-ig*, Lat. *ullo-* already quoted, and this with reason; for a diminutive of 'one' still leaves the idea of 'some.'

But our own term *oth-er* is itself only a comparatival form of *one*, standing for *on-er*. I was first led to this view by the recollection that our language, while it shares with the Greek and the Norse a strong love for the asperate *th*, also habitually interchanges this letter with an *n*. Thus the θ of μεγ-εθ-ος, αυξ-αθ-ειν, corresponds to the ν of τεμ-εν-ος, *mag-n-us*, *pig-n-us*, λαμβ-αν-ειν, *sper-n-ere*; the θ of παθ-ος to the ν of πεν-ομαι;[1] and of course if θ be convertible with ν, *a fortiori* with νθ: so that the forms ιδρυνθην, αμπνυνθην, from ιδρυω, αναπνεω, and πενθ-ος, βενθ-ος, by the side of παθος, βαθος, have nothing in them that is very strange.

In Anglo-Saxon again, the plural of the indicative present ends in *as*, but that of the subjunctive present has *on* or *an*, and the past tenses also prefer *on*. Similarly a Norse nom. *ann-ar* (= *alter*) forms a fem. ac. *asra*, a dat. s. *öðru*, a dat. pl. *öðrum*, &c.; and a nom. *mas-r* 'man' stands by a gen. *mann-s*.

But it is not only in the Norse that our 'other' is represented by two forms, one with a liquid, *annar*,

---

[1] L. and S. deny the connexion of these two words, holding that παθ-ος belongs to πασχω. But why may not all three be of one stock ?

the other with an asperate, *œra* or *ö̆ru*, &c. In the provincial utterance of Lincolnshire the original *n* has been preserved. Thus a friend from that part of the country supplies me with the following phrases, which may be heard, he says, any day :—

'Was it A. or B. who told you?' Ans. '*I don't know which, but it was toner.*'

(Speaking of two pigs.) '*Toner a mun* (I must) *sell, but which on 'em a hardlins know.*'

'*It was toner* (= either) *Mrs. P. that I met, or toner* (else) *Mrs. O.*'

Let me add, what it is not beneath the dignity of philology to record, that a youngster, F. S., aged two, seeing one day on the dinner-table a second pudding to his delight, exclaimed in my hearing, '*Oh, 'nunner pooin!*' while his elder brother, H. S., at the same age had given a preference to another intelligible variety, '*nudder.* It may further be noted that the theory which finds in the *ali* of *aliqui-*, &c. an equivalent of 'an' or 'one,' has its proof in the Norse form *ein-hver*, which Grimm himself (D. G. iii. 38) translates by the very word *aliquis*; and of course the Sw. *en-hvar* and Dan. *en-hver*, though now signifying 'quisque,' are the same word. The neuter form of the pronouns, *ett-hvart, et-hvert*, prepares us for the German *et-was*, which again = *ali-quid.*

This brings me almost to the Greek ἕτερο-, which however stands apart from all its congeners, as having an asperate. But this very peculiarity furnishes the strongest confirmation of the present theory, for among the various forms of the first numeral the Greek ἑν stands alone in this particular. I thus at any rate escape from the difficulty which Grimm meets by simply cutting the knot, telling us that ἕτερος had originally in all probability no asperate (iii. 636). That the asperate in these two words very possibly superseded a digamma I readily admit, seeing that the archaic Latin *oeno-*, the Lith. *wiena-*, and our own *one* virtually begin with this sound. It should also be noticed that both ἕτερο- and ἑν- agree in a common vowel, and that the interchange of a dental liquid and a dental tenuis is of the most ordinary occurrence. One result of this derivation is that ερο- alone, not τερο-, constitutes the comparatival suffix; but this is what I gladly accept.[1] If my explanation of ἕτερο- be correct, the leading sense of the word is 'one of the two,' which in our Greek lexicons is given indeed, but is commonly relegated to the last place. To test this little matter I run my eye over our best lexicon, and find that in twenty-three adjectives compounded with ἕτερο- the word 'one' is essential to their translation: ἑτερ-αλκεσ-, -αχθεσ-, -ήμερο-, -βαρεσ-, -γλαυκο-, -γναθο-, -ζηλο-, -θαλεσ-, -θηετο-, -ελινεσ-, -κωφο-, -μαλλο-, -μασχαλο-, -μερεσ-, -μολιο-, -πλοο-, -πορπο-, -ρροπο-, -σκιο-, -οστομο-, -ουατ- one-eared, -φαεσ-, -οφθαλμο- one-eyed; and I might add ἑτερο-ποδ- 'one-footed,' ἑτερο-σκελεσ- 'one-legged,' for a person who has an imperfect leg or foot may well be so called. Of course in all these adjectives the notion expressed, viz. 'one,' is 'one of two.'

The Latin *iterum* seems to claim a place among the words which have been under discussion, and this claim is perhaps confirmed by the form of the German *wieder*. At any rate those who would derive *iterum* from the pronoun *i-* 'this' (Dr. Donaldson for one),

---

[1] See the eleventh of these papers.

have overlooked the fact that the signification of the words repudiates the theory. A derivative from such a pronoun would signify 'hither, citerior.' The logical connexion of *iterum* with ἕτερος, Sansk. *itara*, is satisfactory, as well as that of form. Still a doubt hangs over the question when we find, devoid of all comparatival suffix, the Old Germ. *ita* 'again,' the Anglo-Sax. prefix *ed-* 'again,' the Welsh prefix *ad-*, and the *ad-* of like power in the Latin *ad-mone-* 're-mind,' *a-gnosc-* 're-cognise,' as well as the English *a-cknowledge* and archaic *a-cknow*, for here we come across representatives of the Greek ἀνα. The Danish *atter* and Swedish *åter* are simply corruptions of an older *achter*, a variety of our *after*.

I conclude this part of the subject by collecting, chiefly from the D. G., the various forms that represent the Latin *altero-* :—Sanskrit *antara-* and *itara-*, Old Prus. *antar-s*, Lith. *antra-s*, Lett. *ohtr-s*, Old Slav. *utoryi*, Greek ἕτερο-, Latin *altero-*, Goth. *anþar*, Old Fris. *other*, Old Sax. *other*, *oðar*, *odar*, Ang.-Sax. *oðer*, Saterl. *ar*, *or*, Eng. *other*, Old Germ. *andar*, Mod. Germ. *ander*, Dutch *ander*, Norse *annar*, Swed. *annan*, Danish *anden*.

But the form *tother* must not be passed over. When it means 'the other' it is not difficult to account for the passage of *th* into a mere *t*, as such change is only in harmony with the law in Greek, which writes θρίξ and τρίχος, but not θρίχος. This *tother* (also *poper* in Old English, as quoted above) is exactly one with the Greek θάτερον for τὸ ἅτερον. But for the most part the form *tother* (Scot. *tither*) has an article preceding it; and then the *t* is due to what Mr. Whitley Stokes calls Provection, having been transferred from the end of the preceding word, just as in *for the nonce*, in place of *for then once*. In other words, *the tother* would be more correctly divided *thet other*, precisely as *the tone* should give way to *thet one*. In fact, in the older writers *tother* is rarely found, I believe, except with a prefixed 'the.' In this form, for example, Jamieson gives one quotation from P. Plowman, two from R. Brunne, and four from Scotch authorities. I have noted fourteen occurrences of the phrases *that oon*, *that othur*, one or both together, in the metrical parts of the Canterbury Tales. Thus in the Knightes Tale, v. 477:—

> 'Of whiche two Arcita higte that oon,
> And he that othur highte Palamon.'

And, again, the Life of St. Edmund the Confessor (Trans. Philolog. Soc. 1858) has in v. 477:—

> 'Nis pat on lipor younj: pej heo ne lore pat oper also.'

In Greek too το θατερον probably originated in τοῦ ἀτερον, the θ before the asperated vowel representing the final dental of the original pronoun. I feel the more entitled to defend the division τοῦ ἀτερον,[1] because Greek MSS., like Latin MSS. in similar cases, write such words as the article in immediate connexion with their nouns; the division, which is seen in our printed books, being due to editors alone.

I here assume that *thet* or *that* is an older form than *the*, and so discard the common doctrine that we have in the final *t* of *that* a neuter suffix. Indeed

---

[1] So Bopp (§ 155): 'Aus dem Zeugniss der verwandten Sprachen erkennt man dass τό ursprünglich τοr oder τοῦ gelautet habe.' (See also note 13 to § 349.)

such a theory is inconsistent with the fact that the pronoun *that* (like *what*) is capable of being used in connexion with words which are distinctly not neuters, e.g. *that man, that woman*. The original form I believe to be rather *then*,[1] or *than*, the *n* having subsequently passed, as it so often does, into a *t*. Thus in *then-ce, when-ce*, &c., or, as they were once written, *thenn-es, whenn-es*, the *es* is a genitival suffix signifying 'from,' precisely as in τοθ-εν, for so I divide the word, just as I wrote τοθ-ατερον above. The idea of any neuter suffix is, I think, to be rejected, among other reasons, because suffixes to imply negation are in themselves improbable; and again in *ut-ero-*, 'which of the two,' ποτ-ερο-, the root-syllable has a claim to the dental. The ν of αγαθον and *m* of *bonum*, as I have elsewhere explained, are no exceptions to the general law which rejects suffixes of mere negation.

With this preface I next proceed to the adverbial forms which signify 'or,' taking first those of the Teutonic family, as exhibited by Grimm (D. G. iii. 274, § c). But here I would suggest a caution against a prevalent error, that of attaching too much weight to antique as compared with later forms. A safer course is to give a preference to fuller forms over shorter, so long as one is sure that the greater length is not due to the addition of a new element. Thus while the Gothic *dippdu*, Old Germ. *edo, eddo, erdo, odo*, &c., and Ang.-Sax. *oððe*, Norse *eða*, and Latin *aut* exhibit no final *r*, we are justified in regarding, as so far purer forms, the Modern Germ. *oder*, and the Swed. and Dan. *eller*. The greater fulness alone is an argument in favour of

---

[1] See my paper on Pronouns of the third person.

this view, but the question is at once decided by the necessity for a comparatival suffix in order to express the required idea. Similarly when we compare the varieties *edo, eddo, erdo,* we are bound to give a preference to the last; and of the Middle Germ. varieties *ode, oder, alde, alder,* while *oder* and *alde* have each their own superiority over *ode,* the highest claim belongs to *alder,* which differs but slightly from the Modern Germ. adjective *ander.* That *aut* is an abbreviation of *alter* (Fr. *autre*), seems to be commonly admitted; nor need we be surprised at the abbreviation, when we find such abundant evidence of the gradual absorption of the comparatival suffix in general in all the Teutonic branches (D. G. iii. 589—596), whenever the irregularity, so-called, of the formation prevents any resulting confusion with the positive. Grimm indeed seems to limit this truncation to the adverbial comparatives, but our old English writers extend it to adjectives. Thus Shakspere (Othello, iv. 3) talks of '*mo* women,' '*mo* men,' and Chaucer abounds in such phrases as (C. T. 9,293) 'Bet is quod he a pyke than a pikerell;' and we still use *less* in place of *lesser*.¹ So the Latin, besides *aut,* exhibits an abbreviated comparative in the first part of *ma-velle, ma'lle,* which corresponds to our Ang-Sax. *má,* and in *sat* for *satis.* The Keltic family takes the same liberty in its irregular comparatives, as for example the Breton in *mâd* 'good,' *gwelloch* or rather *gwell* '·better ;' *drouk* 'bad,' *gwasoch*

---

¹ In the old language other instances are found, as *leng* in place of the fuller *lenger* (for *longer*); for example in St. Edmund the Confessor (published in the Society's volume for 1858), v. 366: 'per hit gan dæsche adoun: hit nolde no leng abide;' and again, v. 510; 'He answerede him þe leng þe wors.

or rather *gwas* 'worse.' So too in Welsh the corresponding forms are *gwell* and *gwaeth* rather than *gwellach* and *gwaethach*, and in this language indeed there are some twelve other comparatives that have undergone the like curtailment.[1] The etymology of the Gothic *þiþþáu*, which Grimm places at the head of the series of words representing 'or,' had been the subject of a previous discussion in p. 60 of the same volume, but the writer with good reason seems to attach no great value to his own solution of the problem. The view taken in the present paper of course requires that the numeral 'one' shall constitute the first element, and accordingly it agrees closely with the Gothic form of this numeral, *áin*, making allowance for the passage from the dental *n* to the dental *th*, which we have already seen in this word. The final *áu* of *þiþþáu* corresponds no doubt to the final vowel of the old German *eddo*: and, as this appears to have lost an *r* belonging to the comparatival suffix, so the Gothic may be presumed, like οὕτω for οὕτως, to have lost an *s*, which in that dialect represents the German *r*; and *ás* is the very form which Grimm assigns to the comparative of Gothic adverbs (D. G. iii. 585, and with two examples 596 B. i.).

Our own particle *or*, as proved by its German equivalent *oder*, has suffered the same compression as *gaf-fer* for *grandfather*, as *gam-mer* for *grandmother*, as *where* (= *quo*) from *whither*, as *where* in Somersetshire for *whether*, as Scotch *smure* for *smother*, as the Danish *far-broder* (i.e. 'patruus,' or

---

[1] See also Grimm, D. G.

father's brother). But better evidence cannot be found than that which the Old Frisian forms offer, where the ordinary adjective *other*, besides the fuller forms, has a gen. *or-a*, a dat. *or-em*, an acc. *or-ne* (Richthofen's Altfriesisches Wörterbuch, v. *other*), and again *or-half*, as well as *other-half*, corresponding to the German *anderthalb* '1½.' The word *eith-er*, so much used as the correlative of *or*, one is tempted at first to regard as a mere variety of *other*, especially as the first syllable *eith* coincides, as nearly as is to be desired, with the German *ein* 'one.' But the German *entweder*, which in use corresponds to our particle *either*, is no doubt, as Grimm suggests, deduced from *ein-weder*, the *n* of which, in my view, has thrown out an excrescent *t*.[1] If so, we have what is nearly an equivalent of the Latin *alter-uter*, the sole difference being that, while the Latin attaches a suffix of comparison to both elements, the German with a wise frugality is satisfied with the presence of a single suffix of this nature. Care however should be taken not to confound the English *either* which corresponds to the Latin *alteruter* with that other *either* of our language which had the power of *uterque*, and in Anglo-Saxon was written *æghvader* (Grimm's D. G. iii. 55, § c.), or in shorter form *ægder*. From Modern English this latter form has disappeared; and the German *jeder* which represents it has given up its legitimate sense *uterque* for the more general *quisque*. An early example of our *either* = 'both' occurs in the Life of St. Kenelm, as published by the Philological Society (v. 355):—

'For rijt as heo þe vara radde : out berste aiþere hire eje.'

---

[1] See the Tenth of these Papers.

The forms *an* and *ne* remain. Already Grimm claims *an* as a word which belongs to the class of *alter*, influenced no doubt by the forms of the Germ. *ander* and Norse *annar*. But if this be right, and for one I have no doubt about it, the process probably was this: starting from a form *anner*, out of which *alter* grew, first the *r* was lost, in accordance with the law which governs irregular comparatives, which gave *anne*, a form actually in use in interrogative clauses to denote 'or;' and then this *anne* by the loss of its tail became *an*, and by decapitation *ne*, whereas the received doctrine has been that *anne* is compounded of *an* and *ne*. The only awkwardness in these results is that we are making *aut*, *an*, and *ne* the same word, whereas in use they must not be altogether confounded. Neither *an* nor *ne* can ever be allowed to act as substitutes for *aut*, nor the reverse. On the other hand, though *an* and *ne* may at times be interchanged, there are idioms in which this licence would not be admitted. This theory, by which *an* and *ne* are regarded as corruptions of a fuller *anne*, has its parallel in the theory (see above) which deduces both *que* and *et* from a fuller *quet*.

I feel that what I have here written will scarcely find acceptance with one class of philologers,—I mean those purists who expect roots and the derivatives from roots to take one and one only form, whereas in truth no language is so strictly homogeneous. Practically one finds every language surrounded by a cluster of what are called dialects, out of which the written language has borrowed no small number of elements. Thus our own language exhibits root-words sometimes in a triple variety, as *bag*, *bay*, and *bow*,—words in origin all one, yet in use far from interchangeable, for it would require an interpreter if one came across such a statement as: 'He put a few clothes into his carpet *bay*, made a *bag* to his friends, and started for a voyage across the *Bow* of Biscay.' It is matter for less wonder then, if, starting from a twofold numeral, *an* (*a*) and *one*, we find a variety in the root-syllable of its derivatives, as *any*, *other* (*or*), *else* (A.S. *ell-es*), *eleven*, (*el-leven*), *either*; while the German has *ein-ig*, *and-er*, *od-er*, *et-was*, *ei-lf*; and the Old Norse goes so far as in the same noun to give us a nom. sing. *ann-ar* and a dat. pl. *öth-r-um*.

Still I find myself supported by the authority of Bopp as more than once expressed, as § 19, vol. i. p. 33: 'Die Spaltung *einer* Form in verschiedene mit grösserem oder geringerem Unterschied in der Bedeutung, ist in der Sprachgeschichte nichts Seltenes;' and again in § 516, vol. ii. p. 389: 'Hierbei hätte man zu berücksichtigen, dass in der Sprachgeschichte der Fall nicht selten vorkommt, dass eine und dieselbe Form sich im Laufe der Zeit in verschiedene zerspaltet, und dann die verschiedenen Formen vom Geist der Sprache zu verschiedenen Zwecken benutzt werden.'

IX.

ON PLURAL FORMS IN LATIN WITH A SINGULAR MEANING, AND ESPECIALLY ON VIRGIL'S USE OF *menta*.

ONE of the most serious hindrances to a right understanding of the Latin vocabulary is the doctrine, often propounded, that the poets by some strange licence might use a plural for a singular. But, whenever such an assertion is made, the only safe conclusion is, that the true meaning of the singular has been misunderstood. *Castra* occupies a prominent place among such words, but it is not an easy matter to decide what was that meaning of *castrum* which justifies the translation of *castra* as 'a camp.' Tradition supplies no evidence to guide us, and so we are driven to etymology. Now *castrum* in its final letters agrees closely with *rastrum, rostrum, claustrum, plaustrum;* and there can be no doubt that of these the first three are derivatives from the verbs *rad-ere, rod-ere, claudere*. *Plaustrum* as to form stands in the same relation to *plaudere*, but the connexion of meaning is somewhat obscure. Perhaps the explanation is this. We know that the old roads of Italy were narrow; and hence it was important that a large and heavy vehicle should so far as practicable give early evidence of its approach. Thus in the present day when a carriage of any kind enters a long lane, too narrow for the passage of another vehicle in the opposite direction, it is found a useful practice on entering the lane to blow a horn; and thus it becomes a sort of law of the road, that the giving such a signal carries with it for the time a right to the sole use of the passage. Again, especially at night time, it is found expedient for a waggon to be provided with a set of bells. Now a clapper or two boards incessantly striking against each other is a cheaper way of effecting the same object; and *plaustrum* ought etymologically to signify 'a clapper.' It is true that even then the clapper is not the waggon. Still the sound of the clapper would be good evidence of the approach of the waggon, and thus there is no wide jump from the one idea to the other. The *vallum* or palisade of a rampart, for example, is only part of the rampart, which includes the mound and the ditch; but, to an advancing army, the *vallum* from its superior height was the first object seen, and so at last came to signify the whole of the rampart.

If then we apply the preceding evidence to *castrum* we are brought to a syllable *cad* as the root; and here we come across what are too commonly regarded as independent words, *cadere* and *caedere*; but these are in fact as closely allied as our *rise* and *raise*, our *lie* and *lay*, or, what is nearer to the purpose, our *fall* and *fell*. In fact, *fal*, the root-syllable of these two English verbs, is the analogue of the Latin *cad*, for a Latin c has often supplanted a labial; and indeed the corresponding πετ of πιπτω has preserved the original consonant; but a classical p under Rask's law should be represented in our language by an *f*. Other examples of a Greek π, a Latin k (q), and an English *f* corresponding to one another, are seen in τισυρες, *quattuor* (Go. *fiduor*), Eng. *four*, and doubly so in πιμπτος, *quin(c)tus*, with the proper name *Quinctius*, *fifth*. Again, a *d* in Latin, Greek, and even English, is often interchangeable with an *l*. Thus to take what in form is precisely parallel, the familiar noun *calamitas* was written, we are told, by Pompey, as *kadamitas*. I have said that this word thus quoted in illustration is identical in form. I may go further, for it is also of the same stock, as *calamitas* speaks of a something supposed to issue from the stars, a blight falling upon a crop.

Nay, the change from *cad* to *fal* is also to be traced in Greek and Latin in this very root, for σφαλλειν and *fallere* mean strictly 'to cause to fall, to trip up:' hence ·the frequency of the combination *fallere pedes*. And again, in our own language, although the orthodox course is to make *fall* an intransitive verb, in country life 'to *fall* a tree' is at least as common as 'to *fell* a tree.'

My belief then is that in military language, and among the Romans military language was familiar to everyone, *castra* meant generally 'trenching tools,' the ordinary axe, and besides these the pickaxe, spade, &c. This view is confirmed by the fact that the verb *castrare* 'to cut,' has not merely the notion of *emasculare*, like our own verb as applied to horses, but is applicable in the general sense of the verb cutting, and so is used in connexion with such accusatives as *arundineta, uites, arbusta, caudas catulorum*.

One advantage that results from this theory is that the phrases *mouere castra* and *ponere castra* receive an intelligible explanation, whereas with the translation *castra* 'a camp,' we are reduced to an absurdity, for even the trees of an abattis, after serving the purposes of one camp, are never carried on to the next station to perform the same duty. The tools, however, form an important part of a soldier's plant; so to say; and when an army arrived at the close of a day's march, they would be the first things to be taken from the *impedimenta*. Yet after all there is a gap in the theory; for although trenching tools are essential to the making of a camp, and although the phrases *mouere castra* and *ponere castra* already obtain in this way thoroughly satisfactory translations, yet there is a wide difference between the tools employed and the resulting camp. This gap I propose to bridge over by the suggestion that the *castrorum metator*, in laying out the proposed form of a camp, marked the outline by having the tools themselves deposited as he went along where they would presently be needed. On the completion of this duty, the figure would be duly represented to the eye by the series of tools.

But the use of a plural form to denote a singular idea is so inconvenient, that when the use of the word in the singular with its original meaning has passed away, there is an irresistible tendency to call the singular again into service with the new meaning hitherto limited to the plural. Hence *castrum* 'a fort,' at last established itself, and still more the diminutival *castellum* 'a little fort.' It should be noted, however, that in the connexions *castrum Inui* (Verg. Æn. vi. 766), *castrum Mineruae* (Apulorum) of the Itineraries, and *castrum Mineruae* (Brutiorum) of Varro (ap. Probum ad Verg. Ecl. 6), the word is of a totally different origin and meaning. We have now a noun belonging to the same family with the so-called adjective but rather participle *castus* 'pure,' and the sb. *castu-* 'purifying.' These evidently point to a verb, and the verb really exists in *cārēre* (*lanam*) 'to card wool,' that is, 'purify' it, for Varro is no doubt right when he explains the term (L. L. vii. 92, p. 339, Spengel's ed.) by *purgare*, and connects it with *cārēre*. In Greek the root is represented in the adjectives καθ-αρο- and κεν-ο-. In this view *castrum* is 'a place of purification,' 'a shrine,' and so identical in power with *delubrum* from *lau-ere*. Again this second *castrum* has also its derived verb *castrare* 'to purify,' whence *castrare uina saccis* 'to strain' wine, of Pliny, and perhaps *castrare libellos* of Martial (i. 36). In the latter passage there may possibly be a *double entendre*.

Nay, that *plaustrum* itself did not in origin mean 'a waggon' is shown by its use as a plural in not a few passages, where evidently a single waggon was before the writer's mind, as: *Modo longa coruscat Sarraco ueniente abies atque altera pinum plaustra uehunt* (Juv. iii. 256); *Ipse uides onerata ferox ut ducat Iazyx per medias Histri plaustra bubulcus aquas* (Ov. Pont. iv. 7, 9); *Tardus in occasum sequitur sua plaustra Bootes* (Germ. Arat. 139). In other passages the notion of a single waggon seems, if not decided, yet preferable, as in: *Tardaque Eleusiniae matris uoluentia plaustra* (Virg. Georg. i. 163); *Dicitur et plaustris uexisse poemata Thespis qui canerent agerentque* (Hor. Ep. ii. 3, 275); *Ruris opes paruae, pecus et stridentia plaustra* (Ov. Tris. iii. 10, 59). Thus *plaustra* itself belongs to the class of words here under consideration. Yet already in Plautus, Cato, and Cicero the singular *plaustrum* was in use with the meaning of a single waggon.

Another word in which the true meaning of the singular is commonly missed is *furca*. This word is in fact a compression of a trisyllabic *for-ic-a*, the first syllable of which is seen in the verb *for-a-re*, and virtually in *fod-ere*, for the *r* and *d* are interchangeable in these words, just as in *auri-* sb. 'the ear,' and *audi-* vb. 'hear.' Our own language also shares the interchange, for the root, in obedience to Rask's law, appears with a *b* in *bore* and *bod-* of *bodkin*, whether we use this noun with Shakspere in the sense of 'a dagger,' or in reference to the little instrument which belongs to a lady's workbox. Then as regards the meaning of *furca*, there can be little doubt that we should translate it 'a prong,' seeing that *bi-furco-* and *tri-furco-* mean 'two-pronged' and 'three-pronged.' It was at first then only as a plural that it could be employed to denote 'a fork.' Some of our dictionaries indeed venture to give as the original meaning of *furca* 'a two-pronged fork,' quoting in proof Virgil's *furcasque bicornes*, which however rather points the other way; for if the noun already denoted a two-pronged instrument, the epithet *bicornes* would be superfluous. However, the phrases *Furcae* and *Furculae Caudinae* for the fork in the road near Caudium were established at a time when it was still necessary to use a plural to denote 'a fork.' So Plautus (Persa, *ad fin*.) has, 'et post dabis (manus) sub *furcis*,' where later writers would have said *sub furca*. It is true that in the Casina (ii. 6, 37) we find, 'ut quidem tu hodie canem et furcam feras;

but here we may well suspect that the poet wrote *furcas*, and that the singular was an adaptation to later usage introduced in after-time. Such changes may be proved to have taken place in the text of both Plautus and Terence, just as has happened to the plays of Shakspere.

The nouns *forceps*, *forpex*, and *forfex* have suffered much in the hands of our modern lexicographers, who have followed the guidance of the author of the book entitled 'Varronianus.' The writer of that work thought he saw in the first part of these words the adverb *foris*, and he was disposed to deduce the final syllable from the several verbs *cap-io*, *pect-o*, and *fac-io*. But in truth the three forms are only dialectic varieties of the same word. From *forc-* of *furc-a* it was thought desirable to form a derivative by the addition of the diminutival suffix *ec*. I say diminutival, because Pott has clearly shown that the suffix *ax* of Greek substantives adds the notion of little; while the identity of the Greek *ax* and Lat. *ec* is proved by the forms *murex*, *sorex*, *pellex*, *podex*, corresponding to μυαξ, ὑραξ, παλλαξ, πυνδαξ. But the power of the suffix is also sufficiently determined by the three words *cimex*, *pulex*, *culex*. Now in the case of *furca*, the addition of a suffix *ec* would have led to an unpleasing form, *forc-ec-*, and hence, to soften the sound, a labial was substituted for one of the offensive gutturals; and so arose the three varieties, *forc-ep-*, *forp-ec-*, *forf-ec-*. But as *forcep-*, standing for *forcec-*, could only mean 'a small prong,' it required a plural to denote the more complex instrument consisting of two claws. Thus *forcipes*, as 'a pair of pinchers' for the extraction of teeth, is used by Lucilius: *uncis forcipibus dentes euellere* (ap. Charis. i. 74); but the later writer Celsus in the same sense habitually uses the singular. The word is also used as a plural for the 'blacksmith's pinchers' in Cato; but here again both Virgil (Geo. iv. 175, and Æn. xii. 404) and Ovid (Met. xii. 277) have *tenaci forcipe ferrum* or *ferrum forcipe curua*. It was from the consideration of this special use of the pinchers that some etymologists would derive the word from the adj. *formus* 'hot' and *cap-ere*. But the connexion with *furca* is confirmed by the fact that while Pliny (ix. 31, 51) ascribes to the crab *brachia dentioulatis forcipibus* (al. *forficibus*), Apuleius (Apol. p. 297, 4) speaks of the *furcae cancrorum*.

The plural *uolsellae* is used of a pair of tweezers by Varro in the proverbial phrase, 'pugnant uolsellis non gladio:' and also by Martial; but for Celsus the singular has supplanted the plural, so that the word follows the example of *forceps*, and is used in the same sense.

Again the familiar noun *rastro-* (*m.* or *n.*) I may safely assume to have meant originally 'a single tooth of a rake,' or 'a scraper with but a single point or edge.' Hence Terence, Virgil, and Ovid agree in the need of a plural to express the more complicated rake with many teeth. Still, as these were permanently combined in one instrument, it was found in the end convenient to use the word in the singular, and as such it occurs in the later writers, Pliny and Seneca.

Another example is *bigae*, which is of course a contraction of *biiugae*, and so being an adjective requires a noun *equae* to complete the meaning, 'two mares yoked together for the purpose of drawing a chariot;' and in this form it is employed by Varro, Catullus, and Virgil; but again the unity of the combination becoming fixed, eventually later writers, Tacitus Pliny Suetonius and Statius, exhibit *biga* as a singular. Precisely the same fate attended the use of *quadrigae*, 'four mares yoked together for drawing a carriage,' for the word is a plural in Cicero and Virgil, but is exchanged for a singular *quadriga* in Propertius Pliny Martial and Ulpian. If it be here objected, that Virgil and Propertius being contemporary might have been expected to use both of them either the singular or the plural, a legitimate answer seems to be found in the consideration, that the higher style of Virgil's poetry would justify, if not require, the use of the older form.

An eighth example is *cassi-*, the plural of which denotes 'a net,' in Virgil (speaking of a spider's web) and Ovid generally; but the singular with the same meaning is found in Ovid (A. A. iii. 554) and Seneca. Hence it seems reasonable to suppose that the singular word originally meant 'a single mesh of a net.' At the same time it must be admitted that many little nets are at times united to form one large net.

Ninthly, *folles* as a plural, like our own equivalent in form and meaning *bellows*, is the only shape known to Cicero Virgil and Horace, and this agrees with the fact that the instrument consists of two flaps; but Livy (xxxviii. 7) Persius and Juvenal have in the same sense the mere singular.

As *litera* originally meant but a single character of the alphabet, a plural was necessary to denote 'words or writings;' yet Ovid and Martial have the word in the singular with the sense of a letter or epistle.

It was once the fashion in school books to say that

limina was used poetically for the singular, meaning 'a threshold.' This error however has long been thrust aside, as it is known that a door has two *limina*, the *l. superius* or 'lintel,' the *l. inferius* or 'threshold,' the word signifying what carpenters call 'a tie,' and being derived, not indeed from *liga-re*, which would have given *ligamen*, but from a lost *lig-ĕre* which has also produced a noun *lictor* (not *ligator*). Still in not a few instances the singular is used to denote a gate or entrance.

Currus is another word as to which our lexicons are unsatisfactory. It is clear that in not a few passages the plural of this noun is used in speaking of a single carriage, as in Virgil (Æn. x. 574), 'Effunduntque ducem rapiuntque ad litora currus;' and Ovid (Met. ii. 6), of the chariot of the sun: 'Vasti quoque rector Olympi non regat hos currus.' Again the same poet (Trist. iii. 8, 1) has: 'Nunc ego Triptolemi cuperem conscendere currus.' So in Lucan (vii. 570): 'Mauors agitans si uerbere saeuo Palladia stimulet turbatos aegide currus.' Further, that *currus* did not in itself mean a carriage, is shown by Virgil's use of the word in speaking of the plough (Georg. i. 174): 'Stiuaque, quae currus a tergo torqueat imos.' Now the phrase *regere currus* has a special fitness, if *currus* means strictly 'a wheel,' for it is the wheel which a driver has to look to. Further, it is probable that mere rollers came into use before carriages. Moreover, the word *roll* is but a variety of *whirl* and *hurl;* and the last word in Scotch is a synonym for wheel in the term *hurl-barrow* (Jamieson). Nay in Scotch *hurler* by itself means 'one who drives a wheelbarrow;' and the simple verb *hurl* is applicable alike to the driving a wheelbarrow and to a ride in a carriage (Ib. supplement). For the latter use I quote from the same; 'If a frien' hire a chaise and give me a hurl, am I to pay the hire? I never heard of sic extortion.' Even when *hurl* has the sense of the Latin *torquere* (hastam), we have the notion of the circular movement which with the sling and Roman *jaculum* preceded the casting forward; but *cur* of *curro* is the equivalent of the *hur* or *hir* of our *hurry*, *hurl*, and the Dorsetshire *hir-n* (A. S. *yrn-an*). Hence I do not hesitate to claim for the Latin *curro* the original notion of revolving rather than that of running. Such will well suit the repeated phrase in Catullus (64, 327, &c.): 'Currite ducentes subtegmina, currite fusi;' and Virgil's similar use of the verb (Ecl. iv. 46): 'Talia saecla suis dixerunt Currite fusis . . . Parcae.' So also in those passages which speak of the potter's wheel, as Horace's (Ep. ii. 3, 22): 'Currente rota cur urceus exit?' No doubt the mere notion of running or quick forward movement is far more common; but it is most unphilosophical to decide the question of priority by mere number. Nay, it is generally to be suspected that the older the meaning of a word the fewer should be the examples. From all this I conclude that mere circular movement was first denoted by the root, and secondly that the onward circular movement as of a rolling stone was the idea which preceded that of simple running; so that we have here a mimetic word, an imitation of the sound heard in rapid *whirling*.

The word *septentriones* at the outset could only have been used as a plural; and such was still the form in favour with Cicero and Caesar; but Virgil

Ovid Pliny and Vitruvius have the singular; and this variety was only the more requisite, when names were required alike for the *Ursa major* and *Ursa minor*, where Vitruvius employs the terms *major* and *minor septentrio*. It seems indeed a somewhat violent proceeding for Virgil to have retained the singular form, when by *tmesis*, as it is called, he gives an independent position to the numeral in *Talis Hyperboreo septem subiecta trioni Gens* (G. iii. 381). As to the etymology of the word, two different accounts are recorded by Festus. That which would deduce it ' a septem bobus iunctis quos triones a terra rustici appellant,' has little internal evidence to support it. I cannot but give a preference to his second statement, ' Quidam a septem stellis,' for *tara* is the Sanskrit for a star, and indeed is still preserved in several of the vernacular languages of India. For the Latin I would assume a form *ter-iones* with that masculine diminutival suffix *ion*, which is well known in *matell-ion-*, *senec-ion-*. An *e* rather than an *a* is supported by the familiar *stella*, i.e. *ster-ula*, or rather *ster-el-a*.

I have thus dealt with *castra, plaustra, furcae, forcipes, forpices, forfices, uolsellae, bigae, quadrigae, casses, folles, literae, limina, currus, septentriones;* and these examples are sufficient to establish the principle that, when an object consists of two or more like parts, a word, in itself denoting one of these parts, is first employed as a plural to denote the compound, but eventually is supplanted by the singular, which then also denotes the compound.

With this premised, I call attention to the use of a plural *menta* in the Æneid: *Nosco crines incanaque menta Regis Romani primám qui legibus urbem fundabit*, &c. (Æn. vi. 810). Now the ordinary meaning of *mentum*, 'a chin,' will not avail here, for we need not stop at the English phrase 'a double chin.' My own conviction is that the first meaning of *mentum* is 'a jaw,' and thus the plural *menta* would denote 'both the jaws,' that is 'the mouth,' or rather in the present passage those parts on which the beard grows, both above and below the opening expressed by the word mouth.

How readily words of the same stock are employed to denote 'the jaw,' whether upper or lower, the mouth made up of both jaws, the chin, the beard, the cheeks, the gums, is well seen in those which begin with the syllable γεν or *gen*. Thus in Greek we have (1) γενυ- sb. f. to which our lexicons assign the meaning of 'under-jaw,' and in the pl. 'both jaws, the mouth with the teeth;' (2) γενειον 'strictly the upper jaw, but usually the part covered by the beard, the chin, and later the jaw, the cheek;' (3) γενειαδ- sb. f. 'a beard,' and in pl. the 'cheeks;' (4) γναθο-. (= γαν-αθο-) sb. f. 'the jaw, mouth;' but strictly the 'lower jaw;' (5) γναθμο- sb. m. 'the jaw;' (6) Lat. *gena-* 'cheek;' (7) *dens genuinus* 'a cheek-tooth or double tooth;' (8) *gingiva* 'the gums;' (9) Welsh *gên* 'mouth, jaw, and chin;' (10) Fr. *gan-ache* 'lower jaw.' Next, with the changes of consonant to be expected, (11) Sanskrit *hanu*, 'the jaw;' (12) Gothic *kinnu*, 'chin;' (13) Old Germ. *kinni;* (14) Eng. *chin;* (15) Lith. *zanda-s* 'jaw;' and then, with a labial in place of the *n*, (16) Germ. *gaumen* and Eng. *gums*, together with (17) Sanskr. *jamba* 'the chin;' (18) γαμφηλαι 'jaws of lion,' &c. 'beak of bird.'

But, as has long been pointed out, especially by Buttmann in his Lexilogus when treating of μέλας and κελαινος, a guttural often slips into a labial, probably by a passage first into *gu* or *gw*, then into *w*, and then into *m*. We must therefore connect with the preceding family of words (19) the Latin *mentum*, (20) the French *menton* of the like meaning, and also (21) Germ. *mund*, (22) English *mouth*, (23) the Gr. μυστακ- sb. m. 'upper lip or moustache,' as also (24) μασταϰ-, sb. f. 'mouth, beak, upper lip.' And this with the more confidence when we find (25) a Welsh *mant* 'a mandible,' whence *is-fant* 'lower jaw,' and *gor-fant* 'upper jaw.'

But it behoves the philologer never to be satisfied until he come to a verb as that from which the other parts of speech are deduced. Now the one among the many meanings attached to γενυς, *mentum*, &c. which most readily connects itself with action is 'the jaw,' as the instrument of mastication; and the Latin verbs *mand-ere* and *mand-uca-re* at once present themselves with the desired meaning and a suitable form, for as the Latin *scāla* stands to the verb *scand-ere*, precisely so *māla* to *mand-ere*. Indeed the combination *nd* and *l* are frequently convertible, and the Latin seems generally to have a predilection for the liquid *l*. Thus the verb *mŏl-ere* 'to grind,' has long been held to be of the same stock with *mand-ere*. Many too of the allied languages exhibit the form with an *l*, as Greek μυλη and Latin *mola* 'mill,' with pl. μυλαι as 'the grinders,' or to use the Latin phrase the *dentes molares*. So we have Lith. verbs, *mal-u*, *mal-in-u* and *mald-in-u*, Russ. *melju*, Irish *meil-im*, Goth. *mal-an*, Germ. *mahlen*. (See Bopp's Glossarium Sanscritum, v. *mrid*.)

But Buttmann in his Lexilogus (§ 48, on ουλαι, p. 198) justly observes that stamping or pounding was a process older than grinding, and so he finds the earlier sense in the Latin sb. *mall-eo-* m., and the Latin verb *mulca-re*. To these we must add the Sanskrit *mridā* or *mardā* 'dust,' the Gothic *malma* 'sand,' and *mulda* 'dust,' as also our own *mould*, whether applied to earth well broken up or to brown sugar, and the German *malm-en*, *zermalm-en* 'to crush.'

The Greek verb μαλ-ασσ-ω too is said to have signified originally to beat and so make soft, as in dressing leather, or, we might add, in making a beef-steak tender.

The same scholar treats the Greek verb αλ-ω and the nouns ουλαι and αλευρον as of the same stock. And if this be just, we must add to the family the nouns ουλα n. pl. 'gums,' and ολμο- m. 'a mortar, kneading-trough, the hollow of a double tooth,' &c. The doctrine that crushing preceded grinding is confirmed by what we see in the familiar verb *mord-e-* 'bite,' of the Latin compared with the Sansk. *mrid* or *mard*, which is translated '*conter-ere*.' Hence too we see that the Latin *mort-ario-* n. has been justly claimed as belonging to the family. Further, the Prakrit has *mal* in the place of the Sanskrit *mard*.

Hence *mordere* and *molere* are of the same stock; while as to form, we have a precise parallel to the connexion between *ardere* and *alere*, for the notion of elevation is the original idea in both these words, as also in the adjective *arduus* (see p. 173); and if *ardere* happens to be limited to the action of flame, so also *alere flammam* is a familiar combination. But I am here reminded of a doctrine which I put forward some thirteen years ago as to the etymology of the verb *obsolesco*. To the arguments I then adduced I have now to add other evidence, and as the matter is of some importance I will put together all that I have to say upon the subject.

Those who would connect the verb with *abolere* and *exolescere* fail to explain the appearance of the *s*, for *obs* in place of *ob* can only be defended when the simple verb begins with a thin consonant, *p, c*, or *t*, a principle which extends to the two other prepositions which end in *b, ab* and *sub*. Accordingly, I at one time was tempted to connect the root of *obsolesco* with the *sol* of *solium*, 'a seat,' *consulere* (old form *consol-* or *cosol-*) 'to sit together (in deliberation),' so that *obsolesco* should contain in itself the same metaphor as our verb 'supersede.' But I have now no doubt that the idea of dirt belongs to *obsolesco*, and that it is of the same stock with *sordes*. I am led to this conclusion, first, by the habitual union of the two words, as 'Ut eum, cuius opera ipse multos annos esset in sordibus, paulo tamen obsoletius uestitum uideret' (Cic. Verr. ii. 1, 58); 'Splendetque (uirtus), per sese semper neque alienis umquam sordibus obsolescit' (Cic. Sest. 60); 'In homine turpissimo obsolefiebant dignitatis insignia' (Cic. Phil. ii. 105); then in Hor. (Epod. xvii. 46), 'O nec paternis obsoleta sordibus;' and (Od. ii. 10, 5), 'Obsoleti sordibus tecti;' and in Val. M. (iii. 5, 1), 'Candida toga turpitudinis maculis obsoleta.'

In two of the passages just given, the notion of defilement is supported by the appearance of the adjective *turpis*, or the abstract noun derived from it;

and these had no doubt for their physical and original sense that of dirt, whence the idea of moral pollution readily flows. But the word *obsoletus* did not need the aid of *sordibus* for the expression of this idea, for we find *uestis obsoleta* in Liv. xxvii. 34; *uestitus obsoletior* in Cic. in Rull. ii. 5; *obsoletus Thessalonicam uenisti* in Cic. in Pis. 36; and *uestitus obsoletus* in Pseudo-Nep. Ages. 8. Again, the word is opposed to *enituit* in the younger Pliny (Pan. iv.); and in one of the tragedies which bear the name of Seneca (Agam. 976), there occurs the marked phrase *sanguine obsoletus*.

But the matter seems placed beyond all doubt when we come across a verb *obsordesco*, uniting in itself the same two distinct though connected meanings which belong to *obsolesco*, 'to pass out of use,' and 'to become dirty on the surface;' and this on the authority both of an old and of a late writer, so as to prove the great length of life which *obsordesco* enjoyed, viz. 'Obsórduit iam haec in me aerumna miseria' (Caecil. ap. Non. vii. 603, who himself translates the word by *obsolescere*), and 'Ne coma fusa umeris fumo obsordescat amaro' (Prud. Apoth. 214).

Of course the common result of non-use is the collection of dust, rust, mildew, mould, and all those undesirable objects, which the Romans included under their term *situs*, a word which etymologically ought only to mean 'putting down and leaving alone,' as it of course comes from the verb *sinere*.

Several of our modern languages exhibit the same root with the same meaning, as with ourselves in *soil* the verb, *soil* the sb., especially in the form *night-soil*, also in *sullage*, *s(o)lush*, *sully*; but in the last we have a word of French origin, representing *souiller*, by the side of which exists the adj. *sale*. Perhaps after all we come back to the obsolete verb *sol-ĕre* (to sit down), whence *consolere*, for the natural place for sitting in the earliest states of society is the ground, *solum*; and this also is the leading source of what we call dirt. Even the notion of *solēre* 'to be wont,' results from that of permanence, which resides in the posture of sitting, as opposed to locomotion. Hence indeed *suesco* and *consuetudo* are probably akin to *sol* in the sense of 'sit' (cf. the Germ. *sitte*); and we have a parallel in the Latin *mos moris*, which is of the same stock with *mora* 'delay,' and so with the Greek μοση and the verbs μι-μ(ε)ν-ω and *maneo*, as also with our own *manner* and Fr. *manoir*, &c.

But to return to the word *mentum*, I find a little difficulty in three words, which by meaning and partly by form seem to claim connexion with the family of *mol* or *mal* 'crush, grind,' &c. viz. : μασα-ομαι 'chew,' μασσ-ω 'knead' (with its derivatives μαξω, μαγμα), and *maxilla* 'the jaw.' Thus while *mala* serves beyond all dispute to connect *mand-ere* on the one side with *maxilla* on the other; *maxilla* and μασσ-ω imply a form μαγ rather than μαλ. Yet λ and γ seem to be sounds utterly inconvertible, unless indeed we may say that the *y* sound forms an intermediate link between them. Such was my contention in a late paper read before the Philological Society, which compared θυγατ-ερ- and *filia-*; and the argument derives strength from the parallelism seen in the Greek μογις and μολις.

At any rate, the Latin nouns, which having a long vowel before an *l*, form diminutives in *xillo* (or *sillo*), seem to owe the long vowel of the simple noun and the *x* of the diminutive to an original guttural in the syllable which precedes the *l*. Thus *āla* for *ahala*, *paulo-* for *pauculo-*, *tālo-* beside ἀστραγαλο-, *pālo-* beside *pango*, and *tēla* beside *tex-ere*, seem all to claim a lost guttural, which would account for the forms *axilla*, *pauxillum*, *taxillus*, *paxillus*. The loss of the guttural would be exactly parallel to what we see in our own words, *nail, hail, rail, sail, wain* (*waggon*), *rain*, beside the German *nagel, hagel, regel, segel, wagen, regen*; and indeed the Latin *vēlum*, whence *vexillum*, may have grown out of an older *suegelum*, and so be one with the German *segel*. See also the remarks on the Greek noun παρασειον 'upper sail,' in the paper on the German prefix *ver*.

X.

EXCRESCENT CONSONANTS.

ALTHOUGH generally averse to the introduction of new grammatical terms, I have thought it desirable to ask admission for one on the present occasion, because the ordinary term 'epenthesis' seems to have been formed upon a false theory, and so to have misled, as it appears to me, not a few philologers; and among these several who hold a place in the front rank. I especially refer to the three German scholars, Grimm Bopp and Diez. Thus the words 'einschiebung,' 'eingeschoben,' 'einschaltung,' are with them in constant requisition; and in my mind this assumption of an 'inshoving' always raises a presumption that some error lies concealed beneath them. For example, in speaking of certain diminutives (iii. 668), Grimm has to deal with a syllable *in*, which, not seen in the nominative, appears in the oblique cases, and so he is led to regard the *n* as intrusive, viz. in *prentili* 'a small brand,' g. *prentilin-es*, d. *prentilin-e*, &c.; where however it seems more reasonable to suppose that the nom. has lost an *n*, as is admittedly the case with the Latin *ordo ordin-is, ratio ration-is, caro carn-is*. The same doctrine is repeated by him twice in p. 672 and again in p. 678.

In my paper entitled 'Quaeritur' (see below), I refer to Bopp's dealings with the Sanskrit genitives plural, *dsvd-n-ám, trt-n-dm, sánd-n-dm*, the *n* of which he regards as euphonic, while it appears to me to be the genitival suffix, as in our own *Frier-n Barnet*, contrasted with *Abbot's Langley* and *King's Langley*, as also in *Buck-en-ham* (Norfolk), and, what is substantially the same, the county town *Buck-ing-ham*, which originally was nothing more than 'Mr. *Buck's* home or house,' for the largest town had its beginning, and this often in the residence of a single family. Again in Weinhold's Alemannische Gr. (Berlin, 1863), I find (§§ 409, 411) that the nouns *fater, Karl, Heinrich* had two forms of the genitive, *fateres fateren, Karles Karlen, Heinriches Heinrichen*, &c. Besides, if the *n* of *dsvd-n-dm* &c. be not a genitival suffix, there is nothing whatever to represent the idea of genitivity (excuse the word), since *am*, like the corresponding *ων* of Greek nouns, is a mere symbol of plurality.

Diez too (Gr. ii. 201) assigns to the old French perfect of *dire* a form *déimes* (= *diximus*) or 'mit eingeschobeuem *s, déismes.*' But in my paper on the Latin perfect (Philolog. Trans. 1860-1, p. 185), I was led to a very different view, viz. that *deismes* is the more genuine form, seeing that the Latin *diximus* itself grew out of a fuller *dix-ismus*, corresponding to *dix-istis*.

Again it was probably an impression that a consonant was required to prevent hiatus which led the French to sanction the division *aime-t-il*, as though the *t* were a foreign element; but of course we have here what represents the Latin *amat ille*. In *il est* the *t* is silent; but in the inverted form *est-il?* coming before a vowel, it is pronounced; and the same applies to *aimet-il*, as it should have been written.

Those who would insert consonants 'hiatus vitandi caussa,' never stop to explain to us why one consonant rather than another is selected for this ignoble office. But in truth it may be doubted whether any real instance can be found, unless we are to accept such as '*Maria Ranne*' or 'the *Law ran the Prophets*' of London speech. At any rate in a large majority of the instances usually adduced it will be found that the so-called epenthetic consonant is no foreign matter, but either an original part of the word, or else a simple outgrowth from the consonant immediately preceding.

In a paper by Mr. Weymouth (Philolog. Trans. 1856, p. 21), and in Bindseil's valuable, even though unfinished work, 'Abhandlungen zur Allgem. verg. Sprachlehre' (Hamburg, 1838), the true theory, as it seems to me, is given as regards the difference in the position of the organs of speech for the production on the one hand of the nasals m, n, ng, and on the other of the mutes b, d, g. As those writers point out, it depends solely on the position of the *velum palati* whether the one set of sounds or the other is heard. When the *velum* is so placed as to leave a free passage for the air through the nose, we have the nasal; but the moment this passage is closed, the sound passes at once to the allied mute; so that what began as an m may end as b, what began as ng may end as g (*goose, bag*), what began as n may end as d. Such secondary consonants then must be regarded as natural outgrowths, or, to use my new term, as excrescent, rather than intrusive, as intrinsic, not extrinsic.

But it is not with the nasals alone that there is this tendency to pass from one consonant to another. Whenever the organs of speech which are employed

EXCRESCENT CONSONANTS. 207

in the production of two consonants lie near one another, a passage from one to the other is apt to occur. But it is especially from the dental series that excrescent consonants proceed; and this was perhaps to be expected, as this class of consonants occupy a middle place, and so have an affinity for the labials on the one side, and gutturals on the other. Precisely as, when we throw great force into the sound of an *n* at the close of a syllable,—for instance, to take a vulgar example, but not the less valuable on that account, in pronouncing the words *gown* or *drown-ed*,—there is a strong tendency to produce what would be written as *gownd* or *drownd-ed*; so if we lay a stress upon an *s* there naturally results a following *t*, and hence a Roman intending to say *pos* found that he unintentionally uttered *post*.

I propose then to take into successive consideration all the following combinations, in which for convenience the alphabetical order is preferred: *ct, ft, ht (cht), lt, nt, pt, rt, st; bd, gd, ld, nd, rd;* λθ, σθ, ρθ, σθ, φθ, χθ; *cs, gs, ns; lz, rz; pf; mb, mp, ng, rn.* In treating these combinations I must be brief; but throughout my view is that the second of the two consonants is excrescent.

1. Ct: *plecto*, cf. πλεκ-ω, *plico, simplex; nect-o*, cf. *necesse, necessarius*, &c., αναγκη; *flect-o; pect-o;* γαλα for γαλακ, but gen. γαλακτ-ος, with Lat. *lac*, also *lacte* as a nom., g. *lact-is;* cf. Ang.-Sax. *meol-oc* and our *milk;* ιητ-ερος, with *iec-ur* and ηπ-αρ; κτειν-ω, with καιν-ω, εκανον, κεκονα; κταομαι κεκτημαι beside παομαι πεπαμαι, for the consonants κ and π are here interchanged as in κοτερος, ποτερος, &c.; νυκτ-ος, *noct-is* compared with νυχα, νυχιος (see p. 69).

The Latin nouns in *etum* had an older form in *ectum*, as shown clearly in the case of *uirectum, dumectum*, aft. *uiretum, dumetum*. In these, however, *um* alone, in my belief, is the suffix, so that *carect-um, frutect-um, salict-um*, &c. come from *car-ec-, frut-ec-, salic-* (n. *carex, frutex, salix*), throwing out at the same time an excrescent *t*.

Indeed generally this passage from a *c* to *ct* is apt to be followed by the loss of the guttural, so that the *c* seems itself to have been transformed to a *t*; but whenever the preceding vowel is found to be long, it would probably be safer to assume the existence of an intermediate form with *ct*. Thus *diutius* by the side of *diu* leads me to suspect that the base of the latter word was *diuc-*; and, indeed, I have elsewhere (Tr. Philolog. Soc. 1856, p. 320) given my reasons for believing that all nouns of the fourth declension once ended in *uc*, so that *genuc-ulum* is a regular diminutive from *genu(c-)*, and the adj. *metuc-ulosus* duly formed from *metu(c-)*. Hence I hold *diutius* to stand in place of *diuct-ius*, which exhibits an excrescent *t*.

Otium again, for this form (not *ocium*) has the exclusive support of inscriptions, I am strongly inclined to regard as a shortened form of an obsolete *oct-ium*, and this again as a decapitated variety of *uoct-ium*, from the root of the verb *uŏc-are* 'to be empty,' and the adj. *uoc-iuo-* 'empty,'—two words which, following the best authorities (Bergk, Zeitschrift f. Alterthums-W. 1848; Mommsen, Corp. Inscr. i. p. 70, b. *ad fin.* &c.), I am bound to write with an *o*, not an *a*. As regards meaning, such an etymology has all in its favour; and I cannot but prefer it to Prof. Aufrecht's suggestion (put forward, however, with much hesitation), that it may come from *auere* 'to be happy,' an idea substantially the same as Corssen's (Kritische Beiträge, p. 17), who would connect it with the Sanskrit root *av* of various meanings, 'iuuare, tueri, ualere, gaudere,' &c. out of which he seems to give a preference to 'tueri,' so that his *autium* would be directly opposed to *bellum*, peace to war.

The long *e* of *sētius* by the side of *sĕcus* and *sĕquius* also receives its due explanation, if it be considered as standing for *sectius* with an excrescent *t*. Much has been written on the origin of these words, as by Corssen (Beiträge, p. 5), Fleckeisen (Rhein. Mus. viii. 227), Schweizer (Kuhn's Zeitschrift, viii. 303). My own view is that we must start from a theoretic adj. *sequis* 'second' from the verb *sequi*. This word I find entering into the formation of *sesquis* 'one and a half,' Germ. *anderthalb*, which we cannot but treat as a compression of *semi-sequis*, when we place it by the side of *sestertius*, i.e. *semis-tertius* 'two and a half,' Germ. *drittehalb*. But the words *alter* and δεύτερος, the ordinary words signifying 'second,' are in form comparatives. Hence a neuter comparative *sequius* has nothing in it to offend; and *secus* itself I also hold to be a variety of the same word, having lost its *i*, precisely as *minor* and *minus* have (see p. 122). On the other hand, the meaning of 'other or otherwise' accords well with the uses of the words in question, as in the common phrase *haud secus*, and such passages as :—

'Ideo nihilo 'sse mihi uidentur sētius quam sómnia' (Plaut. Men. v. 7, 57);

'Quid sēquius aut quid interest dare te in manus ; . . ?' (Trin. 130);

P

where I readily accept the simple emendation of *sequiust* for *secutus est* of the MSS. A very different but I think not very satisfactory etymology of *setius* is given by Corssen (Beiträge, p. 11).

As to the derivation of *nitor nixus*, which Corssen deals with in the same work (p. 20), but I think not very happily, all is smooth, if, following the guidance of the old Latin grammarians themselves, we start from the sb. *genu-* 'a knee,' or rather from its older form *genuc-* as heard in the Greek γνυξ, the Latin *genuc-ulum*, afterwards *genic-ulum*, corresponding to our own *knuck-le*, Germ. *knock-el-n*, to say nothing of the Germ. *knicks* 'a courtesy.' Thus the original meaning of *niti* is 'to kneel,' and its secondary sense of 'straining' or 'striving' arises from the idea of employing the knee as a fulcrum in many muscular actions, as for instance in cording a trunk. The old form *gnitor*, given by the grammarians, and the participle *nixus*, together assure us that *nitor* has lost two gutturals, and must have been corrupted from a fuller *gnictor*, where we have almost the same form as in *genic-ulum*, and what strictly corresponds to the Germ. *knick-s*, excepting indeed as to the *t*, which I claim as an ordinary outgrowth. Forcellini for once seems to have gone wrong, and to have missed the original meaning of the verb *niti*, so that it may be worth while to give evidence on the subject, which frotunately is easy to find. Thus Festus has, '*Nixi* di appellantur tria signa in Capitolio ante cellam Mineruae *genibus nixa*.' So we have in Plautus (Rud. iii. 3, 33), 'Ambae te obsecramus *genibus nixae;*' in Virgil (xii. 303), 'Impressoque *genu nitens* terrae;' in Livy (xxvi. 9), 'Matronae *nixae genibus* orantesque;'

in Ovid (Her. xxi. 100), 'Et de qua pariens arbore *nixa* deast;' in Seneca (Thyest. 60), 'Quem *genu nixae* tremuere gentes;' Germ. (Arat. 67), 'Dextro namque *genu nixus* diuersaque tendens Bracchia.' And if this be not enough we have the fact that the constellation called by the Greeks Ἐνγόνασιν has for its Roman name indifferently *Ingeniculus* and a simple *Nixus*. Thus Cicero (Arat. 373) has, 'Flexo confidens corpore *Nixus*,' and again (N. D. ii. 42), '*Engonasin* uocitant *gembus* quia *nixa* feratur;' while Ovid (Met. viii. 182) writes, 'Qui medius *nixique genu* est anguemque tenentis;' and Manilius (v. 645), '*Nixa genu* species et Graio nomine dicta *Engonasi ingenicla* inuenis sub imagine constana.'

In closing this long section on the combination *ct*, I deem it but right to add that Corssen asserts that an original *o* never disappears before a *t*, while he admits that when a *c* has superseded an earlier *g*, as in *autor autumnus* from *augeo*, it is not so protected; but a doctrine in itself so arbitrary has found little support with other scholars.

2. Ft: see paper on *post* and *after* (p. 121). To the examples there given add *tuft* by Fr. *touffe*, Scotch *tuff*: *-schaft*, the suffix of German nouns, freund-*schaft*, fiend-*schaft*, contrasted with our friend-*ship*, &c.; *laught*-er from *laugh*.

3. Ht (cht, ght): Ang.-Sax. *liht*, Germ. *licht*, our *light*, compared with Lat. *luc*-; so *miht, macht, might* with the Ang.-Sax. verb *mag-an*; *niht, nacht, night* (see *noct-* above); Germ. *specht* by the side of Lat. *pico-* and our wood-*pecker*; *acht-en* and *veracht-en*, the analogues of ὀπτ-εσθαι ὑπερ-οπτ-εσθαι; *fechten*, *fight*, compared with *pug* of the Latin *pugnus*

pugna pugil and πυξ; *gelacht-er* by the side of *lach-en lache;* and the whole classes of German adjectives in *ig* and *icht*, as *beinig* and *beinicht*.

4. Lt: βελτ-ιον βελτ-ιστο-, compared with *bello-*, *mel-ior*, and our *well; alt-er* by the side of *alio- ali-qui-;* and *ult-ra, ult-ro, ult-erior, ult-imo-*, as contrasted with *sup-ra, por-ro, sup-erior, min-imo-*; but forms connected with comparatives and superlatives will be discussed more fully in the following paper. Add *salt* with Lat. *sal;* Germ. *falte* compared with *pal* of the Latin *palma, palam, pl-ic-a*, &c.

5. Nt: as βεντ-ιστο- by *bono-* and *bene;* λεοντ-ος by *leon-is;* S. *ant-ara* 'one of two' by Norse *ann-ar*, our *one*, Sc. *ane*, and the so-called article *an;* Lat. *int-ra, int-ro, int-erior, int-imo-, int-er, int-us*, from *in; cont-ra, cont-ro*, from *con*, but see following paper; Germ. *ent-zwei, ent-gegen*, where *ent* stands for the prep. *ein* or rather *en* = Lat. *in; ent-weder* 'either,' formerly *ein-weder*, where *ent* stands for the numeral *ein* 'one;' *ent* the prefix, Lith. *ant*, the analogue of the Greek ανα; the Germ. *eigent-lich, nament-lich, bescheident-lich*, &c.; Fr. *loint-ain*, from *loin*, cf. *prochain*, from *proche;* Lat. *tegument-um, cognomentum*, &c. from *tegumen, cognomen*, &c. The *t* also of imperfect particles I hold to be an outgrowth from the preceding *n*, so that in the crude form *scribent-i- scriben* is an old substantive like the Lat. *unguen* (whence *unguent-um*), and still more like the German so-called infinitive *schreiben*, while the final *i* is probably a remnant of the preposition, or rather in this case the postposition, *in*. We ourselves, by the way, once wrote *i* for *in*, as in the Shakaperian phrase, 'By the second hour i' the morn' (*Antony and Cleopatra*, iv.

7, 4). In this way the Latin participle will be brought into agreement with the Keltic forms, as the Welsh *yn myned* 'iens,' more literally 'in itione,' and with our old phrase *a-going* for *an going*, of precisely the same power. To these I add from Mr. Weymouth's paper *tyrant.* by τυρ-αννο-, and *ancient;* the latter in both its senses, as an adj. = Fr. *ancien*, and as a sb. = our *ensign*.

6. Pt: πτολεμο-, πτολι-, πτυελο-, πτερνα-, compared with πολεμο-, πολι-, πυελο-, περνα-, and Lat. *perna-*; πτυ-ω compared with Lat. *spu-o*, Eng. *spit;* τυπτ-ω, ῥιπτ-ω, θαπτ-ω, ὑπτ-ιος, Lat. *subt-us, subt-er;* but as to these see next paper.

7. Rt: *heart* by Lat. *cor*, and καρ; *uespert-ino-* from *uesper-;* *fert-ili-* from *fer-;* *mort-i-* from *mor-* 'die,' as well as *sort-i-, part-i-, art-i-* (but see next paper); Germ. *juchert* or *juchart*, representing Lat. *iuger-*. In such words as *braggart*, I have long been inclined to think that the *t* is excrescent, and that the syllable *ar* is a diminutival suffix, one with the *er* of *fresh-er* 'a little frog,' and of *hamm-er, dagg-er, fing-er*, and the Germ. *mess-er*. The Latin in the same way was in the habit of forming contemptuous terms for men, by means of a diminutival suffix, as *toc-ulion-*, and the Greek too, as πλουτ-ακ-, φεν-ακ-, λαλ-αγ-. If such explanation be just, it must apply also to such words as *slugg-ard, cow-ard*, &c.

8. St: *crast-ino-* from *cras;* *prist-ino-* from *pris*, i.e. *prius;* *rust-ico-* from *rus;* *Ligust-ico-* from *Ligus;* *Libyst-ico-, Libyst-ino-*, and *Libyst-id*, from *Libys;* οστ-εον by the side of *os ossis;* *ost-ium* from *os oris*. Here let me add that the Greek στοματ- is but a decapitated οστ-ομ-ατ-, and so of the same stock with the

Latin *os oris*. In ον-ομ-ατ- the Greek has preserved the root-vowel *o*, which is lost in the Latin *nomen* and Germ. *namen*. Again an excrescent *t* is seen in the Latin *post*, as also in *post-ero-*, *post-umo-*, in *extero-*, *ext-erior-*, *ext-umo-*, *ext-ra-*, *magist-ero-*, *minist-ero-*, *dext-ero-*, *sinist-ero-*, *dext-imo*, &c. (see the next paper); in *ust-ula* from *ur-* (*us-*) 'burn ;' and probably in *agrest-i-*, *caelest-i-*, *terrest-ri*, *siluest-ri-*, *domest-ico-*, *modest-o-*, for in these words I am inclined to believe we have derivatives from lost words with a neuter suffix in *es*. Thus *modesto-* and the verb *modera-ri* seem to point to a noun *modus moderis* as once co-existing with the noun *modus modi*, just as *glomus -eris* stood by the side of *globus-i*, and so led to the formation of *glomerare*. Precisely in the same way Pott (E. F. i. 235, note, ed. 1859) contends, with reason, that μενοεισής, which is commonly derived from the neuter noun μένος, implies a form μένος of the second declension; and he treats in the same way εἰδοποιός and τειχοποιός. So too one must, I think, assume a masculine αἷμο-ς to explain such forms as αἱμοβαφής and αἱμο-ω, rather than, as is usually done, refer them to the neuter αἷματ-.

Add to the preceding list first *arbust-um* from *arbos*. The common doctrine that this is an abbreviation from *arboretum* is clearly an error, for *arboretum* itself is for *arbor-ect-um*, and so contains the diminutival suffix *eo*, of which there is no trace in *arbust-um*. It is under the same wrong view that some hold *frutectum* to stand for *fruticetum*, *salictum* for *salicetum*. Such a doctrine would lead us into an endless series; for if *salictum* is for *salicetum*, then, as *salicetum* must have grown out of a form *salicectum*, we must again assume a fuller *salic-icetum*, and then a *salic-icectum*, and so *ad infinitum*.

The names of female agents, *tonstrix, defenstrix, persuastrix*, and the noun *tonstrina*, come from masculine nouns in *or, tonsor, defensor*, and *persuasor*, though the last is no longer to be found. The disappearance of the long *o* of *tonsor -ōris* might have been a difficulty, had we not the undoubted case of *doctr-ina* from *doctor*. Our *sister*, Germ. *schwest-er*, has the same suffix, *er*, as *pater, mater, frater*, and that probably a diminutival suffix of affection; while *or* has obtained a preference in *sor-or* (for *sos-or*) and *ux-or*, solely through the influence of the vowel in the preceding syllable, *o* and *u*. The pronoun *ist-o-* I would divide so as to leave *o* alone to the suffix, as in *ill-o-* and *e-o-* (*eum, eam*, &c.); but my reasons I must reserve for a more convenient occasion, as the argument would run to a great length. *Vest-i-* comes from a root *uen* or *ues*, as seen better in the Greek Ϝεσ-νυμι, ημφι-Ϝεσ-μαι; but *i* alone belongs to the suffix, as also in *part-i-*, where it is a corruption of *ic*, as seen in *part-ic-ula-*.

Cust-od- I also claim as one belonging to this class, giving to it for its original meaning 'door-keeper.' The first syllable I believe to be an earlier and truer form of *os* (*oris*), except that, like *ost-ium*, it has thrown out a *t*. The disappearance of the initial guttural is what is already familiar in *ubi, unde, uter*, from *cubi, cunde, cuter*. The second element *ŏd* I compare with the corresponding part of θυρ-ωρ-ο- πυλ-ωρ-ο-, which Buttmann deduces from ὁρα-ω, and I think with reason, so as to make them signify 'door-watcher, or door-warden.' But a ρ is at times represented by a Latin *d*, as in *caduceo-* by the side of the Doric καρυκειο-. Even ὁρα-ω itself is of the same stock with the Latin *uide-o*, as proved by its aorist Γειδον, Γιδειν. Nay, I must also claim as one with the root of ὁραω, and so with that of ειδον, *uideo*, our own *ware*, *wary*, and with an excrescent *d*, *ward*, *ward-en*, and the French *guard-er*, &c. together with our own *regard* 'look back.' The etymology of *custod-* here proposed corresponds to that of *aedi-tumus* or *aedituus*, from *tu-eor*, or, as I am inclined to assume, an older *tum-eor*.

In French we have also instances that belong to this class, in *estre*, now *être*, by the side of the Ital. *essere*, in *naitre* for *nascere*, &c.; as well as in the old French perfect *distrent*, by the side of *disrent*, now *dirent*. Possibly we owe to this principle the personal ending of our verbs, as *lovest*, where an *s* alone seems justified by the older branches of the Indo-European family. So in German we find *morast*, *palast*, *axt*, *einst* (see 'German for the English,' by Sonnenschein, &c.), as also *obst* supplanting an older *opaz*.

9. Bd : μολυβδ-ο-, which in this respect stands half-way between the Latin *plumbo-* and our own *lead*. The Latin *uerber-* I believe to be a compression of an older *uer-eb-er-*, and again the Greek ῥαβδο- to have come by decapitation from a form Fαρ-αβδ-ο,[1] so that the root-syllables are virtually the same, and the suffix which immediately follows it. 'Ροφ-ε-ω (for σορ-οφ-ε-ω) is of course one with the Latin *sorbeo* (for *sor-ob-eo*);

---

[1] Those who are alarmed at this theory of decapitation are invited to compare the Greek ῥαξ (ῥαγ-) with the Latin f(a)rag-um 'a (straw-) berry;' and indeed with our own *berry*, in which two weak vowels, ε ι, have superseded the strong vowels, α α.

but in Greek by the side of the compound ἀναρροφαω we find also ἀναρροιβδ-εω. 'Εβδομο- when contrasted with the Germ. *siebente* seems to have an excrescent δ. The Latin verb *ped-* might well appear in Greek as βελ- or βεν-; but we find βδιν-νυμι, βδελ-υσσω, and an adj. βδελ-υρο- (see Rd below). The Fr. *coude* was written in the sixteenth century as *coubde*, and so establishes its identity with the Latin *cubito-*.

10. Gd: μυγδα by the side of μυγα; and it seems likely that Γημητηρ passed through Γδημητηρ on its way to Δημητηρ.

11. Ld: here Diez (i. 194) supplies most of the following examples: Span. *valdré*; Prov. *foldre* (= old Fr. *fouldre*); *toldre* = *tollere*; Old Fr. *mouldre, resouldre, pouldre*, now *moudre, resoudre, poudre*. The Latin *corulus* passed first into *colurus* (r being supplanted by an *l*, and in the following syllable the converse); then *colurus* produced *couldre*, which is now *coudre*, a word which is therefore the genuine analogue of our *hazel*; Germ. *baldrian* = *valeriana*; Du. *helder* = Germ. *heller*. Add to these our own *ald-er* = Lat. *al-nus*, where the English *r* represents the Latin *n*, just as is the case with *order* (Fr. *ordre*) compared with *ordon-*. So our old *alder-first* and *aller-first* correspond to such German compounds as *aller-beste*. Lastly, αλδ of αλδ-αινω, αλδ-ησκω some scholars identify with the Latin *al-o*.

12. Nd: ανδ-ρος for ανερ-ος; ενδ-ον and ενδ-ος by the side of εν; in Latin *mand-are, pre-hend-ere*, both from *man* of *man-u* 'hand,' for the *m* and *h* in these words represent each other, much as in Greek do μεν (whether the particle or the root of μον-ος) and εν- (nom. εἰς); *tend-ere* by the side of *tene-re*; *in*, the

Lat. prep. leads to *ind-e* 'down' (see p. 70), and also appears with a *d* in *ind-igeo*, *indu-perator*, *endoter-cisus*, &c. The pronoun *is, ea, id* had for its base *in* (see p. 70), and hence *ind-e*, of which *e* alone belongs to the suffix with the notion 'from' (see the following paper); so, *ken* or *kun* being the base of the relative, we have *und-e* (orig. *cund-e*), 'whence.' The Latin gerund *scribend-um* I hold to be in its first part one with the form *scriben* already spoken of (p. 212) as equivalent to the Germ. *schreiben*. In the French language instances abound, as *cendre, tendre, Vendredi, viendrai, tiendrai, moindre, gendre*. So the Spanish has *pondré, tendré, vendré*; the German, *niemand, abend, and-er, mind-er, hund, Mailand* for Milan, &c.; English, *yond, beyond, mind, sound* (sb. and adj.), *thund-er, gand-er, kind*, as well as *kin* (= *gen* of *genus*), *compound*; while our *Henry* (*Henricus*) appears in Scotch as *Hendrick*; and conversely *bind, mind, find* appear without a *d* in the Dorsetshire *bīn, mīn, fīn*. The Latin words *cale-, palam* and *palma*, &c. *polle-* 'weigh,' *praepolle-* 'outweigh,' exhibit an *l* in the root-syllable, and an *l* is often interchanged with an *n*; but in Latin there is a tendency not to be satisfied with an *n*, but to add to it an excrescent *d*, the more so perhaps as the Latin is also fond of an interchange between *l* and *d*. Be this as it may, we find by the side of the words just mentioned *cando*, at least in compounds (*accend-o*, &c.) and derivatives as *candela, pando, pendo*, with *pondus*. Again, *m* and *n* being freely convertible, the Latin *gemere, tremere*, and an obsolete *abemere* 'to take down,' have led to the French *geindre* as well as *gémir, craindre* as well as *crémir*, and *aveindre*.

As regards the Latin verbs which end in *ngere*, it is

not altogether certain that the *n* is non-radical. Although the Latin *iugum, coniugium*, the German *joch*, and English *yoke* plead strongly in behalf of a mere guttural as ending the root-syllable, yet the Sanskrit gives us a form *yun-aj-mi* as the equivalent of the Latin *iungo*, which seems to imply that *yun* was one form of the root. This view seems to be confirmed by the fact that the French writes *joind-re* where the Latin has *iung-ere*; and similarly *astreind-re, feind-re, peind-re, ceind-re, oind-re*. As a *d* interchanges alike with *n* and *l*, it is no strange matter that we find the Latin *uad-ere* leading on the one hand to the French *all-er*, and on the other to the South Italian *an-are;* but here again the ordinary dialect prefers *and-are*.

13. Rd: an *r* and a *d* are often convertible, as is shown abundantly in Sanskrit and occasionally in Latin, for example, as was just observed, in *caduceo-* (m.) from the Doric καρυκειο- (n.), in *cust-ŏd-* (see above) compared with πυλ-ωρ-ο, &c. Hence we should be the less surprised at a *d* growing out of an *r*, as in *cor cord-is* and καρδ-ια by the side of κεαρ κηρ-; *ord-ior* by *or-ior*; Latin *mordeo-* by the side of *mol-* 'grind,' Lith. *mal-*; *burd-en* from *bear*; *murd-er* from a root—Lat. *mor-* and Sanskrit *mar* or *mri*; *gird* by the side of the Latin *giro-* (written commonly *gyro-*); French *tord-re* by the side of Latin *ter-* 'turn' and *torque-*; our *haggard*—German *hager*. The Latin verb *pēd-* may well have had *pĕd-* for its base, just as *scrīb-, dīc-, nūb-* are lengthened from the simpler forms *scrĭb-* (cf. *conscrīb-illo*, Catul. xxv. 10, and γραφ-), *dĭc-* (*mali-dĭco-*) *nŭb-* (*pronŭba, conŭbio-*, νεφελη); and then this *pĕd-* might have for its Greek analogue πεπ-, but we find πεδ-. Again, *l* and *r* being convertible we have

the equivalent forms *al-ere* and αιρειν (αρ-); but from *alere* come *ard-uus* and *ard-ere*. So also *obsordesc-* and *obsolesc-*. (See the following paper.)

14. Λθ: αλθ-ω, αλθ-ησω, αλθ-εσσω are said to be of the same stock with the Latin *al-o;* but should perhaps be connected with our *heal*. In either case the θ is excrescent.

15. Νθ: ανθ-εσ- from an old root αν- 'blow' (cf. α-η-μι), which the Sanskrit retains; ενθ-εν, of which the first εν alone belongs to the root, and the second εν alone to the suffix (see the following paper). As ν and θ are readily interchanged, for example, in ε-μαθ-ον compared with μεν-εσ-, με-μν-ημαι; in our *oth-er*, the compar. of *one*, in the Norse *ann-ar* and its pl. dat. *öth-rum;* in the Old English plurals *loveth* and *loven*, and the Old English adverbs *henn-en* and *heth-en*, I hold that the right way of explaining such forms as μανθανω by the side of εμαθον, βενθ-εσ- by that of βαθ-εσ-, τερεβινθο- by that of τρεμιθο-, is to consider that ν before the θ in μανθανω, &c. corresponds to the θ of εμαθον, &c.; and that the θ which follows the ν is excrescent. What I here say of νθ I say also, *mutatis mutandis*, of λαμβανω, περδω, &c. compared with ελαβον, *ped-o*, &c.

16. Ρθ: ορθ-ο- and ορθ-ρο- 'dawn' from ορ of ορω ορνυμι; δαρθ-ανω by the side of *dor-mio*, our *dr-eam* and *dr-ow-sy;* πορθ-μο- root πορ- as seen in πορ-ο-, πορ-ιζω, corresponding to our *fare;* αρθ-ρο- (n.) and αρθ-μο- form αρ- 'join;' σκαρθ-μο- from σκαρ- of σκαιρ-ω 'skip;' τερθ-ρο- (n.) 'an end' compared with τερ-ματ-; ενερθ-εν from ενερο-.

17. Σθ: εσθ-λο- = Doric εσ-λο-; Fεσθ-ητ = Latin *uest-i-* from a root εν or εσ; οπισθ-εν compared with

οπισ-ω; ευτοσθ-ι with ιττοι. Again, as θ and σ are convertible, τυπτομεθα has substituted a θ for the σ of the Doric τυπτομες, while τυπτομεσθα has preserved the σ, out of which a θ has grown. So ιθ-ματ- 'a road' and ισθ-μο- co-exist; μαθ-αλλιδ- 'a sort of cup' and μασθ-αλιδ-; εσθ-ιω by the side of es-se es-ca. The Greek σθεν-εσ- too is probably of the same stock with our *sin-ew*, as also with the Greek noun ιν- (nom. ις) of the same meaning, or rather Fιν-, for this noun and *uir-* of the Latin *uires* seem to owe their digamma to an old form σFιν-.

18. ΦΘ: the θ of φθεγγω, φθειρ, φθινω, φθανω, φθονος, as compared with πολις, πολεμος, can scarcely be other than excrescent. In the adj. ελευθερο- we virtually have ελεφθερο, which there can be little doubt is one with the Latin *libero-*, the *b* of which represents the φ of the Greek word as usual. Consequently the θ is excrescent. As for the ε of ελευθερο- it is not a mere euphonic vowel, as is commonly taught. On the contrary, *libero-* has lost what the Greek has retained. At the same time, both have suffered decapitation, *loebero-* (I prefer dealing with the older form) standing for *sol-oeb-ero-* or *sol-ūb-ero* (for *oe* and *ū* seem to have had the same sound, as they now have in Dutch). Thus we come to what is almost identical with *sol-ub-ili-*; and ελευθερο- may well have grown out of ιλευθερο-, the asperate having eventually disappeared in consequence of the neighbouring θ. The Latin *ub-er-* originally 'a stream,' as is shown by the *ubera mammarum* of Lucretius, as well as by the common phrase *ubertim lacrumare* and the use of *ubertas* for 'a flow of words,' is immediately related to the verbs *um-esco uu-esco*. Hence the genuineness

of the labial is established; and consequently a preference should be given in Greek to ουφαρ over αυθαρ, the latter having probably grown out of a fuller form ουφθαρ.

19. Χθ: διχθα τριχθα for διχα τριχα; αχθ-ομαι by αχ-ισ- and the Sanskrit *sah*. The *g* of the Latin vb. *rug-io*, as in *leones rugiunt*, should have for its Greek analogue a χ; and accordingly we have βρυχ-ω and βρυχ-αομαι; but we also find ροχθ-ο- 'roaring;' and again by the side of ορεγ-ω there stands ορεχθ-εω. In ιχθυ- and εχθ-ρο- the θ is probably excrescent.

20. Cs, Sc, Gs, Sg: the sibilant being often interchangeable with a guttural, we find that the guttural on the one hand often throws out a sibilant, and conversely a sibilant a guttural. Hence *cum* ξυν and συν; κοινος and ξυνος; μιγνυμι μισγω, *misceo*, *mis-tus*, and our *mix*; *augeo* and αυξανω with our *wax*; εκ and εξ in both Greek and Latin; ξηρος and σκιρρος; ιξος and *viscum*. Thus the second of the two consonants in the four combinations seems to be excrescent.

21. Ns: by the side of χην the German has *gans* and the Latin has *ans-er*, which, like our own *gand-er* and the German *gäns-er-ich*, was in strictness applicable only to the male bird, *er* being a male suffix, as in the German *kat-er* a 'tom-cat.' The prep. ανς for ευν has probably only an excrescent σ attached to the ordinary prep. εν.

22. Rz, Lz, Tz: as in German *herz*—*cor*; *kurz*—our *short*; *schmerz*—*smart*; *salz*—*salt*; *malz*—*malt*; *katze*—*cat*; *ratze*—*rat*; *hitze*—*heat*; *zu*—*to* and *too*; *zwei*—*two*.

23. Pf: in German, as *pfad*—*path*; *pfahl*—*pale*;

pfand — *pawn*, &c.; *apfel* — *apple*; *stöpfel* — *stopper*; *tropf-en* — to *drop*.

24. Mb: μεσημβρια for μεσημερια; μεμβλωκα for μεμολωκα; French *chambre* from *camera*-; *humble* from *humili*-; *nombre* from *numero*-; *combler* from *cumulare*; Spanish *nombre* from *nomine*; *hombre* from *homine*; *hembra* from *femina*. Again, as *n* and *m* interchange, we have in Greek ανδεν- — Latin *imbu*; Italian *and-are* with Latin *amb-ul-are*, and with German *wand-el-n* and *wand-er-n*; Greek γαστ-ερ-, Latin *uent-er-*, but English *womb*, Scotch *wemb*, the last used of the belly generally; English *loins*, German *lende*, but Latin *lumbi*. Add with a silent *b*, which however was probably once pronounced, our *lamb* = German *lamm*, our *thumb* — German *daum*.

25. Mp: Latin *templum* and *extemplo* with *extempulo* by the side of τεμενεσ-, all from a root τεμ- 'cut,' whence τεμν-ω; *temp-os-*, *temp-era-re*, &c. from the same root. Other familiar examples from Latin are *sumpsi*, *sumptus*, *ademptus*, *contempsi*, *hiemps*; while in English we have the equally familiar Thompson, Simpson, Hampton. To these add the English *hump* with a dim. *humm-ock*; *stump* by the side of the German *stumpf* and a dim. *stumm-el*. Again, as *m* and *n* interchange, we have Latin *tund-* — our *thump*; as *m* and the guttural *n* (*ng*) interchange, our *stamp* = *stingu-*, better known in *ex-stingu-* 'stamp out' (fire), *di-stingu-* 'stamp differently.' *M* seems to have a stronger affinity for *b* than for *p*. Thus if we find an excrescent *p* making its appearance in the middle of words, the preference given to it over a *b* seems in some measure due to the influence of a following *s* or *t*. At any rate, it is for the most part in such com-

pany that the *p* presents itself. At the end of words a *p* is the less strange, since medials in this position are habitually pronounced as tenues.

26. Ng: in the simple *strong, long*, the final is but a nasal *n*, but takes to itself a distinct guttural sound in *strong-er, strength, longer, length*.

27. Rn: if the *n* of the German *fern* 'far' had been a suffix, it would not have passed into the comp. *fern-er*. I am disposed then to regard the *n* of *stern* also as excrescent. In the cases of *mourn, burn* vb., *burn* sb., *turn*, it is of course clear that the *n* is no part of the root, seeing that we have the Latin *maere-*, *bur-* of *com-bur*, and *bustum*, our dim. *br-ook*, and *ter-* in Latin; but whether it be excrescent or the remnant of a suffix it is difficult to decide. In the case of the vb. *burn*, the German *brenn-en* and our own *brand* seem to be evidence that the *n* is referable to a suffix.

In putting together these examples I have omitted some classes of words which might well have been inserted, because the question involved some matters which required a full discussion. Many of these will appear in the next paper. On the other hand some apology may perhaps be thought due for inserting examples of processes so familiar as what is seen in ανδρος and μεσημβρια. The purpose was completeness.

XI.

ON FALSE DIVISION OF SUFFIXES.

THE number of suffixes in verbs, nouns, and particles has been unduly multiplied, as it seems to me, through various errors, which I propose to consider under several heads. First of all many of those which are supposed to be independent of each other are simply varieties of the same. Thus there is no substantial distinction between the neuter substantives of the Latin and Greek languages which take for their consonant an *s*, *r*, *n*, or *t* with various vowels, as τερ-ασ- τεραγ-ος, ονοματ- ονοματ-ος, σθεν-εσ- σθεν-ε-ος, ἡπ-αρ- ἡπατος, ὕδ-ωρ, ὕδατ-ος; *opes- -eris, frigos- -oris, uber- -eris, rob-ur- -oris, fulg-ur- -uris, ungu-en- -inis, nom-en- -inis.* Whether such a form as ονοματ- grew out of an older ονοματ-, itself deduced from an earlier ονομαν- by the outgrowth of a τ, is of little moment for the present question. The free interchange of the four consonants just enumerated appears partly from the words themselves, and is further confirmed by the appearance of ονομαινω by the side of ονοματ-, as also by such changes as appear in σωφρον- and σωφροσ-υνη, and the Latin pl. *femina* by the side of *femur*.

In the same manner there is no substantial difference in the liquid suffixes of the German *fess-el* (f.), *deg-en* (m.), and *mess-er* (n.), for these liquids are apt to interchange, so that we ourselves have as equivalents for two of them *fetter* and *dagger*.

A second cause through which the number of suffixes is unreasonably increased is the confusion by which a compound suffix is taken for a simple one. Thus in τεμ-εν-εσ-, *fac-in-os-*, and the oblique cases *it-in-er-is*, *iec-in-or-is*, two distinct suffixes have been united. The *en* or *in* of these words may have been due to a secondary verb, as seems probable in the case of the first, since the form τεμ'ν-ω is in common use. The same is possible in the case of *fac-in-os-*, for the Latin language also has many secondary verbs in *in*, as *sper'n-o*, *po(s)'n-o*, &c.; corresponding to our own *reck-on*, *op-en*, and the Greek μανθ-αν-ω, λαμβ-αν-ω. On the other hand, the nouns *ungu-en-*, *fem-en-*, *nomen-* also possess such a suffix. But this is a matter which may be left open. When the vowel before the *n* disappears, as in *uol-'n-es-* (from *uello*), *pig-'n-os-* (from *pango*), there is a still greater tendency to consider *nes* (*nos*) as a simple suffix. So also I believe that the *ion* of *opinion-*, &c. is one with the *ig-on* of *vertigon-*, *origon-*, and so the analogue as regards suffix of such German nouns as *ver-ein-ig-ung*, a word which might have been represented by a Latin *per-un-i-on*. Indeed the Latin actually possesses the simple *un-ion-* 'a little one,' sometimes applied to a single one in a necklace of pearls, sometimes to a single one in a rope of onions. Our own language too abounds in cases where a compound suffix is not seen to be a compound. Thus English grammars speak of *ling*, *lock*, *let*, *kin* as though they were simple, when in fact they are all shortened forms, standing severally for *el-ing*, *el-ock*, *el-et* or rather *el-ick*, and *ick-in*. That *el* is itself a suffix of diminution is abundantly proved by such substantives as *nozzle, speckle, thimble,* as well as the adjectives *litt-le, mick-le*; while *ing* alone is seen in *farth-ing* 'a little fourth,' *tith-ing, lord-ing*; *ock* or *ick* in *butt-ock, rudd-ock,* or *ridd-ick* (Jennings) 'a redbreast,' *fist-ock* 'a little fist,' as once used, *mamm-ock,* and no end of words in the Scotch dialect. I have purposely passed by *hillock* and *bullock,* because here an *l* might have been by some claimed for the suffix. The suffix *et* is seen in not a few words, as *cygn-et, sign-et, gimb-et, emm-et;* but this suffix is probably a corruption of an older *ock* or *ick.*

It is not however denied that nowadays *let* and *ling* are often added to a word *per saltum.*

Another fertile source of error lies in the habit of what Mr. Whitley Stokes calls 'Provection,' a word which may well take a place in the nomenclature of Philology. He applies this term to what occurs in such a phrase as *for the nonce,* where the *n* has been unduly transferred from the preceding word, the more correct form being *for then once* 'for this once.' Similarly *the tone, the tother* grew out of *that one, that other.* What is seen here in distinct words also applies to the prevalent error of treating ματ in Greek and *men* in Latin as simple suffixes, for ονοματ-, *nomen, tegumen,* and *tegumentum* should be divided ον-ομ-ατ- or ον-υμ-ατ-, g(o)n-om-en, *teg-um-en, teg-um-ent-um.* That ατ in the Greek noun and *en* in the Latin are in themselves suffixes is shown by the words already given, ηπ-ατ-ος and *ungu-en-.* On the other hand, *um* is sufficiently familiar in *bell-um,* &c. and virtually in the Greek εργ-ον, &c. Again, that μ does not belong to the suffix of αιματ- seems to be proved by its appearance in αἱμο-ω, which implies a sb. αἱμο- (m.). I have elsewhere (Philolog. Trans. 1856, p. 341) given some of my reasons for believing that the suffix *um* of Latin neuters had in origin a guttural rather than an *m*. In our own language the guttural asperate *ough* is often pronounced as a labial asperate, as *rough*, *cough*, &c. So in different parts of England we have at the present day the three terms *shock*, *shoof*, and *sheaf* applied to the same object. On this view there is nothing strange in the fact that *bellum*, *apium*, and *Ilium* should lead to adjectives *bellic-us*, *apiac-us*, *Iliac-us*; or that *apium* and *allium* should in German take the forms *eppich* and *lauch*, in English *leek*; and conversely that the Greek πυνδαϰ- and Latin *podec-*[1] should in English be represented by *bott-om* as well as *butt-ock*.

It is strange to find Madvig in his 'Bemerkungen' (Brunswick, 1844) putting forward the doctrine that an accusative case in Latin has no true suffix, the final *m* being, he says, a mere euphonic addition, while the ν of Greek accusatives he disposes of in the most summary manner by calling it ἐφελυστιϰόν. Thus he says, 'The accusative is only the theme "euphoniously modified."' In this way he accounts for the identity of such forms as nom. *lignum* and acc. *lignum*. My own conviction, as I have said, is that *bellum* has grown out of an older *bell-ogh*, which eventually passed also into *bello*, so as to enter the second declension.

---

[1] More strictly *fundo-*, but this I hold to stand for a fuller *fundoc-*. How readily a suffix *oc* may pass into a more *o* is seen in the Scotch *winnock* and our more corrupt *wind-ow*, *haddock* the fish, also called *haddow*. Indeed the suffix *ow* of our language, which to the ear is but an *o*, has perhaps always grown out of a guttural.

If what I have said be true, the adjective *bellio-us* was in origin a mere genitive, 'of war,' though in the end compelled to undergo inflection, precisely as happened to the genitive *cuius* of the relative, which at one time the Romans had the courage to decline as *cuius a um*.

I proceed to other cases of what I regard as Provection, in which the letter *t* plays a very important part, while *o* and *b* also occur; and in order to suggest a doubt as to the propriety of the division usually put forward, I place by the side of each suffix examples which exhibit no *t*, *c*, or *b*. Thus to *tion* of *lectio*, *aratio*, I oppose *ion* of *legio*; to *tat* of *bonitat-*, *at* of *sat-iat-* and *uolunt-at-*; to *tela* of *tutela*, *ela* of *querela*; to *itia* of *auaritia*, *ia* of *miseria*; to *itie* of *canitie-*, *ie* of *desidie-*; to *tudon* of *multitudon-*, *udon* of *hebetudon-*, and *edon* of *dulcedon-*; to *ti* of *morti-*, *i* of *torqui-*; to *tut*' of *seruitut-*, *iuuentut-*, *ut* of *salut-*; to *itio* of *seruitio-*, *io* of *remigio-*; to *tro* of *claustro-*, *aratro-*, *ro* of *fulc-ro-*; to *ta* of *nauita*, *a* of *incola*; to *tu* of *partu-*, *conuentu-*, *u* of *man-u-*, *ac-u-*, *portic-u-*. These for substantives; and then for verbs: to *ta* or *ita* of *ducta-*, *clamita-*, *a* of *sona-*, *tona-*; to *tita* of *lectita-*, *ita* of *clamita-*; to *tula* of *ustula-*, *ula* of *ambula-*; to *tilla* of *cantilla-*, *illa* of *sorbilla-*. So for adjectives: to *terno* of *sempiterno-*, *erno* of *hiberno-*; to *turno* of *diuturno-*, *urno* of *diurno-*; to *tili* of *aquatili-*, *uolatili-*, and *bili* of *amabili-*, *flebili-*, *utibili-*, *nobili-*, *uolubili-*, *ili* of *riuali-*, *facili-*; to *bundo* of *saltabundo-*, *querebundo-*, *nitibundo-*, and to *cundo* of *iracundo-*, *uerecundo-*, *rubicundo-*, the mere *undo* of *sec-undo-*, *regundo-*, *oriundo-*; to *tiuo* of *captiuo-*, *iuo* of *uociuo-*; to *tico* of *aquatico-*, *ico* of *ciuico-*; to *ceo* of *rosaceo-*, *eo* of *aureo-*; to *cio* or *tio* of *tribunicio-*, *io* of *regio-*; to *ceri* of *alaceri-*, *uoluceri-*, to *beri* of *luguberi-*, and to *teri* of *compesteri-*, the simpler *eri* of *ac-eri-*; to *cero* of *ludicero-*, *ero* of *pig-ero-*, *rub-ero-*; to *tero* of *dextero-*, σοφωτερο-, *ero* of *supero-*, ενερο-; to *timo* and τατο of superlatives, *imo* and ατο of *minimo-*, μεσατο-. So also for diminutives, whether substantives or adjectives: to *culus a um* of *sermunculus, sororcula, corpusculum, breuiculus, ulus a um* of *regulus, barbula, scutulum, hilarulus*.

Now in all these the error called Provection has been at work. In other words the *c, b, t,* assigned to the suffix, belongs properly to the preceding syllable. The foundation of my argument is of so extensive a character that here I can do little more than refer to the two papers 'On the Representatives of the Keltic Suffix *Agh* or *Ach* "little," in the Latin Vocabulary,' in the Transactions of the Philological Society for 1856, pp. 295—354, and to the preceding paper, 'On English Diminutives,' pp. 219—250. Of the former of these a summary was also given in the second appendix of my Latin Grammar. The result will be found to be, that, while I find the suffix *ag* in its full form in *plag* of *plango*, in *frag* of *frango*, in *strag* of *strag-es, stragulus*, whence *straui, stratum*, in *uorag* of *uoragon, &c.*, and but little changed in *trah* of *traho traxi*, the vowel is modified in *frug-* of *fruges* by the side of *fruor* and *fructus*, in *fug-* (for *flug*, cf. the Germ. *flieh-en, flucht*). On the other hand the medial *g* is exchanged for a tenuis in *orac-ulum, lauac-rum, verec-undus, ridic-ulus, uoluc-ris, inuoluc-rum*; or retained, but with the loss of its vowel, in *sparg-*, *terg-, merg-, uerg-*. A second change I assume is the passage of αχ into αφ, as in γ(α)ρ-αφ-ω by the side of χαρ-αχ- (χαρασσω, cf. ταραχη from ταρασσω). Our own *laugh*, with its written guttural but sounded labial, when contrasted with the German *lach-en*, is another distinct example, and one the more valuable as it is taken in the act of transition. But a Greek φ has generally for its Latin analogue a *b*. Hence *scrib-o;* and indeed the Greek language itself at times exhibits a β, as in θορυβος by the side of ταραχη, and also in τριβω from a root τιρ. Indeed, the Latin also must once have had a secondary verb, *ter-ib-* or *ter-eb-*, by the side of *ter-*, for so only can we account for the nouns *trib-ulum* and *tereb'ra*, as also for the forms *tri'ui, tri'tus*. In this way I would explain the Latin *mir-ab-ili-, dol-ab-ra-, fl-eb-ili-, ten-eb-ra-, illec-eb-ra-, cr-ib-ro-, (g)n-ob-ili-, uol-ub-ili-, sol-ub-ili-,* and the vb. *gl-ub-*.

The assumptions I am making may appear to be over-bold, as I claim not merely a change of the consonant, but a change without limit for the vowel. But it should be observed that the change of vowel obeys something like a law, inasmuch as the assumed vowel is, in a large majority of instances, that which is one with, or if not so, still in keeping with, the root-vowel; and this doctrine of vowel-assimilation demands attention for perhaps all languages. As an instructive example, I point to a family of substantives in some of the chief Indo-European languages, where the leading idea is that of a living creature small or young, viz. πωλος 'a young horse,' *pullus* 'a young horse or a chicken,' παλλαξ 'a young man,' *pellex* literally 'a young woman,' but employed as a euphemism for 'a concubine,' *fillie* 'a young mare,' *pollock* a Scotch term for 'a young fish or crab.'

So far I have taken into consideration the use of the suffix *ag*, &c. in Latin and Greek verbs only. But it also plays its part in the formation of nouns, both substantives and adjectives; and here I was encouraged in the outset of the inquiry by finding that Pott had demonstrated by a large induction that *ax* is a Greek suffix of nouns signifying 'little,' while I also found *ec* performing the same duty in Latin and the Slavonic language, and our own too has clear representatives of the same suffix, which take a great variety of forms, but all proceeding, I think, from an original *ock*, as *bullock*. The Latin nouns *cim-ec-* 'a bug,' *pul-ec-* 'a flea,' *cul-ec-* 'a gnat,' are unmistakeable diminutives, although the primitives have ceased to exist. But with us, as with the Greeks and Romans, the guttural passes into other sounds. As they gave admission to γραφω and *scribo*, so the German has *grab-en*, and we both *grub* and *grave*. Hence I cannot but treat the *f* of *calf, half, turf* (for which the Scotch has a simple *toor*) as standing for *af* or *oof*, and so a diminutival suffix.

But not unfrequently with us a final guttural disappears altogether, though at times it leaves for the eye its ghost, in the shape of a silent *y* or *w*. Thus we have *shad-ow* for 'a bit of shade,' *haddow, window*, by the side of *haddock*, and the Scotch *winnock, way, day, say, any, honey*, corresponding to the German *weg, tag, sagen, einig, honig*.

With this evidence from our own island, I venture to put forward the startling doctrine, for those at least who now hear it for the first time, that all the vowel conjugations of the Greek and Latin verbs, and all the vowel declensions of their nouns, have grown out of older forms, with the guttural suffix *ac* or *ag* more or less modified. Hence I account for the eighteen Latin neuters in *aculo-* or *acro-*, as *sub-lig-ac-ulo-*, *lau-ac-ro-*, for the *ab* in the four hundred adjectives (I give this number after duly counting them) in *ab-ili-*, as *mirab-ili-*; also for the frequentative participles, over sixty in number, such as *plorab-undo-*, *contionab-undo-*, *gemeb-undo-*. Here the suffix is fitly employed, since we also, as Dr. Johnson points out in his 'Grammar of the English Language,' employ our diminutival *el* or *le* in the formation of iterative verbs, as *sparkle, gamble*, or *gambol*.

On the principle here put forward, the vowel verbs of Latin should exhibit some traces of the same meaning; and I see such traces first in such verbs as *frica-re, laua-re, tona-re*, all of which deal with actions which are commonly repetitive, while the simple verbs *lauĕre* and *tonĕre* are not unknown to the older language, and *frictus fricui* again implies a consonant verb *fric-*. Moreover, as in the Slavonic languages verbs fall into two classes, which their grammars call 'momentary' and 'continuative,' so the Latin vowel verbs, where they fail to mark iteration, are distinctly employed for what is akin to this idea, that of continuity, as in *stare* (for *set-a-re*, as opposed to the simple *set*, seen in *si-s(e)t-o*, which denotes the momentary act of stopping); in *sede-, iace-, pende-*, as opposed to *sid-, iac-, pend-*; in *uide-* 'see;' in *s(e)c-i-* 'know,' from a lost *sec-*, corresponding to *seh* of the German *sehen* 'to look at.' Here, however, the original meaning was probably of a physical character; and, if so, we should identify the root with *sec* of *sec-are* 'cut,' in which case we should have what is parallel to *cerno* 'I sift or separate,' and to *uideo* as compared with *diuid-o* 'I separate.' But both Greeks and Romans, though without the simple verb *sco* (σεκ), have deduced from it, by the addition of the very suffix we are discussing, a secondary *sek-ek*; which, offensive by its repeated guttural, led to the substitution of a labial for one of them, and so supplied the Greek language with its σ'κεπ-, and the Latin with its *s'pec-*.

As to nouns, the adjective *rosac-eo-*, to take this as representing a class, when compared with *aureo-*, receives its explanation so soon as we look upon *ros-a-* as having grown out of a fuller *ros-ac-*, which is nearly identical with the Greek diminutive ῥοδ-ακ-. Similarly *tribunic-io-* may well have been deduced from an older *tribun-oc-*, or *tribun-ic-*. In the adjective *aprug-no-* from *apero-*, the guttural happens to have been preserved. Similarly *ciuic-us* and *bellic-us* have, in the *us* alone, the suffix which constitutes them adjectives; this suffix being probably, as I have already hinted, one with the ordinary suffix of the genitive as seen in the Greek σωματ-ος, &c.

I have not so far appealed to an argument which seems to me of much weight, that, in all languages, diminutives have the habit of supplanting the primitives from which they sprang. Thus *fratello, sorella*, in Italian, *soleil, abeille*, in French, *sparr-ow* in English, and *sper-ling* in German, though evidently in origin diminutives, stand now alone in their respective languages; and again the primitive *stare*, of which *star-ling* is the diminutive, is almost obsolete.

What has been said of Latin substantives is equally applicable to Latin adjectives; and strangely enough the whole Latin vocabulary fails to present us with a single[1] original adjective of monosyllabic form, all such simple adjectives having been superseded by words which have assumed a diminutival suffix. Consequently all are disyllabic, or still longer. There is one apparent exception to this assertion in *trux trucis*; but this is only a compression of *tor-uc-* with the guttural suffix in unusual purity, and even this had by its side the double diminutive *tor-u-o-* for *tor-uc-o-*. This general formation of diminutival adjectives seems to be the result of something like a feeling of modesty, a desire to keep within due bounds. The Romans would not say without qualification that a thing was absolutely long. It was 'somewhat long,' 'rather long than not,' or, as in familiar English we say, 'long-ish.' Thus in Latin *breuio-ulo-* is the more correct division, *breui-* itself being but a curtailment of *breu-ic-*. So we also have adjectives in our *yell-ow, shall-ow, holl-ow, call-ow*.

But it is common for a c to give place to a t, as has been more than once noticed in these pages (see pp. 75, 227); and this especially in the case of diminutives. Hence in *breuit-er*, *er* alone is strictly speaking the suffix, which probably grew out of an older *es*, if we may argue from the general habit of the language. Now, when Plautus wished to give to the Greek adverb ἀνευσχημως[2] a Latin dress, he wrote *ineusceme*. But the Greek οὕτως had also the shortened form οὕτω, so

---

[1] Except perhaps *par*, which however has a pl. *par-i-a*.
[2] Trin. iii. 1, 24 (see my paper on Ritschl's Plautus, Philolog. Trans. 1860-1, p. 178).

that the loss of the *s* was no violent proceeding; and I venture to suggest that as the Greek suffix ως was reduced to ω, so my assumed Latin suffix *es* was to *e*, as seen in *ineusceme, docte*, &c. Nay, we may go one step farther, and identify the assumed suffix *es* with ως, the *ē* with the ω, since the Latin had *certo, uero*, &c. as adverbs by the side of *certe, uere*; and the same interchange of these long vowels is seen in ἀπάτωρ and πατήρ, οἰκήτωρ and οἰκήτηρ, *Anio* and *Anienis*. Thus I am disposed to contend for the identity of the three adverbial suffixes *er* (for *es*) of *breuiter*, *e* of *docte*, *o* of *vero*, both with each other, and with the Greek ως and ω of οὕτως, οὕτω.

The cases of *canit-ie-, auarit-ia-* are also cases where a *t* has superseded a *c*, and indeed the forms in *ic, canicie-, auaricia-*, have good manuscript authority, though not the best, and they are to the present day preserved in the Spanish vocabulary. Nay, the comparatives *tristic-ior, iustic-ior, laetic-ior* so frequently present themselves in manuscripts of the second order in place of the orthodox *tristior, iustior, laetior*, that it seems to be a safe conclusion that such forms were in provincial use. (See the paper already referred to, p. 346.) Thus we have direct evidence in favour of the forms *tristic-, iustic-, laetic-*, from which *tristic-ia, iustic-ia, laetic-ia* would be duly formed.

What has been said of these words applies of course to the classes represented by *bonit-at-, multit-udon-, seruit-io-, nauit-a-*. So also as regards the frequentatives in *ita*, as *clam-ita-*, it may justly be contended that *it-a* is a double suffix of diminution standing for *ic-a*. Indeed the verbs *uell-ic-a-, fod-ic-a-, mors-ic-a-* have preserved the guttural. No doubt the frequentatives in *ita* form a very large majority; but these are matters, as I have said before, not to be decided by numbers; and further, there was a special reason why many of them should prefer to substitute *ita* for *ica*, as having already a preceding guttural, as *clamita-* for instance, *agita-*, and *quaerita-*; I say 'many,' after counting over three hundred so constituted, and a combination of three hundred might well lead to something like a law for the others.

The same applies to the so-called supines, or nouns of the *u* declension, which have a short vowel before the *t*, as *fremitu-*, *gemitu-*, *crepitu-*; as also to such nouns as *position-*, *exposition-*. Indeed in *ration-* we know, from our own verbs *reck* and *reck-on*, that a guttural is the more genuine letter. So again with the noun *sation-* a guttural may be claimed as having preceded the *t* on the strength of our verb *sow* with its final *w*. For *condition-* and *dition-* the case is clear, as the older forms are now known to have been *condicion-* and *dicion-*. Lastly in *red-it-u-*, *ad-it-u-*, &c. the *t* is an original part of the root, as shown by the forms *it-er*, *ex-it-io-*(n.), *in-it-io-*, *com-it-*, *ped-it-*, &c.; and the old verb *per-bit-ere*, &c.

In many cases, however, the appearance of a *t*, no way belonging to the suffix, seems to admit of its true explanation in the theory that it is excrescent. I refer to such forms as *lect-ion-*, *cant-ion-*, *capt-ion-*, *assertion-*, *ust-ion-*, *gent-i-*, *mort-i-*, *uest-i*; *cant-u-*, *iact-u-*, *quest-u-*, *part-u*, *salt-u-*; *iuuent-ut-*, *uirt-ut-*, *senect-ut-*; and the verbs *lect-ita-*, *ust-ula-*, *cant-illa-*. But not so in *capt-iuo-*, &c. for such an adjective denotes the belonging to the class of men *capti* or things *capta*, so that a perfect participle is called for, which is not the case with the nouns in *ion* and *u*, for these speak only of an act in progress, not of an act completed.

But there remain for consideration the cases in which a *t* is preceded by a long vowel, as *aration-*, *uolatili-*, *aquatili-*, *aquatico-*. All these I would explain on the same principle which was applied (p. 208) to *ōtio-*, *diūtius*, *sētius*, viz. that the older forms had a *c* before the *t*, and that the *t* itself was an outgrowth from this *c*, the several words being deduced from *ar-ac-*, *uol-ac-* (cf. *uoluc-ri-*), and *aqu-ac-*.

Again, I am disposed to transfer from the suffix to the verb the *t* which precedes *or* in the names of agents, as *arat-or*, *act-or*, *duct-or*, *rapt-or*, *past-or*, *cant-or*, *sart-or*, the *or* itself being only a variety of *uir*, just as the Welsh has *barf* 'beard,' *barf-wr* 'barber;' *mor* 'sea,' *mor-wr* 'sailor;' *pryn-u* 'to buy,' *pryn-wr* 'a buyer;' *pechod* 'sin,' *pechad-wr* 'sinner' (one of course with the Lat. *peccat-or*). And these Welsh forms are, I believe, generally regarded as containing the word *gwr* 'man.' But if I thus treat *t* of the above Latin words as excrescent, what is to be done with the Greek names of agents, such as οικητωρ, οικητηρ? My answer is simply this, that they should be dealt with in precisely the same way, the τ being attached to what precedes. One advantageous result of this view is that the French forms such as *taill-eur*, *brass-eur* become intelligible; and further that the Teutonic branches fall into agreement with the classical languages as regards nouns in *or*, *er*, like our *sail-or*, *dealer*, and the Germ. *küf-er*, *geb-er*, &c.

I have yet to deal with comparatives and superlatives, and to justify the division σοφωτ-ερο-, δεινοτ-ερο-, alt-ero-, sinist-ero-, ποτ-ερο, σοφωτ-ατο-, δεινοτ-ατο-, *ult-*

imo-, int-imo-, &c. (p. 120), as contrasted with the prevailing habit of assigning the *t* to what follows. What I subsequently said in the same paper will more than prepare the way for my defence. It may be remembered that, starting from the suffix ιον of Greek, *ior (ios)* of Latin comparatives, I called in aid the doctrine of Bopp, that these two suffixes were apt to lose one of the two vowels, an *i* being lost for *minor* and *minus,* and *secus* as superseding *secius* (cf. p. 122), to which I might have added the Latin *prim-ores* (for *prim-iores*) and the Greek πλε-ον for πλε-ιον, the *ple-ores* of the Carmen Arvale, and *plus* or rather *plous* itself, as a contraction of *pleos,* and lastly the theoretic *op-os*, afterwards *post,* of the same paper. On the other hand, we have but the *i* in *magis, nimis, satis, prist-ino-;* probably also in οπ-ισ-ω, more certainly in πρ-ιν, which, though short in later writers, has often a long vowel in Homer. It has been said indeed that the vowel is 'properly' short; but surely the authority of Homer is for the present question more weighty than that of any number of later poets; and indeed generally it may be asserted that the passage from long to short vowels is more in accordance with reason and with the history of language. Thus πριν may well have grown out of πρ-ιον, i. e. πορ-ιον.

In the same paper I pointed to the fact that both in Gothic and the younger German languages the same appearance, sometimes of *i (e),* sometimes of *o,* is the universal characteristic of comparatives, as *ald-iz-a, minn-iz-a,* together with *frum-oz-a, frod-oz-a* in Gothic, *alt-ir-o (alt-er-o), menn-ir-o (menn-er-o),* with *jung-or-o, frot-or-o* in Old German; and from this I drew what I deemed a reasonable inference, that these

Teutonic suffixes grew out of an older suffix *ios* or *ioz* (*ior*). The Greek and Latin suffixes differ indeed in the one having a *v*, the other an *s* (*r*); but this is a distinction which must not be regarded as affecting their identity, seeing that it is in obedience to a law which subsists between the two languages (see p. 163); and indeed the Sanskrit serves as a connecting link with its fuller suffix *tyáns* (Bopp, V. G. ii. pp. 32, 35), which at the same time accounts for the long *i* in the Greek com-parative.

But, as I said in the former paper, no one can for a moment separate the suffix of Modern German and our English comparatives, as in *ält-er*, *old-er*, *wis-er*, from the *er* of the Old German *alt-er-o*, &c.; nor this again from the classical *ev-ep-oi*, *sup-er-i*, *inf-er-i*. The word '*τ-ερ-ο-* 'one of two,' proclaims its intimate connexion with the numeral *ἐν* 'one,' both by its meaning and by its asperate, for the Greek language stands apart from all its congeners in giving an asperate to these two words. Then as to the change of consonant we have the same in our old *bet-est* from a root *ben*, and, what is still more to the purpose, the Danish has alongside of each other *en* as m. and f., *et* as neuter for the indefinite article, which of course is but the numeral *one*. We are taught indeed that the *t* in this and other words is a neuter suffix; but in fact such a thing as a neuter suffix has no existence, all that characterises a neuter being the loss of some final consonant, and not any addition. A change of *n* and *t* is seen not merely in the Norse participle m. *haldinn* (for *haldins*), f. *haldin*, n. *hald-it*, but also in our own *hold-en*, *clov-en*, as compared with the Scotch *abas-it*, English *clef-t*, and with the

Latin *pos-it-o-*. Of course a classical *t* according to Rask's law should appear in our tongue as *th*, and accordingly the comparative of our *one* is *oth-er*.

Again, so far as regards the Teutonic family, it is the common doctrine, and one which I think cannot be disputed, that superlatives are formed from the comparative, and not directly from the positive. In the French *le meilleur* too this is self-evident; as also in the Lapp *dnek* 'short,' *ânekub* 'shorter,' *ânekumus* 'shortest,' which throw light upon the Latin superlative. The same theory accounts for the forms μεγιστος, βελτιστος, where μεγις, βελτις, following the analogy of Latin comparatives, have given a preference to the σ over ν. It matters little whether we divide these as μεγισ-τος, βελτισ-τος, or treat the τ as excrescent, inasmuch as both τος and ος are well fitted to represent the Greek article, so that βελτιστος will exactly correspond to the French *le meilleur*. Such a position for the definite article is the ordinary construction in the Scandinavian family, and by way of example I give the Danish *patriot-en* 'the patriot,' *dag-blad-et* 'the day-leaf or journal.' Further, it is by adding the definite article as a suffix that the so-called definite declension of adjectives has attained its peculiar form, as Bopp has clearly shown. The Latin superlative, *nouissimus* for example, Bopp divides as *nouis-timus*; but I hold the true division to be *nouist-imus*. Indeed generally it seems to me that the ordinal numerals, as δεκ-ατος, ενν-ατος, εβδ-ομος, *dec-umus*, *sept-umus*, and the forms derived from prepositions, ὑπ-ατος, πρωτος (= προ-ατος), μεσ-ατος (from μεσος, which is probably akin to μετα), εσχ-ατος, *imus* (= *in-imus*), *primus* (= *pro-imus*), *summus* (= *sub-*

imus), *inf-imus*, are safer guides in etymology than the superlatives from ordinary adjectives; and of course the same consideration applies to comparatives. Hence I have no longer any doubt as to the division of *alt-ero-*, *post-ero-*, &c., *post-umo-*, *ult-umo-*, *int-imo-*, &c., in all of which the *t* is for me excrescent, while σοφωτ-ερο-, σοφωτ-ατο-, I regard as more genuine than δεινοτ-ερο-, δεινοτ-ατο-, and standing for σοφ-οκτ-ερο-, σοφ-οκτ-ατο-, σοφ-ο- itself having superseded an older σοφ-οκ-.

The three forms ποτ-ερο-, *ut-ero-*, *wheth-er*, I defend in a wholly different way. In these I hold the dental to be part of the root syllable, representing probably an original *n*, as does also the *d* of *id*, *quid*, and *quod* in Latin, and *t* of our *it*, *that*, *what*, for again I protest against the doctrine that in these letters we have a mere suffix of neuters. I cannot here pretend to do justice to a question which covers so wide a field. My arguments were given many years ago in a paper read before the Philological Society (Proc. iii. 56), and were subsequently more fully developed in a paper attached to my little book entitled 'Alphabet,' &c., where they occupy twenty-three pages. There are also some brief allusions to these papers in the last of these essays. I have here only room for the outline. My argument contends, in the first place, that the third-person pronouns, which for Latin are represented by *hic, iste, ille, is*, and *qui*, together with the two prepositions *cis, uls*, and their derivatives, as also the demonstrative enclitic *ce*, seen in *hic, istic, illic*, with their adverbs, and in *sic, nunc, tunc*, were in origin all of demonstrative power, or, in other words, accompanied the physical act of pointing to an object; secondly, that the root form of these words appears to have been *ken*, the guttural of which is preserved in *cis* and *ce*, also in κεινος and in the modern Italian *chi*, *questo*, *costi*, *quello*, *colui*, while the final *n* also is frequently cropping up. The already quoted κεινος, with its analogues the German *jener* and our *yon*, *beyond*, present it distinctly. Of the forms *hinc*, *inde*, ενθεν, *hence*, *thence*, *whence*, I shall have to speak again; and I have already referred (p. 70) to the occurrence of the phrase Is LOCVS in an inscription, where the long *i* in the nominative seems to point to an old root *in* for the pronoun, as distinctly as in Greek the numeral εις and the preposition εις do to forms εν- and εν. In *isto-* the *n* has given place to an *s*, and that *s* has thrown out an excrescent *t*, while *illo-*, or *olo-* (cf. Virgil's *olli* and the old form *aboloes* for *ab illis*), or rather both *illo* and *ollo* together, point to a form *iol* as an older variety of the root; just as *mag-is* and *min-us* suggest an older suffix *ius*. But *iol* stands to our *yon* much as the Latin *sol* to our *sun*; and indeed the Slavic languages have the older *ono* in preference to *olo*.

Then for the relative and interrogative the evidence is still stronger. I shall not here rely on the fact that in the Tatar languages *ken* is the ordinary form of the relative, as in Finn and Mongolian; while in the first of these it has also the by-form *cu* precisely as the Latin, although at the same time I am satisfied that the German School of Philology is wrong in denying to these languages all affinity with the Indo-European family. But the evidence at hand is enough. The existence of an initial guttural will not be disputed, although it has been lost for *unde*, *ubi*, *uter*, *ut*. Nor is it difficult to establish the claim of the concluding nasal. In the Spanish *quien* it has been preserved, but more commonly it has passed into the allied *n*, and this to an extent but seldom noticed. First the Sanskrit has it in *kim*, a form which has much distressed some philologers. Dr. Guest (Proc. Phil. Soc. i. p. 287) claims *whom* as an old English nominative, and he also refers to such forms as Swed. nom. *hwem*, gen. *hwem-s*, Dan. nom. *hvem*, Fries. gen. *waems*, Du. gen. *wiens*. Then our pronoun *he* is represented in Old Norse for the m. by nom. *han-n*, acc. *han-n*, gen. *han-s*, dat. *hon-um*. So again our definite article *the* takes the two forms of *den* and *en*, and carries the *n* for both m. and f. into every oblique case of both numbers. Lastly, the enclitic *ce*, so familiar in *hic* (*hici-ne*), *istic*, *illic*, and their adverbs, as also in *nunc* (*nunci-ne*), *tunc*, *sic*, has in Umbrian the form *cen* in the abl. of *eiso*, *eizu-c* or *eisu-cen* (A. K. p. 135).

I cannot stop to discuss the *rationale* of the change of meanings by which a mere demonstrative became available for use as a relative or interrogative. The fact is what concerns us most, and no one will doubt that in Greek the so-called definite article was not unfrequently employed as a relative, as by Herodotus when he says, θυουσι τῃ Παρθενῳ τους τε ναυηγους και τους αν λαβωσι; while the German *der* and our own *that* perform both duties, and the same is true of most branches of the Indo-European family.

But the question remains, What is the meaning and what the origin of the assumed root *ken*? As a preparation for this inquiry, I would meet the question by another, What word is best fitted to accompany the act of pointing to an object? and the answer can only be one, a word signifying 'look.' Now *ken* in Scotch and Old English is a verb with this very meaning, and, as I show in a subsequent paper, this word is no way limited to our own island or to the Teutonic family. It is the root of our verb *know* (*kon-ow*), and so lies at the bottom of the Latin *gnosco*, the Greek γιγνωσκω, the Sanskrit *jna*, and indeed extends far beyond these limits, so as to include Chinese itself, for again I repeat my unwillingness to draw an absolute line of distinction between our Indo-European languages and those of the Tatar stock. I go back, then, to the forms ποτ-ερο-, *ut-ero-*, *wheth-er*, and claim the *т* and *th* as representing the *n* of the root κεν.

I conclude this paper by a matter for which this last inquiry was a necessary prelude, the just division of the adverbs signifying *whence*, as ποθεν, ενθεν, οπισθεν, ουρανοθεν, *inde*, *unde*, *hinc*, *illim* and *illinc*, *istim* and *istinc*, *caelitus*, *funditus*, *intus*, &c., *hence*, *thence*, *whence*. I may observe in passing that the use of *intus* in Plautus in the sense of 'from within' is not to be denied. Now the power of the genitival suffix, viz. 'from,' is precisely that which belongs to all these words, and *us* (or) is a familiar form of the genitival suffix, although an older form was probably *ius*, as in *cu-ius*, *nullius* (= *nullo-ius*), λογο-ιο(ς). In the preceding paper I gave evidence that *en* of *Heinrich-en*, *Frier'n Barnet*, and the Sanskrit *sun-u'n-am*, was but a variety of this. I might at the same time have pointed to the so-called adjectives *lin-en*, *gold-en*, as genitives in origin; as also to the *in* of ξυλ-ιν-ο-, *crast-in-o-*, *Roma'n-o-*, as having the same origin and the same power, and even (*pace* Germany) to the Finn, where for the consonant declension *wieras* 'a guest,' *kirwes* 'a hatchet,' *caunis* 'beautiful,' have for genitives *wierah-an*, *kirweh-en*, *caunih-in*, and the Lapp, where *toli* 'a stool,' has a gen. *toli-n*. But if this suffix exist in the adverbs above given, we must divide them as ποθ-εν, ενθ-εν, οπισθ-εν, ουρανοθ-εν, *caelit-us*, *fundit-us*, *int-us*, where θ of ποθ-εν belongs to the root, as does the τ of τοτ-ερο-, the θ of ενθ-εν, οπισθ-εν is excrescent, that of ουρανοθ-εν is a substitute for the χ of ουρανοχ-, while *caelit-us* stands for *caelic-us*, and the *t* of *int-us* is again excrescent. As in οπισθ-εν, &c. the ν is often dropped, leaving but οπισθε, so *ind-e* and *und-e* probably represent an older *ind-us*, *und-us*, for the loss of the *s* would be followed by a degradation of the vowel into ŏ, as in *ipsus ipse*, *magis mage*, *scripserunt scripsere*. Precisely on the same principle the short final of *supernĕ* and *infernĕ* is to be explained, for these words denote 'from above,' 'from below,' so that they are to be regarded as representing lost adverbs *supernus*, *infernus*, and are not to be mixed up with ordinary adverbs in *e* as *recte*, in which the suffix has a very different power. Then as *exinde*, *proinde*, &c. are often cut down to *exim* or *exin*, &c., *illinde*, which analogy suggests, would lead to what is actually found, *illim*, and that, with the enclitic added, to *illin-c*. So also with *hinc* and *ist-inc*; and this view is confirmed by the co-existence of *utrinde* and *utrimque*, or *utrinque*. With us the genitival suffix, as in Latin, has a sibilant, so that the old forms *henn-es*, *thenn-es*, *whenn-es*, are but genitives of a stem *henn*, &c., and thus here too the *n* of the root reappears; and to confirm the assumption that ποθ-εν and our *wheth-er*, *oth-er* have in the *th* a representative of an *n*, we also find in Old English the variety *heth-en*, for what is now written *hence*. I conclude then that in *ind-e, und-e,* as in *ενθ-εν*, the dental mute is excrescent, and the *n* a portion of the root.

A difficulty may suggest itself in the cases of the assumed *ill-inde, ist-inde,* in that *ill* and *ist* alone belong, on my own showing, to the root; but my defence is that in *ill-o-* and *ist-o-* we have reduplicate pronouns. In the Greek *οὗ-το-ς* this is commonly admitted. But the neuter forms *ill-ud* or *ill-ut, ist-ud* or *ist-ut,* suggest a similar reduplication for them; and this admitted a form *ill-ind-e* is no longer an anomaly.

Lastly, let me notice the fact that the word *look* is used whether we point to a near or to a remote object, so that we here have an explanation of the difficulty which may well have occurred to the reader,—I mean that I have been assigning a common origin to words so opposed in meaning as *hic* and *ille*, *citra* and *ultra*, *this* and *that.* Thus we have in Terence *luciscit hoc iam* (Haut. iii. 1, 1), 'it is getting light, look, already;' while, on the other hand, when Virgil (Aen. v. 457) says :—

> 'Praecipitemque Daren ardens agit aequore toto,
> Nunc dextra ingeminans ictus, nunc ille sinistra,'

we find an equally satisfactory exponent of *ille* if we translate the second line by the words :—

> 'Now with his right redoubling blows; now, look, look,
> with his left.'

This paper in a great measure grew out of a desire to deal with questions which presented themselves in the preceding paper 'On Excrescent Consonants,' and so may be regarded as a sort of supplement to it.

XII.

QVAERITVR.

THE SANSKRIT LANGUAGE AS THE BASIS OF LINGUISTIC SCIENCE; AND THE LABOURS OF THE GERMAN SCHOOL IN THAT FIELD—ARE THEY NOT OVER-VALUED?

First Part.

I had thought at one time of placing at the head of this paper 'Doubts of a Non-Sanskritist.' But on reflection it seemed desirable that the title should be more definite. If the words I have actually used be thought by any one to savour of national ill-will, I must give the assurance that nothing could be more remote from my purpose or from my feelings. Those who have to deal with the classical languages must be either blind or ungrateful if they fail to acknowledge the deepest obligations to the scholars of Germany. The editions of Greek and Latin authors that have appeared in England during the last half-century have not been numerous, but even of these a large proportion have been simply reprints of German works. Again, the Lexicons of the two languages that have issued from the English press during the same period are for the most part so thoroughly of German material, that it would have been more creditable if the title-pages had carried the words, 'Translated from the German of . . . . . with some few changes and additions.' Again, if we turn our thoughts to the opposite side of the English Channel, we find no great activity in the sphere of classical, especially Greek, literature; yet what progress is visible there is chiefly due to the energy of German, not French, scholarship, as witness the valuable collection of Greek authors that has proceeded from the press of Didot. Nay, the high and indisputable reputation that Germany has won in this field only renders the duty more imperative to watch lest failure or shortcomings on any side should be kept from notice owing to that very prestige. Further, I wish it to be observed that the term I have used is 'overvalued,' which is quite compatible with an admission of great value; and again, I put what I have said in the form, not of a proposition, but of a question. It is only when that question is answered in the affirmative, or when the arguments put forward in this paper remain un-answered, that the slightest damage can be done to the reputation of the philologers concerned. It would have been simply indecent, if the present writer had expressed his fears in the form of a direct proposition, conscious as he is that he comes to the inquiry wholly destitute of what may at first sight be deemed an essential requisite, a knowledge of the Sanskrit language. Nay, he cannot pretend even to that smattering which may be obtained by a three weeks' study of the language, and which has before now served to float a big book in the English market, a little sprinkling of the Devanagari character, and a judicious use of the hard words Vriddhi, Anuswara, &c., passing for profundity in the eyes of the uninitiated. Such little knowledge as I have is that only which may be acquired in the perusal of grammars and glossaries, and works of like nature.

The question here naturally suggests itself, how it is that I have taken upon myself to enter into a contest for which I am confessedly so ill-equipped; and my answer is that I find the same suspicions which have found a way into my own mind entertained by many others, and those too gentlemen whose position as scholars gives great weight to their opinions, though, like myself, they are wholly wanting in the special qualification, a knowledge of Sanskrit. In every point of view then it seems desirable that the question should be raised. If our fears are ill-founded, it is well that they should be removed, and the road more thoroughly cleared of all obstruction for the Sanskritist. If otherwise, it is surely good for the progress of philological science that the matter should be thoroughly sifted.

I do not propose to enter into the domain of Sanskrit history and chronology, a task for which I am wholly unfitted, especially as those who have the best qualifications admit that it is involved in the greatest obscurity; nor indeed could one expect easily to find materials for accurate investigation in such a literature as that of the Védas. The 'Mantras,' on the one hand, dealing for the most part with the devotional, and the 'Bráhmaṇas,' on the other, with the ceremonial and dogmatic, can scarcely be available for such a purpose. As to the Upanishads or the short appended treatises, I will be satisfied with a second-hand quotation from a work of a learned Hindú, that they 'contain some rude indications of philosophic thought, and, like the twinkling of the stars in a dark night, may occasionally serve as guides in a history of Hindú philosophy. They do not however exhibit any great attempt at method, arrangement, classification, or argument. Even there the poetry predominates over the logic. Bold ideas abruptly strike your fancy, but you find no clue to the associations which called them forth in the author's mind, and search in vain for the reasons on which they are based. Sublime thoughts are not wanting, but they resemble sudden flashes, at which you may gaze for a moment, but are immediately after left in deeper darkness than ever. Nor are they free from those irregular flights of the imagination in which poets with vitiated tastes delight to indulge, setting at defiance all rules of decency and morality.' (Banergea, *Westminster Review*, new series, vol. xxii. p. 463.)

An argument for the antiquity of the Sanskrit language has recently been founded ('Lectures on the Science of Language,' by Prof. Max Müller, p. 204, third edition,) upon certain passages in the Book of Kings and the Book of Job, but it is an argument which, as it appears to me, withers to the touch. All rests upon the statement that four articles imported into Judea in the days of Solomon, viz. the ape, the peacock, ivory, and sandal-wood, are called in the Hebrew text by names foreign to that language, but indigenous in Sanskrit. But it is not an easy matter to prove that a word is indigenous in a language, and the Sanskrit-speaking race on their first entrance into the Indian peninsula (for they are allowed on all hands to have been immigrants), would naturally adopt the native—that is, non-Sanskrit—terms for those objects which are peculiar to the country,

provided indeed they had not already adopted them
in the previous intercourse of commerce. But, passing
over this consideration, let us throw a glance at each
of the four words on which this important super-
structure has been erected. *Koph*, the Hebrew for
'ape,' is, we are told, 'without an etymology in the
Semitic languages, but nearly identical in sound with
the Sanskrit *kapi*.' It is of course implied here,
though not said, that the Sanskrit does furnish a
satisfactory etymology for its *kapi*. To supply the
omission, I turn to Bopp's Glossary, and there find
that *kapi* 'ape,' has for its root the Sansk. verb *kamp*
'tremble,' so that, for some reason denied to us, the
ape was conceived by the Indian mind as 'the
trembler.' Then ivory has for one of its Hebrew
names *shen habbim*, where, as *shen* means 'tooth,'
habbim might well speak of the 'elephant,' and this,
it is said, 'is most likely a corruption of the Sanskrit
for elephant *ihha*, preceded by the Semitic article.'
If, as I suppose is the fact, *ihha* be a misprint for
ibha, the resemblance is even then limited to the
consonant, and we have nothing offered in the way
of proof that this name for the elephant is the
original property of Sanskrit. Thirdly, *tukhi-im*, in
Hebrew 'peacocks,' bears no doubt a tolerably close
resemblance to the Malabar name *togëi*; and this 'in
turn has been derived from the Sanskrit *sikhin* 'fur-
nished with a crest.' Lastly, the Malabar and Sanskrit
name for sandal-wood is *valguka*; and 'this *val-
gu(ka)*,' the Professor says, 'is clearly the name which
Jewish and Phœnician merchants corrupted into
algum, and which in Hebrew was still further changed
into *almug*.' I would submit that at any rate the

word 'clearly' is somewhat out of place in an etymon which involves four assumptions, the aphaeresis of *v*, the apocope of *ka*, a paragogic *m*, and the metathesis of *gum* to *mug*. Even if true, such derivations have scarcely strength enough to serve as the foundation of so large a theory.¹

But the same writer has elsewhere ('History of Ancient Sanskrit Literature,' p. 524), contended that the Vêdas have an antiquity far older than the knowledge of writing. 'The collection of the (Vaidic) hymns, and the immense mass of the Brâhmaṇa literature, were preserved,' he says, 'by means of oral tradition only.' In another passage of the same work (p. 507) he tells us that 'before the time of Pâṇini, nay, even when he himself wrote (sic) his great work, writing for literary purposes was absolutely unknown.' To understand the full force of this proposition, to form an adequate idea of the extent to which the Professor would tax the mnemonic powers of the Brahmans, we must remember that Pâṇini, according to his own authority, was preceded by whole generations of grammarians. In his 'Lectures on Language' (p. 110) he says: ' 'Those valuable lists of words, irregular, or in any other way remarkable, the Gaṇas, supplied that solid basis on which successive generations of scholars erected the astounding structure

---

¹ I leave this as I wrote it, but I subsequently found that Prof. Max Müller had borrowed the whole argument from Lassen's 'Indische Alterthumskunde,' vol. i. p. 538, &c., so that the setting alone was his own. It is true that he himself referred to this passage of Lassen; but his reference was so placed, that a reader might well suppose the argument about 'ivory' alone to have been drawn from Lassen.

that reached its perfection in the grammar of Pâṇini.'
But if the structure be 'astounding,' and 'the perfection of a merely empirical analysis of language,' it seems not to be possessed of much that would be interesting to the mere European scholar, for the Professor concludes his panegyric with the words: 'Yet of the real nature and natural growth of language it teaches us nothing.'

As regards the Vêdas themselves, one can readily imagine that religious feeling and poetical feeling combined may do much to invigorate the powers of memory, while the mere rhythm of verse contributes to lighten the task; but intense indeed must have been the feeling of duty which could induce Brahmans to commit to memory, and there retain, a complete library of the driest grammarians.

The whole argument then carries with it, as it seems to me, its own refutation; and in truth the challenge implied in the words, 'I maintain that there is not a single word in Pâṇini's terminology which presupposes the existence of writing,' has already received a twofold answer from my colleague, Professor Goldstücker ('Pâṇini, his place in Sanskrit Literature,' 1861); first a self-refutation, quoted from the Oxford Professor's own words: 'This last word *lipikara* (a writer or engraver) is an important word, for it is the only word in the Sûtras of Pâṇini which can be legitimately adduced to prove that Pâṇini was acquainted with the art of writing;' and as my colleague observes (p. 17): 'It is obviously immaterial whether another similar word be discoverable in his grammar or not; one word is clearly sufficient to establish the fact.' But he further produces from

Pâṇini's own work an abundant supply of terms which could have no meaning whatever when writing was unknown. Let me quote one more passage from the same work (p. 14): 'As, according to his (Max Müller's) view, Pâṇini lived in the middle of the fourth century B.C. (pp. 245, 301, ff.), it would follow that, according to him, India was not yet in possession of the most useful of arts at the time when Plato died and Aristotle flourished.'

I have entered into these details to show the unsatisfactory condition of the chronology of Sanskrit literature, and at the same time I would suggest the question whether there should not be a little more caution in the acceptance of literary conclusions, even from those to whom the English public has been accustomed to look as authorities above all controversy.

But if we cannot have the advantage of a reliance on literary history, we must be content to examine the internal evidence supplied by the language itself, and the dealings therewith alike of Indian and European authorities. As my own doubts, and I believe those of the friends to whom I have already alluded, were first raised by what appeared to us as most strange, though generally sanctioned, etymologies, I will proceed to produce some of these, limiting myself for the most part to a single class.

Already Max Müller ('Lectures on the Science of Language,' p. 370) himself quotes, as an example of Indian etymology, the derivation of the sb. *kâka* 'crow,' from *apakâlayitavya, i.e.* 'a bird that is to be driven away,' but adds that Yâska, another grammarian, anterior to Pâṇini, considered *kâka* to be an imitation of the bird's note. Whether the Professor himself adopts or rejects this mimetic origin of *káka*, his words do not enable one to say. But be this as it may, in another Sanskrit noun, *kárava*, Lat. *cor(o)vo-*, 'raven,' he steadily refuses to see what, for one, I must regard as a still more exact imitation of the bird's note, viz. *cor cor*. Had he included in his view the Greek κορ-αξ-,[1] he might perhaps have assented to Pott's doctrine (E. F. ii. 506, 507), that αξ in Greek substantives is a suffix of diminutival power, so that κορ alone would be the root. He himself, in his aversion to what he calls by way of disparagement the Bow-wow theory, strives to deduce the whole family, *kárava*, κορωνη, raven, &c. from the Sanskrit verb *ru*, to which he ascribes 'a general predicative power' as expressing sound, 'from the harshest to the softest,' and so applicable 'to the nightingale as well as to the raven,' nay, even to 'the barking of dogs' and 'the mooing of cows.' In a note however he hesitates between this etymon and one from the Sansk. *káru* 'singer.' To the special honour of this last derivation, the raven seems to be about as well entitled as the parrot or the peacock; and the deduction of *kárava* from *ru*, a general term implying 'sound,' would probably be regarded by lawyers as 'void for uncertainty.'

The same objection of excessive generality applies to the whole class of etyma with which I now propose to deal, viz. those of words ascribed to roots of various forms, but with the one meaning 'to go.' Thus the

---

[1] We must not suppose the ancients in their nomenclature to have distinguished with modern accuracy between the raven, the rook, and the crow. (See Mr. Wedgwood's paper on that subject.)

S. *go* (*gau*), the equivalent in power and probably in form of Lat. *bov-*, Gr. βου-, as also of our own *cow*, is deduced by Sanskritists of all classes, Indian and European, from a S. vb. *ga* 'go;' and that this explanation of the word may not suffer for want of company, I may add the S. *ilá* 'cow,' referred by Bopp (Gloss.¹ s. v.) to the vb. *il* 'go.' Now that animals like the 'hare' or 'stag' should receive a name from their marked power of locomotion is, at any rate on the logical side, admissible, and thus we may perhaps be ready to assent to the current etymologies of *hare* (Germ. *hase*), the Latin *lepos-*, and the Greek ἐλαφο-. But the cow is scarcely entitled to put in a claim for such distinctions as against any other living creature. Strangely enough the same pair of words, *go* and *ila*, also signify 'earth,' and these again have the same origin ascribed to them (Bopp, Gl. a. vv.). So also the Gr. γαια passes with Bopp (V. G. § 123) as standing for γαϝια, and so an adjectival offspring of a sb. corresponding to the S. *go* 'earth,' and eventually of such a vb. as *ga* 'go.' In the same section S. *gmá* 'a name for the earth in the Véda-dialect,' is deduced from the S. vb. *gam* 'go.' Nay, our own *earth*, though it comes immediately from our old English vb. *ear* 'plough,' represented in Sanskrit by *ar*, is traced ultimately to the S. *ṛ* 'go' (Bopp, ibid., M. Müller, 'Lectures on Language,' p. 256, and Pott, E. F. i. 218). It would be an interesting fact if such a series of at any rate consistent etymologies

---

¹ I have preferred to draw from this work, although now somewhat out of date and superseded by other works, simply because it comes from the founder of the science.

could be accepted as proofs that the Hindú mind had already discovered the motion of the earth, whether about its own axis or about the sun. But as it seems more probable that then, as now, there existed an inveterate tendency to treat the earth as the one fixed object to which all the movements around us are conveniently referred, we must look for some other explanation of the theory; and accordingly Bopp suggests that the movement of the earth must here be regarded as only 'passive,'—in other words, the *earth* (*erde*) is 'the betrodden one' ('die betretene'). Though it does not visibly move itself, man and beast would be in an awkward predicament for locomotion if there were no earth to move upon. Before leaving the earth, I ought to notice that Prof. M. Müller believes (p. 257) our word *aroma* to be another ramification of *ar* "plough" and *r* 'go,' for does not Jacob say (Gen. xxvii. 28), 'The smell of my son is as the smell of a field which the Lord has blessed'?

From land I pass to water, but the same etymology pursues us. Thus the *Ganges* itself is the Sanskrit *Gangá*, literally the 'Go Go' (M. Müller, ibid. p. 384). So we have S. *salila* 'water' from S. vb. *sal* 'go' (Bopp, Gloss. a. v.); S. *ap* 'water,' the analogue of the Lat. *aqu-a*, from vb. *ap* 'go;' *sarit* 'river,' from vb. *sr* 'go' (M. M. ibid. p. 253); and *saras* 'water,' from the same vb. (ibid.). The last noun is by Bopp translated by the Lat. *lacus*, and declared to be one with the Greek ἶλος (cr. form ἰλεσ-) 'a marsh,' in which case the motion of 'going' seems to disappear. Yet after all Sanskritists may contend that marshland, being half water, half land, has a double claim to a derivation from roots which denote 'going.'

Take next the class of worms and reptiles. Bopp, for example (V. G. § 86, 1), refers the Latin *vermi-* (= *quermi-*) and S. *krimi* to the S. vb. *kram* 'go;' the Germ. *schlange* 'snake' to S. vb. *sraṅg* 'go;' and the Lat. *serpens*, S. *sarpa*, first to S. vb. *srp* 'go,' and ultimately to *sr* 'go.' Had any of these verbs meant 'go by little and little,' the derivation would have been satisfactory, but the meanings given by Bopp in his Glossary to these verbs, as well as to all their compounds, furnish no authority for such an assumption. No doubt in his comparison of the verb *srp* with kindred languages he dwells much on the idea of slow movement in those kindred languages; and again Professor Wilson in his Grammar, though he adds the meanings 'creep or glide,' gives precedence to the general term 'to go.' I cannot but think however that the suffix of *srp* as compared to *sr* and that of the Lat. *ser(e)p-* with the varieties of ἑρ(ε)π- and Lat. *r-ĕp-* (*rēpere*), Eng. *c(e)r-ep* (*crep-t, creep*), Germ. *kr-iech-en*, and with an additional suffix of diminution *cr-aw-l*, represents the idea *paulatim*, as it seems to do in the Lat. *car-p-* (see my paper 'On the Suffix *agh*,' &c. Trans. for 1856, p. 336). When I wrote what is there seen, I expressly stated that I was at a loss for the root *ser-* 'go.' This I now find in the S. *sr*, although I still believe a form *ker*, as heard in *cr-eep* and *kr-iech-en*, to be more genuine than *sr* with the sibilant. I am not deterred from regarding the two roots as substantially one by the fact that as a rule the guttural *k* or *c* of Western Europe is usually represented by the palatal *s* of Sanskrit, not by that which occurs in *sr* and *srp*.

Another class of words, which Bopp is disposed

generally to refer to roots significant of simple movement, are those which denote 'time' ('da überhaupt die Zeitbenennungen meistens von Wurzeln der Bewegung stammen,' V. G. § 69). For instance our word *year*, old Germ. *jár*, together with what he regards as an equivalent in form, the Gr. ὥρα 'season,' is referred by him to the S. vb. *ya* 'go,' but by Lassen and Burnouf it seems to S. vb. *ir* 'go.' Again the Goth. *aivs* (crude form *aiva*) as also its relatives, Lat. *aeuum*, Gr. αιων, is deduced by Bopp, Graff, and Kuhn from S. vb. *i* 'go' (ibid.). The *i* might perhaps not have passed with the ill-informed as forming the kernel of these words; but all is accounted for; the initial *a*, it seems, attains its position through 'Guṇa,' and all that follows the *i* (or *e*) is to be regarded as a suffix. In spite of such a combination of authority I am still disposed to prefer my own etymology of *aeuum* from the Latin *auge-* (for the vowel-change compare the variety seen in the allied αεξ-ω and αυξ-αν-ω), with 'growth' for the original sense, as exhibited in the well-known line, *Crescit occulto uelut arbor aeuo*, 'grows like a tree with growth concealed.' The Lat. *saeculum* is also referred by Bopp (V. G. § 248, Anm.) to a S. vb. *sac* or *sak* 'go, follow.' Further, as he (Gloss. s. v. and V. G. ib.) considers S. *amati* 'time' a derivative from *am* 'go,' so he is also inclined to deduce from the same stem the Latin *annus* (as standing for *amnus*) as well as the Greek ενος. That *amnus* was in fact the older form of *annus* is proved by the derived *sol-emni-s*, but to the derivation from a verb 'to go' I would oppose that other derivation which connects it with the Latin prep. *am* 'round,' German *um*. The very idea of a year implies a circle, and the words *annulus* 'a ring,' and the noun *ănus* with a long vowel, seem to complete the proof. On the same principle the word *year* itself, like *yar-d* 'an enclosure,' and *gard-en*, &c., claims kindred with many words denoting a circle, as χορτο-, *horto-*, χορ-ο-, *cor-o-na-*, *circ-o-*. The initial change between a Gr. χ, Lat. *h*, and a *g* (*y*) in German and English is in accordance with the usual law, as seen in χθες, *heri*, *hesterno-*, *gestern*, *yesterday*.

So much for the alleged deduction of substantives from Sanskrit verbs signifying 'to go.' But in the formation of secondary verbs also the roots *i* 'go,' and *yâ* 'go' are thought by Bopp well fitted to play important parts, as for example in furnishing suffixes by which verbs are converted into passives (§ 739) and causals (§ 740). As regards the former, if *kŏrd yâi*, to take Bopp's own example from the Bengali, have for a literal translation 'I am made' ('ich werde gemacht'), as given by himself, then *gemacht* is by itself already a passive, just as *verloren* is in the Modern German *gehen verloren*, literally 'to go lost.' We too may say 'become detested' or 'become fascinating,' where the distinction between the passive and the active idea turns upon the accompanying participle, not upon the word 'become.' Again, Bopp's illustration from the Latin *amatum iri* is surely not applicable. If the principle for which he is contending be valid, we ought already to have a passive in the indicatival phrase *amatum eo* 'I am going to love,' but this is a mere future of the active. The introduction of a passive of *eo*, whether in the indicative as *amatum itur*, or in the infinitive as *amatum iri*, is only a convenient mode of exhibiting an impersonal verb, equivalent to the French *on va aimer*. The examples of *ueneo* and *pereo*, quoted by Bopp, are at first sight more to the purpose, and he would have done well to strengthen his case by comparing them with *uendo* and *perdo*. Yet after all *uēnire*, standing for *uenum ire*, means probably 'to go into the window,' and so 'be exhibited for sale,' which certainly is more truly the meaning of the phrase than 'to be sold.' So also *uenui est* admits of the literal translation 'it is in the window,' *i.e.* 'is offered for sale.' Again, *perire* 'to come to an end,' like the English *go to the dogs* or the Greek ἔρρε ἐς κόρακας, contains no doubt what is virtually a passive idea; but this arises from the combination with the *per* and the ἐς κόρακας, &c. That 'go' does not carry in itself the idea of a passive is clear from our own phrases 'go to the Bar,' or 'into the Church,' or 'into business.' Curtius (Beiträge, p. 329) goes still farther, and conjectures that the θη which appears in the aorist and future of Greek passives is connected with the S. vb. *yā* 'go,' in which however all resemblance seems limited to the long vowel. I pass then from the passive.

The causal mood of the Sanskrit verb, as well as the tenth conjugation in general, having for their distinguishing character the syllable *ay*,[1] Bopp's mind is divided by a doubt whether this suffix should be referred to the verb *i* 'go' or *i* 'wish.' The latter one would think is far better fitted for the formation of a desiderative mood, which, it seems, is a general appendage to the Sanskrit verb. Nor does *i* 'go' at first sight appear a satisfactory element for the purpose of

---

[1] Of causals some make *ay* the suffix, some *ya*. I believe the former to be right.

constituting a causal verb; but we are assured by Bopp (§ 740) that several Sanskrit words which denote 'motion' at the same time denote 'making.' Whether the particular verb *i* has this convenient privilege he does not stop to tell us. Assuming however that it has, we have before us a strange combination, that roots expressive of 'going' are alike fitted to form passives and to form actives.

But further, although the causative idea is declared to be the character of the tenth conjugation, I find little proof of this in the list of fifty-seven verbs quoted by Professor Wilson in his Grammar, for of all these at the utmost one in five can be explained as containing the idea 'to make.' Thus the first ten in the series are translated by the English verbs 'steal, disrespect, hurt, send, wink, speak, play, be feeble, be able, sound.' I am not then surprised to find in § 772 such a sentence as, 'It deserves however notice that in Sanskrit denominative verbs in *ya*[1] occasionally avail themselves of the causal form without any causal meaning.' My own feeling is that the original notion *paulatim* resides in *ay*, and that it is the Sanskrit variety of that suffix which I have discussed at length in my paper on *agh* or *ag*, the passage of a *g* between vowels (*aydmi*) into a *y* being a common occurrence. On this theory the meaning may well pass into that of frequentative or continuous. But leaving this question open, if we accept that one of Bopp's two explanations which finds in the suffix of the so-called Sanskrit causals or tenth conjugation the root *i* 'go,' we shall have to assign to this use of the word a

---

[1] See note on the preceding page.

somewhat vast domain in the classical and German languages, for Bopp connects with the same type all the vowel-verbs of the Latin, at any rate the first, second, and fourth conjugations of that language (§ 745 c.); all the Greek verbs in εω, αω, οω, αζω, ιζω (§§ 109 a. b. 749, and 762), together with the particular verbs βάλλω, στέλλω, ιάλλω, and ἵημι; and lastly all the weak verbs of the German stock (§ 109). A few of these verbs specially noticed by Bopp himself may claim a few words. We are assured that the Latin *facio* = S. *bháv-dyámi*, literally 'I make to be;' *iacio* = *yáp-dyámi* 'I make to go;' *doceo* = *gñáp-dyámi* 'I make to know;' *rapio* = *ráp-dyámi* 'I make to give' (§ 747). It seems somewhat damaging to this theory that the suffixes *i* or *e* of the Latin, which Bopp himself holds to be the representatives of the S. *ay*, contribute but little to the formation of the causative idea, seeing that *fac-*, *iac-*, *doc-*, *rap-* in themselves already express the full notion of 'making, throwing, teaching, robbing;' as may be seen in the forms *fac-ere*, *iac-ere*, *rap-ere*, and in *fac-tus*, *iac-tus*, *doc-tus*, *rap-tus*. *Yá-p-dyámi* is thought to possess a second suffix of causation in its *p*, so that *yá* 'go' is the real base of the verb; and if this case be doubtful, a causal *p* is declared with greater certainty to be an element in *gñá-p-dyámi* 'I make to know,' *gñá* (or in English characters *jná*) being what Bopp is pleased to call a root-verb, the equivalent of our *know*. But of this *jná* more hereafter. To place Bopp's doctrine clearly before me, I throw aside the equivalent portions *eo* and *dyámi*, and there results the equation, Lat. *dŏc* = S. *jnáp*. No doubt the palatal *j* of the Sanskrit is with reason assumed to be a corruption of a medial guttural *g* or γ. The business then is to prove that *dŏc* is equal to *gnáp*. I make no difficulty about the final consonants, for a Lat. *c* habitually corresponds to a S. *p*. But there still remain three problems for solution,—to identify the *d* with *g*, the short *o* with the long *a*, and to account for the appearance of *n* in the Sanskrit or its disappearance from the Latin. For the first Bopp simply quotes the instance Δη-μητηρ — Γη-μητηρ; on the difference of vowel he says nothing. The difficulty as to the nasal is disposed of by the assurance that for *gñá-ná-mi* 'I know' there occurs an actual *gá-ná-mi*, and that in Persian there exists the form *dá-ne-m* 'I know.' But surely the asserted loss of an *n* from *gñá-ná-mi*, when followed so closely by a second *n*, is but a poor justification for the disappearance of an *n* in *doc* for *dnoc*. For one then I must regard the *doc* of *doceo* as better explained within the limits of the classical languages by *dec* of *deico* (= *dico*) and δεικ-νυμι, by δακ, the root of δι-δασκω, δι-δακτος, and δακτυλος, by the *dic* of *di-dic-i* and *dig* of *dig-itus*. But if I must look to the Sanskrit, here too I find a thoroughly admissible representative in the vb. *diś* 'show,' with that palatal *s* which regularly corresponds to a western *k*-sound; and indeed Bopp himself I find, in his 'Glossary,' regards this root *diś* as one with the root of δεικνυμι and the Lat. *dico*.[1]

---

[1] As some friends well acquainted with Sanskrit were slow to believe that a writer like Bopp could have published such 'extravagancies,' I quote his very words (§ 747): 'Kan ich aber das *c* der genannten Form (*facio*) nicht mit dem skr. causalen *p*. vermitteln, so glaube ich doch dem Lateinischen noch ein anderes Causale nachweisen zu können, worin *c* die Stelle eines skr. *p* vertritt, nämlich *doceo*, welches ich im Sinne von ich mache wissen auffasse und für verwandt mit *dí-śo* (eigentlich ich wünsche zu wissen)

The *p* of *rap-* or *rapi-*, as also that of the S. *rápayámi*, is again treated by Bopp as of causal power, and he finds in his root *rá* 'give' only a variety of *dá* 'give.' Thus 'to give' and 'to cause to give or rob' owe their marked difference of meaning to the causal suffix; not that this is an essential matter with him, for this same root *dá* or *rá* is thought by him to be identical with the S. vb. *lá,* to which simple form is ascribed the double meaning of 'to give' and 'to take,' a mixture of ideas which, if carried out in life, might lead to inconvenient results.[1]

So much for the value to the Sanskritist of his roots signifying 'to go' in the way of etymology; and the stock is no small one. Taking of the ten conjugations the first alone, and again limiting myself to the series which Professor Wilson quotes in his Grammar as 'the most useful verbs of this conjugation,' I find just twenty, viz. 1. *aj* 'to go;' 2. *at* 'to go;' 3. *i* 'to go;' 4. *du* 'to go;' 5. *ukh* 'to go;' 6. *r* 'to go,' 'to gain;' 7. *rj* 'to be straight' or 'honest,' 'to gain,' 'to go,' 'to live;' 8. *kram* 'to go,' 'to walk;' 9. *gam* 'to go;' 13. *vichchh* 'to go;' 11. *char* 'to go;' 12. *dhauk* 'to go;' 13. *pat*

---

und dem gr. ὁδάν, ὁδεύω halte. Ist das *d* dieser Formen aus *g* entstanden (vgl. Δημήτηρ aus Γημήτηρ), so führt doch zum skr. *ǵadpáyámi,* Ich mache wissen *ǵd-ad-mi* ich weiss für *ǵnd-nd-mi*) und zum peru. *dd-na-m* Ich weiss. Als ein Beispiel eines lat. Causals, worin das ursprüngliche *p* unverändert geblieben wäre, erwiese sich *rapio,* im Fall es dem skr. *rápayámi* ich mache geben entspricht, von der Wz. *rd* geben, die, wie mir scheint, nichts anderes als eine Schwächung von *dd* ist. Auch kommt, sowie neben *dd* eine erweiterte Form *dds* besteht, neben *rd* im Vêda-Dialekt *rds* vor. Mit *rd* und *dd* scheint auch ihrem Ursprunge nach die Wz. *ld* identisch, welcher die Bedeutungen geben und nehmen zugeschrieben werden.'

[1] Ibid.

'to go,' 'to fall;' 14. *śad* 'to wither' or 'decay,' 'to go' (with this appended: When the verb means 'to go,' the causal retains the final,—*śādayati* 'he causes to go,' or 'drives'); 15. *sad* 'to decay,' 'to be sad,' 'to go;' 16. *sasj* 'to go;' 17. *sidh* 'to go;' 18. *sṛ* 'to go;' 19. *sṛp* 'to go,' 'to creep' or 'glide;' 20. *skand* 'to go' or 'approach.' I should have made some addition to this list had I included those verbs which only express a more special or limited form of motion, as 'pervade, jump, hasten, run, gallop, approach, wander.'

With such an abundance of verbs to draw from, a philologer should the more hold himself bound to proceed with caution, and so take care that the logical connexion between the root and the supposed derivative should be well-marked. Whether the examples I have quoted exhibit such caution, I leave to others to decide. Lastly, I think it right to repeat that, by confining myself almost wholly to those instances of bold etymology which deal with verbs signifying 'to go,' I avoid the charge of selecting instances favourable to my view. Indeed without some such limitation it would be an easy matter to pick holes in any of the most carefully elaborated philological works, for the most cautious etymologer is apt to be carried away at times by tempting theories. In the next section of my paper I purpose more particularly to consider Bopp's celebrated work, the 'Vergleichende Grammatik,' in its general system.

In the short discussion which followed the reading of the above paper at the Philological Society it was replied on one side that the idea of 'to go' was precisely that which was well adapted to denote an active verb. To this I answer that a vb. 'to go' was equally claimed for the special formation of passives; but in truth the argument seems to me upset by its very generality. What is fitted to denote every form of action is for that reason unfitted to denote any form of action. The very essence of language is distinction or difference. Accordingly the other answer to the difficulties I had raised was that although simple 'going' is commonly assigned as the meaning of the verbs I have quoted, yet in truth each of them originally denoted some special form of going. Such seems to be the feeling of Bopp also (V. G. § 515). I will only reply to this that I took the verbs with the meaning attached to them by the several authorities from whom I was quoting. But over and above this, when the discussion was brought to the individual substantives, I found that the Sanskrit scholars who were present employed in the defence of the Indian etymologies a vagueness as complete as that expressed in the general term 'going.' Thus *go* and *ilá* 'the cow,' and *go* and *ilá* 'the earth,' were said to be well entitled to such derivation, as being in the Indian mind the centres of activity most important to man.

I take the opportunity of making a slight addition to the paper. As *sr*, according to Wilson's Grammar (p. 200), at times signifies 'to go quickly' or 'run,' I am the more justified in attributing to the suffixed *p* of *srp* the power of *paulatim*. At any rate it has no causal power here. Further, if the Sanskrit vocabulary could deduce from a verb signifying 'to run' by the addition of this suffix a secondary verb *srp* 'to creep,' I am justified in connecting our own *cr-ep* (whence *creep* and *crep-t*), as regards its root, with the base of the Dorsetshire *hir-n* = Ang.-Sax. *yrn-an* 'to run;' and that base, *hir*, corresponds of course to the Lat. *cur-* of *curro*. Again, if the S. verb *sal* 'go' is one with the verb *sr* 'go,' we have the analogue of this *sal* in the Greek ἄλλομαι and Latin *salio*, whence *sal tu-s* 'a sheep or cattle *run*.' I am the more inclined to attach some value to this conjecture, because as *fal* of *fallere* 'to cause to fall' seems to furnish the only[1] root for *fors fortis*, so does *sal-* for *sors sortis* 'that which leaps from the urn' (situla), a noun from which has come the verb *sortiri* of the Latin and the verb *sortir* (with a very different power, more akin to the original root) of the French. Lastly, let me observe that if the Sanskritists had been contented to derive *sarit* 'a river' from a root *sr* 'go' or rather 'run,' there could have been little objection, our own terms 'current' and 'watercourse,' Bull's 'Run' and 'runlet,' exhibiting a similar origin. Such terms as *saras* 'marsh or marshland' and *ap* 'water' have not the same justification.

---

[1] I have been somewhat hasty in using the word 'only,' for I find Mommsen (Inscr. p. 268) writing: 'Recte omnino *sortem* derivarunt grammatici quidam a *serie* et *serendo*, ut *fors* venit a *ferendo*.' But I still adhere to what is stated above.

XIII.

QVAERITVR.

Second Part.

It would be to shrink from the task I have undertaken were I not to take into special consideration the great work of Bopp, who appears with something like general consent to be entitled the founder of Comparative Grammar as a science; and the claim upon my attention is only the stronger that his 'Vergleichende Grammatik,' the first portion of which was published in 1833, has been recently reprinted with some changes and considerable additions (1857-60).

Here, as in what I have already said, I shall without further apology for my temerity proceed to state unreservedly the objections that have presented themselves to my mind, not expecting those objections to be accepted as valid, but desirous that they may attract the notice of scholars whose more intimate acquaintance with the subject will enable them to detect any errors I may have committed. The contest is happily one in which the victorious and the defeated must alike be gainers, the one object of both parties being to promote the cultivation of the science of language.

First of all then I find in the very title of the commencing chapter ('Schrift- und Laut-System') what appears to me unphilosophical, viz. the precedence given to writing over sound. Over a large portion of our globe there exist whole races possessed of the faculty of speech, but without any knowledge of written symbols; and indeed no small part of the population even of this country is in this position. But I should have passed over this matter if the error, so to call it, had not told unfavourably on the arguments that follow. The very first paragraph in the chapter gives to three of the vowels a special character, which, as it appears to me, is not due to them. Thus the title of original vowels (Urvocale) is assigned to *a, i, u ;* and this, I believe, on no other ground than that the Sanskrit alphabet had special characters for these when the sounds of *e* and *o* may have been denoted by combinations of the first three, much as the French language employs its dipthongs *ai* and *au* as simple vowels. Had the school of philology founded by Bopp looked upon the materials for oral language as belonging to the domain of physical science, and wholly independent of those other forms of language which are addressed to the eye, such an error could not have occurred. In particular I must repeat the regret, to which I had already given expression in the year 1852, when I drew up the present paper (Proceedings, vol. v. p. 192), that the valuable paper on vowel-sounds which was read by Professor Willis before the Cambridge Philosophical Society (November 28, 1828, and March 16, 1829) seems to have been wholly unnoticed by the leading scholars of Germany. At any rate, when I entered upon the present inquiry, I had never[1]

---

[1] I subsequently found that I had not done justice to German scholars in this remark. In Dr. Bindseil's 'Abhandlungen zur allgemeinen vergleichenden Sprachlehre' (Hamburg, 1838), p. 84, reference is made to Professor Willis's paper, and from the appended

come across the slightest allusion to this paper, or to the principles established in it, in any German writer; yet had read much from this quarter that would never have been written by any one acquainted with the results of Mr. Willis's experiments. Nay, I do not recollect to have seen at that time in any of their prominent works in the field of philology any reference to that physiological organ which may literally be called the *primum mobile* of human speech,—I mean the two *chordae vocales*. Now that Professor Czermak of Prague by his simple apparatus has enabled the inquirer to witness the action of these musical strings in the living man, we may hope that the study of oral language may be placed on its proper basis. It will then be laid down as the first dogma that as vowel-sounds constitute the substance of language (for brevity I drop the word 'oral,' which is the only form here under consideration), so the character of any vowel depends almost wholly on the distance for the time between the *chordae vocales* and the margin of the lips,—in other words, on the length of the vocal pipe,— the position of the tongue being of no moment so long as it does not close the passage of air. So thoroughly definite and mathematical is the character of the physical experiments on which Professor Willis's results are founded, that he has given numerical values

---

note I learn that the paper itself was reproduced in the German language in Poggendorff's 'Annalen der Physik und Chemie.' Still Dr. Bindseil himself seems to have been satisfied with a bare reference, making little or no use of the principle, nor does his work appear to have met with much notice among his countrymen. It stopped abruptly with the first volume, although this contains only a general introduction and a treatise on gender.

to the distances that belong to such of the vowels as are most familiar to English ears. At the same time as the number of points in a line is infinite, so the vowel-sounds pass by imperceptible gradations from the one extreme *i* (the sound in *feet*) to the other extreme *u* (or *oo* in *boot*). Thus it is wholly owing to the imperfection, yet necessary imperfection, of alphabets, that there is but a limited set of symbols for vowel-sound. The number itself is essentially infinite; and it was therefore a subject of amusement as well as regret to hear some few years ago that a conclave of learned philologers was then sitting in London to determine, among other high matters, what was the full number of vowels.

But the vowel-order *i, e, a, o, u* (with the sounds which prevail on the Continent), as resulting from Professor Willis's experiments, would have supplied the German philologers with a principle capable of solving pretty well all the problems that arise in connexion with the vowels, not merely of the Indo-European family, but of language in general. In the paper already referred to (Proc. Philolog. Soc. vol. v. pp. 191—204) I have shown in some detail that it explains the *umlaut* and *rück-umlaut* so-called of German philology, the formation of plurals in English, &c. by what Grimm calls 'motion,'—that is, an alteration of the root-vowel, as in *geese* from *goose*, and generally the assimilation of adjoining vowels so familiar in all the Tatar languages and prevalent to a considerable extent in the Keltic, Teutonic, and Classical languages, to say nothing of others. In page 203 of the paper I gave, from my colleague, Professor Malden, a tabular view, showing the full development of the principle in the changes of Greek vowels and diphthongs. And I have little doubt that the mysterious Guṇa and Vriddhi of Sanskrit are simply results of the same law.

No doubt Bopp has allusions to the principle of vowel-assimilation, but these are altogether incidental. Thus it is only when he passes from the Sanskrit (§§ 41, 42) to deal with the Zend, that he notices some cases where the presence of a y, i, or e affects the vowel of an adjoining syllable, and in § 46 mention is made of a similar euphonic influence belonging to a Zend v (w). But these are matters which should not be treated as peculiarities of the Zend. The philologer is bound to state the law of vowel-assimilation in its broad simplicity.

But there is another point in which Sanskritists seem to have been misled by the habit of looking at language in its written aspect. They ascribe to the Sanskrit, in accordance no doubt with Indian authority, two vowels, r and lr, which at any rate do not present themselves in the vowel-series of the Cambridge Professor. Moreover it is admitted that this vowel r is closely related to the ordinary liquid r. May I propose as the probable solution of the whole difficulty the following?—It is well known that the two liquids r and l often lead to the disappearance of an adjoining vowel; most persons would say to a metathesis of the vowel, a doctrine which I hold to arise from an inaccurate view of the matter, though this for the present is not important. Our own *thorough* for example appears in the two shapes *through* Eng. and *durch* Germ. Again, in our provinces the form *brid* is at times used, where the prevalent language prefers *bird*;

so *pretty* and *perty* coexist. The Latin too has *truc-* and *toru-o-*, and the Greek θρασος and θαρσος, with but little distinction of meaning and no distinction of origin. In such cases it is convenient to have a notation which will readily adapt itself to the two varieties of pronunciation; and on this principle it would not have been unwise to employ such a form as *brd*, *prty*, to represent at once *bird* and *brid*, *perty* and *pretty*. The Slavic languages are not less given to such varieties than others; and accordingly words without any represented vowel occur in the Bohemian vocabulary, as *krt* 'mole,' *krk* 'neck,' *blb* 'blockhead,' *wlk* 'wolf.' Yet Dobrowsky does not on this account class *r* and *l* with the vowels of the language. Possibly the habit of virtually dropping the letters *r* and *l*, as in the case of *bird* in the mouth of a Londoner (*bŏd*), and *talk*, *calm* generally, as well as the Fr. *meilleur*, may have had its counterpart in India, and so have lent some encouragement to the doctrine that they are vowels.

But to return to the ordinary vowels: if a language is limited to three symbols for their representation, it is a matter of course that *a* should have a first preference, because, lying in the middle of the series, it is for that very reason the easiest to pronounce, and consequently the most common; and after *a* the vowels *i* and *u* have the next claim, as occupying the two extremities.

It has also been urged that the Sanskrit alphabet has a special claim to our consideration in its philosophic completeness. But this claim is open to grave doubt, seeing that it appears to have been without any character for the sound, if indeed it possessed the sound itself, that is heard in the initial consonants of our English *thin* and *thine*, *fat*, *vat*, in the two consonants of the Fr. *juge* and the final of the German *einfach*. On the other hand, it appears superfluously rich in its ten asperates, distributed through the so-called gutturals, palatals, cerebrals, dentals, and labials; that is, if our informants be right in pronouncing these asperates as we pronounce the italic consonants of block*h*ouse, log*h*ouse, coac*hh*ouse, bridge*h*ouse, cart*h*ouse, guar*dh*ouse, chop*h*ouse, club*h*ouse. If such be the correct pronunciation, the non-asperate character together with the simple *h* might surely have sufficed. I have also assumed that व (*va* of German Sanskritists) corresponded to an English *w*. But if it really be a *v*, then a *w* is wanting; if it be at one time a *v*, at another a *w*, then we have another defect in the alphabet, two uses of a single symbol. But these very difficulties about the pronunciation seem to be valid reasons why we should select our primary facts from the known sounds of living tongues, rather than draw from alphabets of ancient date, no matter how venerable, in which the problems of pronunciation must to a considerable extent be full of difficulty, if not insoluble.

The second main-heading in Bopp's work is 'On Roots' (Von den Wurzeln). As regards the preliminary discussion which treats of the distribution of languages into classes, I will confine myself to the remark, that as in the preceding chapter, so here again the author appears to have been led astray by the consideration of written language. No doubt the Chinese is to the eye monosyllabic. To the ear not so; for it is well known to those who have learnt to speak the language in China itself, that it abounds in disyllabic and polysyllabic words, whose unity, as with us, is denoted by the possession of a single accent. Thus Bopp is simply wrong in his statement of facts about the Chinese language (§ 108, p. 201, note); and again his definition of the Semitic family as one having disyllabic roots is at variance with the doctrine, now maintained by many of the first Hebrew scholars, that these apparent roots are in truth secondary forms. And indeed the Hindostani furnishes an instructive parallel, for here too it seems the existing verbs cannot be reduced to forms of less than two syllables, until we pass from the limits of the Hindostani to the parent Sanskrit.

I must also point to another instance of error similarly caused. The peculiar notation employed for Hebrew words, in which symbols for consonants play the most important part, and the habit of denoting variations of meaning to a great extent by mere variation of vowels, as *katul* 'killed' with a fem. *ktul-ah*, and *kotel* 'killing' with a fem. *kotl-ah* (§ 107, p. 196), have together led Bopp and his followers to call the consonantal combination *ktl* the root of the verb in question, although this combination is for the ear an absolute nullity. Nor is he himself blind to this inference, for he expressly says: "A Semitic root is unpronounceable." As well might he, with the English words *bind, band, bond, bound, bundle* before him, set down as the root of this English verb the letters *bnd*.

But I pass to a graver matter, and one that affects the whole texture of the book. The German philologer, departing from the course marked out by his Indian authorities, refuses to accept the doctrine that all words are traceable back to verbs. Accordingly he divides the roots of the Indo-European family into two classes. 'The main principle of Word-building in this class,' says he (§ 109 a, p. 203), 'appears to me to lie in the union of verbal and pronominal roots, which together constitute, as it were, the life and soul' (of the language). Poetical escapades of this kind naturally excite a suspicion of weakness in a theory. I propose then to examine this doctrine of pronominal roots in some detail. It is one that is also maintained by Prof. Max Müller in his 'Lectures on Language' (p. 272, &c.). His nomenclature indeed is slightly different from that of Bopp's. To 'verbal' he prefers the term 'predicative,' and instead of 'pronominal' he talks of 'demonstrative' roots; but substantially the two writers agree. As Prof. Max Müller is somewhat more definite than his fellow-countryman in his statement on this subject, I will quote a few lines from him. 'If they (our primitive ancestors),' says he, 'wanted to express *here* and *there*, *who*, *what*, *this*, *that*, *thou*, *he*, they would have found it impossible to find any predicative root that could be applied to this purpose.' And hence he says soon after: 'We must admit a small class of independent radicals, not predicative in the usual sense of the word, but simply pointing, simply expressive of existence under certain . . . . prescriptions.' I accept the challenge implied in the first of these paragraphs, or rather accepted it many years before it was given, for already, in 1847, in the 'Proceedings of the Philolog. Soc.' (vol. iii. p. 56) I put forward the theory that such a verb as our own 'ken' or 'look' as an imperative would supply what was wanted.

In the paper to which I refer the problem was considered in considerable detail, alike from the formal and logical points of view. Thus, as regards the mere shape of the words, I showed that pronouns of the third person exhibited an initial guttural in pretty well all the languages of Europe and Asia from the Atlantic to the Pacific, and from the Mediterranean to the Arctic Sea. On the other hand I produced similar evidence for the presence of a final nasal, and so accounted for the form of the Sanskrit *kim* which is set down as the 'dhâtu' of the relative, but by its final letter has been, I find, a stumbling-block to Sanskritists. In short, I considered that a syllable *ken*, or something like it, appeared to be the basis of pronominal words of the third person, including in that term demonstratives, relatives, and interrogatives, which I held to be of one stock. On the other hand I regard this basis of pronouns to be one with our English verb *ken* 'see.' But of course I could not rely on our English language alone, or even its German congeners. As *ken*, or if it be preferred *con*, is the simple root whence comes our derived verb *k(e)n-ow* or *k(o)n-ow*, in precise agreement with the verbs *bell* and *bellow*, so the root in question virtually exists in all those languages which possess a representative of *know*, as Latin with its *gnosco*, Greek with its γιγνωσκω, and Sanskrit with its *jnâ*. Nay, the Latin itself has traces of the simpler verb *gon*. I refer first of all to the participles *a-gn-itus*, *co-gn-itus*, which come from stems *a-gon-*, *co-gon-*. From *agnosc-* and *cognosc-* we must have had *agnōtus cognōtus*. Secondly, *cătus* 'shrewd' seems to be a participle from a stem *cen*, just as in Greek we find words ending in φατος from φεν- 'kill.' Over and above this I pointed to the suffix *ce* of Latin demonstratives, as *hic, istic, illic, sic, nunc,* &c. and the so-called interjection *en* ' behold,' as exhibiting our root *ken* in two fragmentary varieties, much as a particle of totally different origin yet identical form, the Homeric κεν, takes in Greek the several corrupted forms of κε or κα and αν. Further, as the range I claimed for the pronominal base *ken* extended to the Pacific, so I quoted from the Chinese itself a verb *ken* 'see.' But I failed to notice the simple verb in Sanskrit. Let me now supply this omission by producing the reduplicate verb in *mi*, chi-*ket*-mi 'I see.' This verb Bopp himself identifies as regards root with the Sanskrit verb *chit* 'perceive, know,' and this again with the Zend *chin* (V. G. 109 b 2, Anm. p. 239), so that the change of *ken* to *ket* is no difficulty for Bopp; and I confirm this by the parallel case of the Latin pronominal form *cit-ra, cit-ro, cit-erior, cit-imus*. I am further indebted to Bopp for a knowledge of three other analogues of my verb, *quita* or *kita* of the Philippines, the New Zealand *kitea*, and Malagash *hita*, words also signifying 'to see,' and identified by himself with the Sanskrit *ket* (§ 87 2). Again, the root in its purest form is found in the Keltic family, as in Cornish *gon*, and Old Irish *gen* 'know' (W. Stokes's edition of the Middle-Cornish poem 'The Passion,' notes, p. 94). Lastly, the Lithuanian has the particle *kat* 'see there.' Thus the area of the verb is as extensive as that of the pronoun. On the side of form then there remains nothing to desire; and as to meaning I would ask whether any idea could be in better keeping with pronominal demonstratives than that of 'see,' 'look.' The very word 'demonstrative,' which Prof. Max Müller selects for his definition, suggests this interpretation; and he himself adds that their office is 'to point,' and so determine 'locality.' It would be more correct to say that it belongs to the finger to point and to the voice only to call attention to the finger's direction by uttering the word 'look.' It is with this feeling that the French has formed its *voici* and *voilà*, and of these the latter is often cut down in rapid pronunciation to *v'là*, an abbreviation which is in keeping with what has been seen in our assumed corruptions of *ken*. I have already pointed to Terence's *luciscit hoc iam* and Virgil's *nunc dextra ingeminans ictus, nunc ille sinistra*, as instances where the most graphic mode of translation is to treat the two demonstrative pronouns as practically the imperatives of a verb with the signification of 'look,' repeated if preferred, for both *hic* and *ille* when closely analysed turn out to be reduplicated forms. It may be observed too that our own *lo* is an example of a verb, *look*, cut down to what is little better than a particle. Nay, when we ourselves utter the word *this* or *that*, we do little more than invite the person addressed to direct his eye to some object at which we are pointing, so that in real power these words are equivalent to an imperative 'look.' No doubt the mind is not at once reconciled to the identification of a verb with an adjective, much less to the declension of a verb as though it were an adjective. Yet if the Latin *ecce* 'behold' is a verb, and few will venture to deny it, we have a perfect parallel in such phrases as *eccum me, eccos uideo incedere patrem et magistrum*, as used by l'lautua. For the full details of my argument I must of course refer to the paper itself. But whether my theory be right or wrong, I trust I have said enough to show that Prof. Max Müller's broad denial of the possibility of finding a suitable 'predicative' root is untenable.

On the other hand let us look at the general theory of roots, whether 'verbal' or 'pronominal,' as put forward by the German school. Bopp indeed puts aside for the most part the question of the origin of words, as not falling within the scope of his work, but Prof. Max Müller speaks somewhat more definitely on this subject. Yet his views, I think, will not be found satisfactory to others, and seem not altogether satisfactory to himself, for, after touching on the topic at the beginning of his book, he practically postpones the question to his last chapter, pp. 349—399, and even then he nearly reaches the end of the chapter before he comes to the point. It is only in page 391 that he says: 'And now I am afraid that I have but a few minutes left to explain the last question of all in our science—How can sound express thought?' I find another reason for doubting whether he is a firm believer in his own theory. The said chapter begins with an admirable extract from a work of Dugald Stewart's which spurns with contempt 'that indolent philosophy which refers to a miracle whatever appearances, both in the material and moral worlds, it is unable to explain.' I say then that when Prof. Max Müller transcribed these words, he had not yet given a thoroughly cordial assent to the view of language with which the chapter ends; for he himself, in his distress, practically summons to his aid the *deus ex machina*, first telling us (p. 392) that 'man in his primitive and perfect state possessed the faculty of giving expression to the rational conceptions of his mind,' and then adding that 'that faculty was an instinct, an instinct of the mind as irresistible as any other instinct.' Further in a note he says: 'The faculty peculiar to man in his primitive state, by which every impression from without received its vocal expression from within, must be accepted as an ultimate fact.' For myself, I can only look upon this last passage as a simple admission that he has no solution of the problem to offer, while the preceding assumption, that language is the result of instinct, seems to savour of that indolent philosophy which the Scotch philosopher is quoted to condemn. Again, the assertion that language first came into play when man was 'in his primitive and perfect state,' seems hardly consistent with the tone of the first lecture, in which he led his hearers to anticipate a very different conclusion. That lecture begins with a justification of the phrase 'Science of Language,' and then refers the origin of every one of our sciences to the agency of man, as stimulated by his 'wants,' when society was yet semi-barbarous or half-savage; and his argument further implies that all the sciences, including of course that of language, were things of gradual growth, beginning in what was humble and lowly. All this is surely at variance with his later theory, that 'the 400 or 500 roots' which are 'the constituent elements' of language are 'phonetic types produced by a power inherent in human nature,' and 'exist, as Plato would say, by nature; though with Plato we should add that, when we say nature, we mean by the hand of God.' One cannot but think that such explanations must have been intended for the class of people so well described by Prof. Max Müller himself (p. 364), those 'who prefer the unintelligible which they can admire to the intelligible which they can only understand.'

But before I pass from his Lectures, I take the opportunity of commenting on two other kindred matters. In p. 351, having said that 'man could not by his own power have acquired the faculty of speech, which is the distinctive character of mankind, unattained and unattainable by the mute creation,' he confirms his proposition by a reference to Wilhelm v. Humboldt's writings: 'Man is only man through language, but to invent language he must already have been man.' This is a taking argument, and one that would be thoroughly valid on the assumption that language must have been created, so to say, at one gush, like a metallic casting. But if we include in our view the possibility of a gradual and slow development of the faculty, such as Max Müller himself in his first chapter assigns to the creation of all the sciences, including by implication the science of language itself, the whole difficulty is dispelled. On this theory the human mind and the faculty of speech react each on the other, and thus 'the foundation-stone of what was to be one of the most glorious structures of human ingenuity in ages to come may have been supplied by the pressing wants of a semi-barbarous society' ('Lectures,' p. 5).

But there is another writer, and he not a German, who, as agreeing in one of the two phases of the Oxford Professor's book, claims our attention. In the

'Study of Words' (p. 16) there stands the sentence:
'God gave man language, because he could not be
man without it.' This seems to imply that language
was contemporary with man's creation. May I be
permitted then to ask how this doctrine is to be
reconciled with what I suppose will be allowed on all
hands as a fact, that the primitive language must
have been wholly wanting in terms for spiritual and
metaphysical ideas, seeing that the roots of language
in their first meaning are very generally held to have
a special reference to the material world. Hence, if
the said doctrine be well-grounded, at the very time
that primitive man existed in the most perfect, the
most spiritual condition, he was yet destitute, it would
seem, of terms to correspond with all the sublimer
elements of his mind. In saying that terms for spiritual
ideas are generally traceable to a material origin, I
have in view such cases as the derivation of *anima*
'soul' from *an* 'to blow,' of *spirit* from *spirare* 'to
breathe,' and of *ghost* as connected with *gust*, with
gas, with *yeast* ('Lectures on Language,' p. 387). But
while I take these examples from Prof. Max Müller,
I must demur to his derivation of *soul*, Gothic *saivala*,
from *saiv-s* 'the sea,' and still more to his explanation that 'the soul was originally conceived by the
Teutonic nations as a sea within heaving up and
down with every breath, and reflecting heaven and
earth on the mirror of the deep.' As I have said
before, I am always alarmed when I find poetry doing
duty for logic. Still, in reliance on more sober examples, I venture to affirm again that the late formation of spiritual language is more consistent with
the theory of man's progressive improvement than

with the converse theory of his degradation,—in other words, more consistent with the first phasis of Prof. Max Müller's book than with the second.

The 'instinctive' origin of language, as laid down in the 'Lectures,' might to some minds have suggested the inference that language ought then to be the same for all people in all countries, and that every infant at the outset of its little life would have been possessed of useful speech; but a condition of things so much to be desired is sadly at variance with fact. This difficulty however the author of the theory at once meets by a little corollary to his theory, that 'man loses his instincts as he ceases to want them.' Yet in speaking of his 'demonstrative' roots (p. 272) he seems to imply that the instinctive movement still retains its force. 'The sound *ta* or *sa*,' says he, referring to the Sanskrit pronouns, 'for "this" or "there" is' (note the present tense) 'as involuntary, as natural, as independent an expression as any of the predicative roots.' It must be due to some unhappy idiosyncrasy, I suppose, that I myself feel not the slightest tendency to follow such an impulse, however natural, however involuntary it ought to be. If I want to say 'this,' I say *this*; if I want to say 'there,' I say *there*. I certainly do not say either *sa* or *ta*.

But, admitting for the nonce the new doctrine of pronominal or demonstrative roots, let us consider the purposes to which they are applied by Bopp and the Oxford Professor. In the instances I am about to quote from these two writers I wish special attention to be paid to the habitual, almost universal, assumption, that if the conditions of outward form be satisfied, it is unnecessary to enter into any logical proof of the appropriateness of the idea. As the references on this head to Prof. M. Müller will be but few, those to Bopp numerous, it may be convenient to give precedence to the disciple over the master. In the index to the 'Lectures,' under the word *declension*, I find the proposition that 'most of the terminations of declension' are 'demonstrative roots.' Again, in the text (p. 274), we are told that 'the Latin word *luc-s*' is formed by 'the addition of the pronominal element *s*,' and signifies literally 'shining-there;' and he goes on to say that by adding 'other pronominal derivatives' we get '*lucidus, luculentus, lucerna,* &c.' What these other pronominal elements are, or how they are fitted for the purpose, he deems it unnecessary to tell us. So in p. 221 he says that 'the short *i* of the Sanskrit locative *hridi* "in the heart" is a demonstrative root, and in all probability the same root which in Latin produced the preposition *in*.' He goes on to deal with the formation of the genitive, dative, and accusative, but in a manner so misty to my comprehension that I fail to pick up a single idea, and can solely refer to his book, pp. 221—224.

Bopp starts (§ 105) with the doctrine that the class of roots he calls pronominal 'give origin to the pronouns, to original prepositions, to conjunctions, and particles.' In § 115 he advances a step farther, claiming 'the case-endings as, at any rate for the most part, of like origin.' Looking upon the nouns of language as the *Personae Dramatis* of the World of Speech, he holds that 'the original office of case-suffixes was to express the mutual relations between these "Personae" in respect of place;' and with this feeling he asks 'What class of words could be better qualified to fulfil such an office, than those which at once express personality and the idea of place, whether nearer or more remote, whether on this side or on that?' Accordingly (in § 134, p. 277) the *s* of the nominative is referred to the pronoun *sa* 'he, this, that,' fem. *sd*; (in § 156, p. 320) the *m* of accusative masc. and fem. to the compound pronouns *i-ma* 'this,' *a-mu* 'that;' and the final *t* which presents itself in the neut. nom. and acc. of certain pronouns, as *tat* and *kat* of the Vôda dialect, to the neut. pron. *ta*, Gr. το. Again, in § 158 the suffix *â* of the instrumental case is 'as he believes' but a lengthened variety of the pronoun *a*, and one with the prep. *â* 'to' (Germ. *an*), a meaning however which one might have thought would be more in place in the accusative. In § 164, p. 329, the dative *ê* is said probably to belong to the demonstrative *ê*, 'which *ê* however is apparently only an extension of the stem *a*,'—that is, the very pronoun which has already done duty for the instrumental. In § 179, *t* we are told is the characteristic of the ablative, and 'no one' (I quote his own words) 'who has once acknowledged the influence of prepositions on case-endings, can have any doubt in referring it to the demonstrative stem *ta* "this," which has already in the neut. nom. and acc. put on the nature of a case-symbol, and will presently be found supporting the character of a personal suffix in verbs;' so that Bopp seems to think that the fact of its employment in two duties is a reason for adding a third duty. Most people, I think, would have arrived at an opposite conclusion. In § 184, p. 378, and § 194, p. 393, the genitival suffix *s* is held to be one with that of the nom., and so the same as *sa* 'this,' while the longer suffix *sya* of genitives is the Vaidic pron. *sya*,—that is, a compound of two pronouns, *sa* 'this,' and the relative *ya*. Lastly, the *i* of the locative he identifies, like Prof. M. Müller, with the demonstrative *i*.

I might be charged with a want of fairness to Bopp if I omitted to report an argument by which he defends his theory as regards the nominatival *s* in the masc. and fem. In the declension of the simple pronoun *sa* 'this,' he observes that it is only the nom. m. and f. that present the *s*, the neut. nom. and all the oblique cases having an initial *t*, just as in Greek we have ὁ, ἡ, with a mere asperate, but afterwards το, του, της, του, &c., so that there is a peculiar fitness in the employment of this pronoun for the two forms for which he claims it. However, he subsequently damages his theory by admitting (§ 345) that originally the *s* may have been carried through all the cases and numbers, excepting only the neuters, and quotes the Vaidic locative *sasmin* for *tasmin*, and the old Latin *sum*, *sam*, &c., for *eum*, *eam*, &c. And even this persistence in excluding an *s* from the neuter is at variance with his own statement (ibid.) that the Greek σητες, σημερον, stand for σο-ετες, σο-ημερον, which σο he himself holds to be of the same stock with the Sansk. *sa*.

Thus for all the case-endings it is enough with our author to find some pronoun signifying 'this' or 'that' or 'what,' it matters little to him which, and to defend himself behind the position that case-endings are in their nature of a locative character. He fails to see that the pronouns in question are but pointers;

and define only position, and even then had no definite meaning in the outset of things, until aided by the pointing fingers. He himself indeed admits (§ 371, p. 180,) that the same pronoun originally signified 'this' or 'that,' 'nearer' or 'farther,' the mind supplying the necessary limitation. But while the demonstrative pronouns at most define only the 'here' or the 'there,' it is the special office of case-endings to deal with motion as well as rest, to talk of the 'whence,' and the 'whither,' as well as the 'where.' Nay, if Bopp's system were valid, we might freely interchange all the case-endings.

But I have yet two other objections to offer, which seem each of them fatal to his doctrine. In the first place, the form he assigns to the case-endings is, in most instances, a very late and degraded form. For example, the locative and dative, which I believe to have been of one origin, have assigned to them as suffixes nothing but the vowels *i* and *i* respectively. But the Latin in *i-bi, ali-bi, utru-bi,* exhibits a *b*, and as the Greek habitually has φ as the representative of a Latin *b*, there can be little doubt that the Homeric ουρανο-φι presents the suffix in a more accurate shape than the ordinary Sanskrit locative. There is still another letter to re-establish in its proper position, a final *n*; and Bopp himself admits that ουρανοφιν is the older form whence ουρανοφι was derived. The Latin *nobis, vobis,* by their long vowel, also betray the loss of an *n*, and still more accurately defined is the suffix in the Old Prussian dat. pl. in *man-s* (§ 215, p. 424). Nay, I cannot but suspect that the Sanskrit, in its masc. loc. *tas-min,* has also in the last three letters a satisfactory equivalent for the φιν or *bin,* for, on grounds independent of the present question (see Proceedings, iii. p. 66, note §, and iv. p. 30), I should claim *tas*, rather than *ta*, for the root-syllable of the pronoun, and this view is confirmed by several other cases of the pronoun. So too the Umbrian locative appears to have had a suffix *men* or *mem* (§ 200, p. 400), and the Zend for the dative of the first personal pronoun has *mai-byá*, the long *a* of which would have a satisfactory explanation in the disappearance of a nasal. But, to take a more general survey of the question, I would object to the fragmentary manner in which the school of Bopp pursue the inquiry into the form of case-suffixes. Each case must originally have had a common form of its own, no matter to what declension a noun belonged, no matter what its gender; and again, it is easy to see in nearly every case that the plural and the so-called dual forms (which in fact are but varieties of plurals) contain, in addition to the case-suffix of the singular, a second suffix denoting plurality, either a nasal syllable, as in our *ox-en*, or a sibilant, as in our *cow-s*. Hence in our search for the full forms of case-suffixes we are entitled, and therefore bound, to include all the forms belonging to a given case without distinction of declension, or gender, or number.

Then again, on the other side, Bopp appears to be unhappy in his dealings with his so-called pronominal roots. These also he has robbed, as it seems to me, of a final *n*, which readily interchanged as well with the liquid *m* as with members of its own dental class, *t* and *s*. Thus for the first syllable of the Latin *is-to-* I find a more satisfactory explanation of the *s* than Bopp's own theory (§ 343) that it results from 'a petrifaction' of the nominatival *s* of the simple pronoun *is*. But I go further. In his zeal for pronominal roots he seems positively to invent them, as for example *ma* (§ 368), *u* (§ 1,002), and above all his favourite *sma* (§ 165, &c.), of which he makes a most abundant, but I fear most unsatisfactory, use.

But it is a special office of Bopp's pronominal roots to supply a corps of prepositions, and accordingly he lays himself out for at least an easy solution of the problems likely to present themselves. The ideas of 'above' and 'below,' of 'before' and 'behind,' of 'in' and 'out,' stand in the relation of opposite poles to each other. The metaphor is Bopp's own. Hence the demonstrative pronouns are admirably suited to act as the needful symbols for these ideas, and so, what is particularly convenient, as they signify at once 'this' and 'that,' 'on this side' and 'on that side,' from one and the same pronoun we may deduce prepositions of directly opposite powers (§ 995). Thus from the pronoun *a*, to take that first as exhibiting the most wonderful fertility, with the aid of various suffixes, whose meaning seems to be a matter of not the slightest moment, for he never stops to explain them, we have S. *a-ti* 'over,' S. *a-dhas* 'under;' Lith. *a-nt* 'up,' Germ. *ent*, Lith. *a-t* 'to,' 'back;' S. *a-dhi* 'over,' 'up' (§ 997), with Lat. *ad* 'to;' S. *a-pi* 'over,' 'up' (§ 998), with ἐπι; S. *a-bhi* 'to' (§ 999), with ἀμφι, Lat. *amb* or *am* 'round,' Germ. *bei*, and Lat. *ob*; S. *a-pa* 'from' (§ 998), with ἀπο, Lat. *a-b*, Eng. *o-f* (the hyphens are Bopp's); and (§ 1,007) from *a-pa* itself, through an intermediate *apara-s* 'the other,' cut down to *para*, we have no less than five S. prepositions,—viz. *pra* 'before,' *prati* 'towards,' *pará* 'back,' 'away,' *puras*, and *pari*. Of these again *pra* (insepar.) 'before' has for its cognates προ, Lat. *pro*, Germ. *ver*. Then *prati* (§ 1,008) is represented by προτι and προς; while *pard* 'back,' 'away' (§ 1,009), gives us παρα; and through a second aphaeresis a prep. *ra* 'back' in some other language, which is one with the Lat. *re* 'back.' So much for one extensive family, all the progeny of the tiny pronoun *a* 'this' or 'that,' including too at once απο and παρα, at once *pro* and *re*.

To the S. pronoun *u*, if indeed such a pronoun exist, are to be referred, it seems, S. *u-pa* 'to,' S. *u-t* 'up;' as also the Gr. ὑπο, Lat. *sub*, and the adj. ὑ-σ-τερο-ς, together with Germ. *aus*, Eng. *out*. To meet the little difficulty about the asperate of ὑπο and the *s* of *sub*, Bopp proposes two theories: 'The *s* is either a simple phonetic prefix or the remnant of a recently prefixed pronoun *sa*,' which however, he adds, would be 'here devoid of meaning.'

The S. pronoun *ana* gives birth to S. *anu* 'after,' Old Pruss. and Slav. *na* 'up,' and ava 'up;' also to S. *ni* 'down,' Germ. *nie-der*; also to S. *ni-s* 'out,' and perhaps to the Slav. *i-su* 'out,' 'which may possibly have lost an initial *n*.'—The loss is the more to be deplored, as we lose at the same time all resemblance between *i-su* and its parent *ana*.

Thus Bopp has thoroughly fulfilled the promises he held out, as we have from the same sources words denoting 'above' and 'below,' 'to' and 'from,' 'backward' and 'forward,' 'absence' and 'presence,' 'up' and 'down.' And then how magical the changes.

With this wonderful manufacture by the Bopp school of prepositions and case-endings from pronominal roots, it may be useful to contrast a few specimens which may show the possibility at least of deducing prepositions and case-endings from verbs. Thus, to commence with a quotation from one of Bopp's own followers, we find in the 'Lectures' (p. 221): 'The instrumental (in Chinese) is formed by the preposition *ỹ*, which preposition is an old root meaning *to use*.' So in a little paper of my own (Proceedings, vol. vi. p. 120) it is stated on Premare's authority that the syllable commonly used in Chinese to denote the genitival relation, *tci*, is at times employed as a verb equivalent to the Latin *proficisci*. Again the Sanskrit inseparable preposition *ni*, Lith. *nu* 'down,' is to be identified with the Lat. vb. *nu-*, Gr. *νευ-*, 'lower,' 'hold down,' and the Chinese *ni* 'descend.' In the French *chez*, Ital. *casa*, and in our own *through*, Germ. *durch* and *dur*, we possibly have prepositions formed from substantives,—viz. the Lat. *casa* 'house,' and Germ. *thür*, Eng. *door*, Gr. θυρα. So little is it necessary to invent pronominal roots, as the source of prepositions.

On Bopp's derivation of particles from pronominal roots I must be brief. That words denoting 'yes' should be derived from pronouns signifying 'this' can surprise no one. Thus we assent at once to such a derivation of the Lat. *sic* and *ita* and *si* of the French, &c. But Bopp is bolder; he hesitates not to deduce the S. *na* 'not' and Lat. *ne* 'not' from his pronominal stem *na* 'this or that;' the Greek μη 'not' from his stem *ma*; and the Greek '*a* privativum' from *a* 'this' (§ 372, 1, p. 180). And here again he relies on his old doctrine that as such pronouns are qualified to denote alike 'this' and 'that' ('dieses' und 'jenes'), in the second of these senses they may well represent negation, for what is *there* is not *here*. It is somewhat unfortunate that the pronoun *a* has on his own showing a marked tendency to express presence (§ 366), as *a-tra* 'here,' *a-tas* 'from here,' *a-dya* 'to-day.' Nor is this to be set down as a late innovation in the life of Sanskrit, for its position must have been already well established before the breaking up of the primeval language, seeing that (to use his own illustrations) it is found in the old Irish *a-nochd* 'to-night' of the far west, and in the Ossetic *a-bon* 'to-day' of the far east. But be this as it may, the same pronominal *a*, once firmly possessed of negative power, is deemed by Bopp a fitting symbol for past time. 'I hold the augment,' says he, 'the initial *a* in *a-bhavam* "I was" for example, and so corresponding to the syllabic augment *ε* of *ε-τυπτ-ον*, &c., to be in its origin identical with the *a privativum*, and look upon it as expressing the negation of present time.' Nay even in such forms as *leg-ê-bam* (the division is Bopp's) he once thought the long quantity of the middle vowel was referable to a suffixed augment, but his confidence in this theory was ultimately shaken (§ 527).

Even among the verbs he is inclined to think that his pronouns play a part over and above their use in the personal endings. Of the suffixed τ in τυπ-τ-ω, ν in δακ-ν-ω and δεικ-ν-υ-μι, αν in λαμβ-αν-ω, he speaks with the greatest hesitation, yet still (§§ 494, 495) 'the most probable explanation' is that they are one and all of pronominal origin, their office being 'to convert the abstract of the verb in question into a concrete.' Nay even the so-called connecting vowels, as in φερ-ο-μεν, φερ-ε-τε, must be ascribed, he thinks, to a similar origin

(§ 500), and indeed to our old friend *a*, for the *o* and *e* of the Greek verbs just quoted are represented in Sanskrit by an *a*.

I now leave the pronominal roots with a strong impression on my mind that Bopp has failed to derive from his theory anything that adds to the value of his book. Even in his other division of roots I cannot divest myself of a fear that he has been wanting in caution. In § 109 *b* he gives us a list of thirty-two root-verbs. In looking over these I find at least fourteen which I have little doubt are secondary, that is, derivative verbs, and eight others that have been shorn of their fair proportions, having lost an initial or a final consonant, or both. On the present occasion I cannot deal with more than a few of them, but to avoid all suspicion of undue selection, I will take a batch that follow one another, those which stand 3d, 4th, 5th, and 6th in his series. The verb *ģnṛ̂* (or *jnâ*) is of course the Lat. *gnosc-o*, Eng. *know*, but in these verbs all that follows the liquid constitutes a suffix, while our obsolete English vb. *ken*, or rather *con*, exhibits the simple verb; and, as I have already noted, the Latin participles *a-gn-itus* and *co-gn-itus* are deduced from compounds, not of *gnosc-o*, but of a primary verb *gon*, corresponding to our *con*. The 4th in the series, *vâ* 'blow,' has suffered curtailment of its final consonant, and is really one with the 17th, *an* 'blow,' which has lost its initial consonant, the two being truncated forms of a fuller *van* which appears scarcely altered in the Germ. *wann-en*, and is the parent of our *winn-ow*, *wind*, and *fan*, as also of the Latin *vannus* and *ventus*. This double corruption of *van* to *vâ* and *an* would be exactly parallel to my assumption that the Lat. *ce* and *en* come from *ken*. The 5th *sti*, Lat. *sta*, though very generally set down as a root-verb, has a suffix, or rather the remnant of a suffix, in the *a*. The proof of this I find in the Latin *sist-o* as compared with *gign-o*, γιγν-ομαι, μιμν-ω, πιπτ-ω, for as these are admitted to be reduplicated forms of γεν, μεν, πετ, so *sist* implies a primitive *set*, or something like it. To this primitive I assign the idea of 'stop,' a verb which is itself probably of the same stock, *st-op;* and I quote in support of this translation the familiar *siste viator* or better still *s. aquam* of Virgil, *s. lacrimas* of Ovid, *s. alvom* of Pliny: I say better, because there is in these phrases no trace of the upright position, which eventually attached itself to so many of the derivative forms. I may be asked here whether I propose to connect the assumed root *set* with the *sed* of Lat. *sed-ere*, *sid-ere* (for *seid-ere*), &c. and our own *set, sit*. My answer to this is at present neither yes nor no; but on the logical side I see no difficulty, as we ourselves have the phrase 'to set up,' equivalent to the Lat. *statuere*. Again, if I am asked to account for the fact that *sta-* and its derivatives eventually possessed as an important part of their meaning that of standing or the upright position, I think I see two explanations. First the compound *a-sta-* in Plautus has the simple notion of 'standing up' rather than that of 'standing near,' so that the preposition is *an* (= *ava*), as in *an-hela-re* 'to send *up* a blast of air,' *a-scend-* 'climb up,' rather than the familiar *ad* 'to or near.' It should be noted too that it is precisely before an initial *s* that the Greek ava, commonly reduced to αν, or rather ον, in the Aeolic dialect, becomes further reduced to *a* or *o* (Ahrens,

De Dialectis, 28, 1). The assumption that *astare* was in the end cut down to *stare*, has its parallel in our own truncation of *arise* to *rise*, for *arise* is the original form. This theory further explains in a thoroughly satisfactory manner the prefixed vowel of the Fr. *état, étais, établir*. But independently of this argument, if the original notion of stopping be considered in connexion with man, and it is of man that we commonly speak, the first result of stopping is standing.

The 6th verb *i* 'go,' though found alike in Greek, Latin, and Sanskrit, I believe to be doubly corrupted. Already *it-er, com-it-ium, in-it-ium, ex-it-ium, comes* (them. *com-it-*), *pedes* (them. *ped-it-*), claim a final *t* for the root, and the forms so familiar in Plautus, *per-bīt-ere, inter-bīt-ere, red-bīt-ere, praeter-bīt-ere, e-bīt-ere* (the last in Plaut. Stic. 608, according to the palimpsest), exhibit an initial *b*. I have marked the *i* as long on the uniform authority of Plautus, though Forcellini hastily assigns a short *i* to these words. Then as regards the simple verb, Ribbeck has done well to follow the guidance of Fleckeisen in exhibiting *baetere* as the reading of Pacuvius in vv. 227 and 255. Thus *bat*, the root of *baetere* (as *cād* of *caedere*), is the Latin analogue of βαν in βαιν-ω, and so only a variety of *udd* 'go,' whence the imperfect tenses *uddere*, &c. We have here an explanation of the apparent anomaly in the corresponding French verb, which unites in the same conjugation a stem *va* and a stem *i*,—these, although wholly different in form, being in origin one,—as *je vais, tu vas, il va*, with *j'irai*, &c. These two verbs *sta-* and *i-* may indeed be pointed to as containing the best evidence of the close intimacy between the Greek, Latin, and Sanskrit languages; but it is in Greek and Latin, not in the Sanskrit, that we find the truest forms of the two roots.

If it be replied to what I have here urged, that the Indian grammarians, when they put forward a so-called 'dhâtu,' do not claim for it the honour of being an ultimate root, nay, that they apply this term to the base of any verb, though it be doubly or even trebly a derivative, I still contend that Bopp applies to his words the very name 'roots' (Wurzeln), and that his whole argument implies that the verbs so called are ultimate forms.

It would not be right to be wholly silent on his treatment of matters connected with the conjugation of verbs, but I must limit myself to the use he makes of the so-called verb substantive, whether *as* or *bhâ* 'be,' though I may refer also to similar proceedings on the part of Professor M. Müller. That this verb is employed in the processes of conjugation I of course do not deny, for I have myself sought to explain many forms by means of it. For example, I have contended that such phrases as 'I am a-dining,' 'I am from dining,' 'I am to dine,' are found in many languages besides our own as formulæ of presents, imperfect or perfect, and of future verbs; but then it is in the prepositions *a* (Ang.-Sax. *an*), *from*, and *to* that I find the essential part of the tense-idea. Indeed the very fact of the verb 'to be' entering into all the three phrases is the best proof that it contributes but little to the notation. But Bopp and his pupil proceed with far greater boldness. Thus the latter ('Lectures,' p. 174) tells us: '*Bam* in *cantabam* was originally an independent auxiliary verb, the same which exists in the Sanskrit *bhávami* and in the Ang.-Sax. *beom* "I am".' Again (p. 234) he says: 'In the Latin *bo* of *amabo* we have the old auxiliary *bhû* "to become," and in the Greek futures in σω, the old auxiliary as "to be".' (See also Bopp, § 526 and §§ 648, 656.) This is to give to the past imperfect and the future of the Latin the very same origin, so that the Romans, it would seem, thought it no inconvenience to confound the two opposite ideas of time. Let me note too that the author of the 'Lectures,' by quoting in the one case the first person of the Sanskrit verb and in the other the mere base or 'dhâtu,' gives a deceptive plausibility to his argument, for one sees some resemblance to *bam* in *bhavámi* and some resemblance to *bo* in *bhâ*. My own views on the formation of the Latin tenses *am-ab-a-m* and *am-ab-o* are given elsewhere (Trans. Philolog. Soc. 1856, pp. 308, 309). I will here merely repeat that I find the symbol of past time, not in *ba*, but solely in the final *a* of *am-ab-a-m*, just as I find it in the corresponding vowel of the Latin *er-a-m*, Gr. ην (= εαν) or ε-τιθε-α, and S. *a-bhav-a-m*. I have said that the two German Professors explain the σ of λεξω as the substantive vb.; but according to Bopp it is equally applicable to the aorist ελεξα (§ 542) and to the perfect τετελε-σ-μαι (§ 569). Nay even the κ of εδωκα and δεδωκα is deduced from the same source (ibid.), a change which will prepare us in some measure for a still bolder doctrine, that the strange *k* which appears in the Lithuanian imperative *dúki* 'give,' is also a variety of the *s* of the substantive verb (§ 680). As to the office it performs in this place, as in the others, not a word is vouchsafed.

As a final specimen of the sort of reasoning which is allowed in the explanation of tense-forms, I may point to a passage in the 'Lectures' (pp. 317, 318). From such phrases as 'I have loved,' 'amatum habeo,' it is inferred that the notion of 'habeo' is specially fitted to denote the past or perfect, the fact being that the essence of this idea lies in the dental suffixes of *ama-t-um* and *lov-ed*. And then, as something parallel, the writer quotes a Turkish phrase, which he tells us is literally 'Paying belonging to me,' but practically signifies 'I have paid.' I fear his knowledge of Turkish is not of the soundest, for at any rate the Latin phrase 'soluendum est mihi' and the English 'I have to pay' sound more like future than past tenses.

I shall conclude my comments on the 'Vergleichende Grammatik' with a brief notice of the free use made by Bopp of grammatical figures as they are called, and these too of the very class which the soberer philologers of late years have been disposed to reject as inadmissible, except in rare cases—I mean the figures which imply an extension of words, whether at the beginning or end or within the body. Bopp's much-used terms *vorschlag*, *einschiebung*, and *zusatz*, strengthened occasionally by the epithet *unorganische*, stand in the place of our old friends *prosthesis* (or *prothesis*), *epenthesis*, and *paragoge*. To the curtailment or compression of words no reasonable objection can be made, as it is the general law of language that forms should be abbreviated.

I propose to take the said figures in order.

Prothesis. The initial vowels of the words αϝερ- (V. G. 2d ed. vol. i. p. 550, note), ονοματ- (ibid.

1st ed. p. 311, note), οφρυ- (ibid.), ονυχ- (ibid.), are declared to be inorganic additions. The first of the set is further declared to represent the Sanskrit nr or nara; but unhappily for this doctrine the noun ανηρ- happens to be the example given by Dionysius of Halicarnassus, when he is speaking of Greek words that originally had the digamma; and as this letter w habitually interchanges with an m in many languages, there arises a strong suspicion that Fαν-ερ- has its root in the first syllable, and so is identical with our own *man*. This is further confirmed on the one side by the English corruption of *man* to *one* (pronounced with a digamma) in such forms as *one says* and *no one*, compared with the German *man sagt* and *nie-mand*, and on the other by the Greek compounds τοι-μανωρ and Αναξι-μανδρος compared with στυγ-ανωρ and Αλεξ-ανδρος. 2. As ονοματ- is always held to be one with the Latin *nomen*, and as this, being a derivative from *nosco*, must originally have had an initial *g* (cf. *co-gnomen*, *a-gnomen*), we are driven to an older γον-ομαr-, of which γον alone is radical. Indeed Bopp himself in his Glossary (s. v.) deduces the Sanskrit *naman* from *jnd*. 3. Οφρυ- being compared with the Sanskrit *bhrû* (gen. *bhruv-as*) is pronounced guilty of having in its first vowel something to which it is not entitled. But let us rather compare it with our own *eye-brow*, to which *eye* contributes no small portion of the meaning. Surely then if a reasonable explanation can be given of the Greek word, such as shall include the idea of 'eye,' we shall have what is more satisfactory. Now the most familiar root-syllable for 'eye' or 'seeing' is in Latin *oc* (*oculus*), and in Greek with the usual letter-change οπ (οπτομαι). But before an asperated letter ο₮ will of course become οφ, as in οφ-θαλμος. I suggest then that οφρυ- stands for οφ-φρυ-, or I should myself prefer to say οφ-ρυ-, seeing that the Greek language habitually drops an initial labial when followed by ρ. Thus we have ῥηγ-νυμι rather than ϝρηγ-νυμι, Eng. *break*, and ῥαγ- rather than ϝραγ-, Eng. *berry*. 4. The noun ον-υχ- I have little doubt is to be divided as here marked; and I say so partly on the evidence of the Latin *ungui-s*, *ung-ula*, *uncus*, and the Irish *ionga*, partly because υχ is a well-established Greek suffix, as seen in ορ-υχ- 'dig' (ορυσσω), the sb. δι-ωρ-υχ- 'a trench,' and virtually in ορ-(υ)χ-ο- 'a trench' (especially for vine-planting), and so closely related to the Lat. *or-d-on-*, which has precisely the same for its first and original meaning. Compare too for suffix βοστρ-υχ-, βοστρ-υχ-ο-, βοτρ-υχ-ο-, as well as βοτρ-υ-. Indeed most nouns in *u* have lost a final guttural, as the Latin *genu-*, *metu-*, *anu-*, contrasted with *genuc-ulum* (Eng. *knuck-le*), *metuc-ulosus*, *anic-ula*. I might also have included the suffixes υγ and υκ, of πτερ-υγ-, καλ-υκ-, as of the same origin with υχ. I am myself too further moved by the long-established belief in my own breast that words with an initial *n* have generally suffered decapitation.

. *Epenthesis.* This doctrine is called in aid by Bopp not unfrequently, but especially when dealing with the genitive plural of certain vowel-ending Sanskrit nouns (§§ 246, 249), which he says 'insert a euphonic *n* between the ending and the stem.' Among the instances he gives of this 'inshoving' are. *aśvá-n-ám* 'equorum,' *trí-n-ám* 'trium,' *sūnú-n-ám* 'filiorum.' And he notes it as something very remarkable that the Zend, the Old German, Old Saxon, and Ang.-

Saxon exhibit a similar peculiarity. Surely then he ought to have asked himself whether this *n* may not be the substantial part of a genitival suffix. Had he done so he would have found, I think, abundant evidence in his own and other cognate languages. I have myself long been satisfied with this explanation of the *en* of the German compounds *mond-en-licht, has-en-lage*, and our own *earth-en-ware, Ox-en-ford, Buck-en-ham* and its equivalent *Buck-ing-ham*, as well as the adjectives *wood-en, lin-en, silk-en*, &c. And then again we have *in* as a genitival suffix in Gaelic, as *bo-in* from *bò* 'cow.' It is the more remarkable that Bopp should have failed to hit this explanation, when he himself interprets (§ 248) the *sám* of the Sanskrit *té-sám* 'horum,' *tá-sám* 'harum,' as containing a double suffix, of which *s* represents the genitival element so familiar in the singular. Secondly, in § 97 and again in § 727, note, he further teaches that while a final *n* in Greek has often originated in a final *s*, such interchange is confirmed by the Prakrit. On this view *té-s-ám* and *atvd-n-ám* would go well together.

Again, as an *n* is ever apt to become silent before an *s* (cf. εις, χαριεις, τυφθεις, *cosol, toties*), it would have been more prudent perhaps, when dealing with the suffix of the dat. pl. in Old Prussian, *mans*, not to have considered the *n* as inorganic, on the sole ground that *mas* would agree better with the Sanskrit *bhyas*. His illustration too from the Latin *ensis* and *mensis* beside the Sanskrit *asis* and *mâsis* involves a similar assumption.

But we need not hunt up particular instances, when we find a wholesale manufacture of epenthetic vowels established by A. Kirchoff in the 'Zeitschrift'

(l. 37) and K. Walter (ibid. xi. 428). Thus ερεβινθος and οροβος and the Old German araweiz of like meaning are convicted of having stolen the vowel which follows r on the sole evidence that the Lat. *ervum* exhibits no such vowel. Ηλεκτρον cannot be entitled to the vowel ε, because forsooth the S. *ark* 'shine' proves the original root to have been *alk*. Again, the Greek having the two forms ορογυια and οργυια, the former is declared to have a vowel that does not belong to it, in spite of the evidence of ορεγ-ω. Nay, even the long vowel of αλ-ω-πεκ- is 'eingeschoben.' Walter's argument turns chiefly on the assumption that forms ending in *rk*, *lk*, *rg*, &c. are ultimate roots. Thus, according to him, ωλακ-, Fωλακ-, αυλακ-, αλοκ-, all varieties of the same word, signifying 'furrow,' come from a root *valk* = Fελκ-. Now my own conviction, founded on a long and wide examination, is that such verbs are all of them secondary. I do not believe in his suggestedde rivation of αυλακ- from Fελκ-; but if it were true, the Latin *uel-* (*uello-*) exhibits the verb in a simpler form. But it is enough to place beside each other such pairs of words as *talk* and *tale*, *hark* and *hear*, *pluck* and *pull*, *sparg-* and *σπειρ-*, *terg-* and *τειρ-*, *calo-* and *heel*, *stirk* and *steer*, *holk* and *holl*, both Scotch verbs signifying 'to dig,' the latter of which is one with the Latin *col-* 'dig.'

Paragoge. Bopp's instances of 'unorganische Zusatz' are numerous, but I shall be satisfied with quoting the Latin *genetric-* 'mother' and *iunic-* 'heifer,' which are declared to have a *c* of this character, inasmuch as the Sanskrit *janitrí* (§ 119) and *yúni* (§ 131) have no such letter. The Greek vocative γυναι by the side of γυναικ-ος, &c. might have suggested the possibility of

x

a final *s* being lost; and, again, the Latin vb. *nutri-re*, being a denominative from *nutric-*, has suffered the same loss.

His use of *Metathesis* however is carried to the greatest extreme. Indeed, the term 'Umstellung,' which is his name for this 'figure,' incessantly presents itself to the eye. I am one of those who believe the doctrine implied in these words to be carried to an unjustifiable extent by even the more sober of philologers; but I will here confine myself to three examples selected from Bopp's book, which I cannot but expect all persons will agree with me in condemning. In § 308, p. 60, he takes in hand the Gothic adj. *hanfa* (nom. *hanf-s*) 'one-handed,' and first pronounces *ha* to represent the *ka* of the Sanskrit *éka* 'one.' This assumed, he holds the residue *nfa* to stand for *nifa*. By transposition of *nifa* he then gets *fani*, which would correspond no doubt with all accuracy to the Sanskrit *pâni* 'hand.' This taken altogether must be admitted to be a strong proceeding; and a German philologer, in discussing a Gothic word, would have done well to cast an eye for a moment on the other Low German and kindred dialects. Had Bopp done so, he would have found at home that for which he travels to the far East, viz. Old Norse *hnevi* 'fist' and Lowland Scotch, not to say Yorkshire *nieve*, Nay, Walter Scott ('Guy Mannering,' xxiv.) has: 'Twa land-loupers ... *knevelled* me sair aneugh or I could gar my whip walk about their lugs;' and, to quote from a more Southern dialect, Shakspere has: 'Give me your *neif*' ('Midsummer Night's Dream,' iv. 1), and: 'Sweet knight, I kiss thy *neif*' ('Henry IV.,' Part II. ii. 4).

In vol. i. 580, note, attention is drawn to an Armenian noun signifying 'man,' of which the crude form is said to be *aran*. Of this the initial vowel is first discarded as a mere phonetic prefix, and then by 'Umstellung' *ran* is identified with Sanskrit *nar* or *nṛ*. Would it not be simpler and quite as justifiable to affirm that the Armenian *aran* was formed from the Sanskrit *nara* by reading it backward?

Lastly in his Glossary s. v. *nakha* 'nail' we have the words: 'hib. *ionga* fortasse litteris transpositis e *nioga*.' The Greek ον-υχ- should have prevented this statement.

In terminating my remarks on Bopp's somewhat free and bold use of 'grammatical figures,' I must be permitted to throw out the hint that if by any possibility the Sanskrit forms just compared with the classical have been advanced to a dignity which is beyond their due—in other words, if they are, after all, the more degraded of the two—then all the difficulties which have presented themselves disappear. From the objectionable figures prothesis, epenthesis, and paragoge, we should pass respectively to aphaeresis, synaeresis or crasis, and apocope. In plainer English, instead of assuming words to grow and extend themselves, we should have nothing but abbreviation, a principle which seems to recommend itself to the common sense of every one. A man need not be much of a philologer to account for the abbreviation of *caravan, forecastle,* and *cabriolet* to *van, foxel,* and *cab*.

In concluding these remarks, the length of which find their only excuse in the importance of the subject, I must be permitted to say that I have written in no spirit of hostility either to Comparative Grammar or to the Sanskrit language. On the contrary, fully believing that the science must be benefited when the philologer extends his views over many languages, especially in the older varieties, but to the exclusion of none, I sincerely trust that some of our own classical scholars will apply themselves with independence and diligence to the study of Sanskrit. My chief object in the present paper has been to check that slavish sequacity which has long interfered with the advancement of linguistic science, and I lay down my pen with something like a conviction that my readers will not so readily give their assent to such propositions as the following. Prof. Max Müller tells us ('Lectures,' p. 167) that 'His (Bopp's) work will form for ever the safe and solid foundation of Comparative Philology.' Again (p. 216), 'Comparative Grammar has well-nigh taught us all it has to teach.' And another writer, if indeed it be another writer (*Saturday Review*, Jan. 10, 1862), speaks of Comparative Grammar as 'a science which has always prided itself on the exactness and almost mathematical precision of its method.'

XIV.

POSTSCRIPT.

I HAD hoped that the arguments put forward in this paper would have drawn out some reply in print from the Sanskritists in Germany and England. Six years have now passed since it was printed. But, with one exception, they have been silent. That exception is Prof. M. Müller, who, in the second series of his 'Lectures' (pp. 13, 14), says:—

'But while we are thus told by some scholars that we must look to Polynesia and South Africa if we would find the clue to the mysteries of Aryan speech, we are warned by others that there is no such thing as an Aryan or Indo-European family of languages, that Sanskrit has no relationship with Greek, and that Comparative Philology, as hitherto treated by Bopp and others, is but a dream of continental professors;' to which he appends as a note:—

'See Mr. John Crawfurd's essay *On the Aryan or Indo-Germanic theory*, and an article by Professor T. Hewitt Key, in the Transactions of the Philological Society, "The Sanskrit Language as the basis of Linguistic Science; and the labours of the German School in that field—are they not overvalued?"'

Now the word 'others' is a plural, and the note

naturally suggests the idea that Mr. Crawfurd and Mr. Key are included in the term. But Prof. M. Müller well knows that I have always accepted the Sanskrit language as a member of the Indo-European family, the study of which is important for linguistic science. Indeed, although my other engagements have rendered it impossible for me to acquire any direct acquaintance, much less a thorough acquaintance, with the language, I have read largely and with care what others have written on the subject; and have not unfrequently employed the knowledge so attained in the explanation of Latin words[1] and Latin grammatical forms. I therefore here call upon him to withdraw or to justify his assertion. Perhaps he will think this the more necessary, when I tell him that a friend, well known not more for accurate and refined scholarship than for caution and urbanity, on reading the above passage from his 'Lectures' made the remark : 'I call that a *suggestio falsi*.'

But while this volume is going through the press, the 'North American Review' (Oct. 1867, p. 521) brings me a paper written in a very different spirit, and claiming the more attention, as report from several quarters ascribes it to a distinguished Professor of Yale College.

After reading this article, I rise with the satisfactory feeling that my inquiry into the doings of German Sanskritists has not been in vain, for the last paragraph of the review, so far as concerns my criticisms of Bopp, runs :—

---

[1] As in the explanation of the Latin words *temere* and *temerare*. (See Trans. Philolog. Soc. for 1866.)

'In a considerable portion of the criticisms which Professor Key makes upon his (Bopp's) works, the majority of comparative philologists, we believe, of the German or any other school, would be free to join, yet without abating a jot of the admiration and gratitude which they pay to the founder of their science.'

Again, in p. 530, he says:—

'In two respects, especially, his (Mr. Key's) objections are to be regarded as valuable protests, requiring to be well heeded, against modes of etymologizing which are too common among Sanskritists: namely, the over-ready referral to a Sanskrit root, of doubtful authenticity and wide and ill-defined meaning, of derivatives in the various Indo-European languages; and the over-easy persuasion that the genesis of a suffix is sufficiently explained when it is pronounced "of pronominal origin."'

And he then goes on to say:—

'As regards the former point, we think our author entirely justified in casting ridicule upon the facile derivation of words meaning "water," "earth," "cow," and the like, from alleged Sanskrit roots claimed to signify "go."'

Soon after he adds:—

'As regards, again, the use of pronominal elements in explaining the genesis of grammatical forms, we deem Professor Key's interpellations not less in place.'

And at the close of the same paragraph there occurs:—

'Meanwhile, no one is to be blamed for feeling a kind of indignant impatience at seeing this and that ending complacently referred to such and such a pronominal root, as if no further explanation of it were necessary to satisfy any reasonable person.'

So far then we agree; but there are points as to which he expresses somewhat vaguely a difference of opinion.

It has been however often said that if two opponents were brought together face to face, an amicable discussion would result in a belief that their differences were far less than at first supposed. This is a truth which applies, I believe, to the present case; and perhaps a few additional words may lead to the same result.

The reviewer opens his argument (p. 521) with a statement that 'the change of ground and of point of view which philological science has undergone during its later history amounts almost to a revolution, and naturally provokes the opposition of ancient opinion and of the prejudices engendered by it;' and he includes me among the 'conservative spirits who are under such influence.' I think that few readers of the present volume will think that he has been happy in his theory that I am scared by innovations in linguistic matters.

Again, in p. 535 he observes that while the labours of the German school are overvalued by some, they are 'undervalued by those who, on account of faults of detail, reject the whole method, as well as by those who, having the acuteness to detect such faults, yet lack the sound learning and enlightened judgment which should enable them to adopt the method wherever it is truly valuable. And we fear that our author is to be ranked in the latter class.'

How he jumps to this conclusion I do not see. In

the first place, it is scarcely correct to say that the objections urged by me are only 'faults of detail.' Many of those objections deal with the backbone of Bopp's work, as, for example, his assumed explanation by pronouns of the case-endings of nouns, as to which the reviewer fully coincides with me. His space did not allow him, he says, to discuss more than a few of the difficulties raised by me; and thus it happens by a strange piece of good fortune for me that in every one of these he is at one with me, except that he cannot altogether go with me in questioning the existence of pronominal roots as a separate class; but he does not enter into any particulars as to the ground on which this qualified dissent is based.

Nor is it enough to say that he was confined by want of space, for he deals with several minor matters which affect myself, but have little bearing on the main question. Thus it is a very unimportant matter whether I am right or not as to spelling 'asperato' with an *e*, which he attributes to 'a whim or a false theory.' Perhaps he may change his view when he calls to mind the grammatical terms *spiritus asper* and *spiritus lenis*, or the Greek adjectives δασύς and ψιλός, applied in the same senses. Again, his linguistic peace of mind is sadly disturbed when he finds that I have the courage to assume that Finnish has a close relation as regards pronouns and grammatical forms with the Indo-European family. Not long ago it was deemed an over-daring act to claim a connexion for the Keltic with this family; and the time will come when even Germans will be startled on coming across a European race whose inflections for the dual and plural of the verb run:—

Dual: *molsoimen, molsoiten, molsoikan.*
Pl. *molsoime, molsoite, molsoin ¡*
forms which bear a strange resemblance to what is seen in Greek grammars. Still greater perhaps their surprise when they come in pronominal declensions to :—
mo 'of me,' *to* 'of thee,' *so* 'of him.'
And again, when they find that as the Persian uses the letters *m, t, s*, as suffixes to substantives with the meaning of 'mine,' 'thine,' 'his,' so precisely as suffixes of the same form the language I speak of presents them with,—

parne 'son,'   *parnam* 'my son.'
nipe 'knife,'   *nipat* 'thy knife.'
aija 'grandfather,' *aijabs* 'his grandfather.'

And the matter will perhaps be clenched, when they see before them *mocum, tocum, socum*, identical in meaning, still more than in form, with the Latin *mecum, tecum, secum*.[1]

The language in question is the Lapp, one so nearly akin to Finn that the admission of one as in any way cognate with the Indo-European will insure the admission of both. The one can only enter the privileged gate arm in arm with the other. Thus it is no such absurdity as the reviewer supposes, to draw arguments from the Finnish, so far at least as concerns the pronouns.

But although I find *ken* and *cu* as the two leading forms of the Finnish relative, and so appeal to them in support of my theory as to the origin of the third-person pronouns, that theory remains intact, even if

---

[1] See Mr. Wedgwood's paper, Trans. Phil. Soc. 1856, p. 1.

such additional evidence be put aside. For the Sanskrit testifies in my favour, and the other members of the Indo-European family as well. To this side of my argument the reviewer has nothing to oppose.

I had forgotten to state how the reviewer treats that portion of my paper which is directed against Prof. M. Müller's views. A few words will suffice on this head. After demurring to my implied assumption that 'accusations made to lie against these two (Bopp and Max Müller) will attach to the whole cause they represent' (p. 528), he soon turns to my dealings with the latter (p. 529), saying:—

'As regards our author's other antagonist, Professor Max Müller, it is only in England that modern philology is looked upon as so identified with his name, that a blot on the one must be presumed to sully the other.'

And then after general compliments to this writer he concludes thus:—

'A notable example of his characteristic weaknesses is offered in his theory of phonetic types instinctively produced as the beginnings of human speech; a theory which forms one of the counts of Professor Key's indictment, and which we should not think of defending in a single point from the latter's hostile criticism. Rarely is a great subject more trivially and insufficiently treated than is that of the origin of language by Müller in the last lecture of his first series.'

Let me conclude then, in the absence of all other replies to my inquiries as put in the paper entitled 'Qvaeritvr,' with a statement that I am thoroughly ready to subscribe to the articles of linguistic faith in the Bopp school, so far as the reviewer states them (in pp. 549, 550), with this one qualification, that all or nearly all these truths had been discovered before Bopp entered the field of philology.

'Bopp and his school have shown, beyond the reach of cavil, that the branches of Indo-European speech have sprung from a single stock; that they are not independent growths, upon which certain common elements have been ingrafted. They all count with the same numerals, call their individual speakers by the same pronouns, address parents and relatives[1] by the same titles, decline their nouns upon the same system, compare their adjectives alike, conjugate their verbs alike, form their derivatives by the same suffixes.'

On the other hand I hold that Sanskrit does not at present deserve the high rank assigned to it in linguistic science, and this partly because no one has yet attained to a knowledge of the language at all comparable in accuracy to that which the students of the two classical languages have reached; secondly, because as yet the Vedic language, which alone can pretend to a rivalry in antiquity with Greek, has so far been but little studied; and thirdly, because Sanskrit literature has no basis for linguistic study comparable in clearness of ideas to the Iliad and Odyssey.

Farther, I believe that in pureness of grammatical forms both Greek and Latin have often a marked superiority over Sanskrit. But the true course for the philologer is to study all these languages so far as the limited opportunities of each permit, and one at least of them thoroughly.

---

[1] I have myself done something to complete this theory by the identification of the Greek θυγατ(-ερ-) with the Latin filia. (Trans. for 1866.)

ADDENDA, CORRIGENDA, ETC.

Page 6, line 24. For -ανα-κοκκυ- read ανα-κοκκυ-.
Page 6, line 28. For -ραψῳδε- read -ραψῳδε-.
Page 13, *line* 1. Add after 'Secondly,' 'the notion of "back" enters into *adim-* "take back or revoke," as used in Dig. xxxviii. 4, 1, §§ 3 and 4: "Assignare autem quis potest (libertum) quibuscunque uerbis uel testamento uel codicillis uel uiuus. Adimere autem assignationem etiam nuda uoluntate potest."'
Page 47, *line* 27. For 'uninteresting,' read 'interesting.'
Page 49, *line* 4. Insert before 'also' the word 'comparo.'
Page 64, *line* 31. Add: 'So Sallust (Jug. 18, 5) speaks of certain immigrants in Africa, who arriving by sea "alueos nauium inuorsos pro tuguriis habuere;" and in this way accounts for the shape of the Numidian huts: "Adhuc aedificia Numidarum agrestium, quae mapalia illi uocant, oblonga *incuruis* lateribus tecta quasi nauium carinae sunt." The same meaning of the adjective is seen in "duratur nasus *incuruus*, coguntur ungues adunci, fit bubo Pamphile," Apul. Met. 3, 213.'
Page 66, *line* 28. Add: 'So too in the French *anévrisme*, "an aneurism."'

Page 82, *line* 1. For *erbitten*, read *erbittern*.
Page 89, *line* 19. For 'Garnet,' read 'Garnett.'
Page 107, *line* 31. For *verchieben*, read *verschieben*.
Page 113, *line* 23. For παρασσηνο-, read παρασσηνο-.
Page 115, *line* 4. Add as an additional paragraph:
'So far I have dealt with the Latin *per* in the formation of compound verbs and compound adjectives; but even in the ordinary use of the word in connexion with substantives the sense of "over" is placed beyond doubt; and this more particularly in the text of Livy, as first (i. 26, 13): "Is (the father of the surviving Horatius) transmisso per uiam tigillo uelut sub iugum misit iuuenem;" secondly (xxvii. 32, 35): "Ibi equus pilo traiectus quum prolapsum per caput regem effudisset;" thirdly (xliv. 19, 9): "Antiochus .. ponte per Nilum facto transgressus .. obsidione Alexandream terrebat;" fourthly (x. 19, 21): "per uallum, per fossas irruperunt;" fifthly (xxvi. 6, 2): "elephantos trausgredientes in ipso uallo conficiunt. Quorum corporibus quum oppleta fossa esset, uelut aggere aut ponte iniecto transitum hostibus dedit; ibi per stragem iacentium elephantorum atrox edita caedes." So Madvig in his text; but in his preface to vol. ii., part 2, he writes: "Recipienda fuerat Ussingii coniectura: 'ibi super stragem iacentium.' Caedes hominum per stragem elephantorum edita nihil est." I think I may now assume that there is no need for the conjecture of Madvig's collaborateur. But the same use of *per* is seen in Catullus (20, 9): " Quéndam municipém meum dé tuo uolo pónte Ire praecipitem in lutum pér caputque pedésque, &c.;" as also in Caesar (B. G. iii. 26, 5): "Hostes desperatis

rebus se per munitiones deicere intenderunt." Perhaps too I ought to add from Plautus (Poen. 5, 12, Geppert's ed.) : "Ita repleuero atritate atr(at)ior multo ut siet Quam Aegyptini qui cortinam ludis per circum ferunt." In the passages so far quoted the notion of "over" seems alone admissible; but there are many others in which the same translation is at least as satisfactory as that by "through;" for example in "Quó Castalia pér struices sáxeas lapsu áccidit," (Liv. And. 36 Ribb.); "Dubii fauentem pér fretum introcúrrimus," (Naev. 59 R.); "Perque agros passim dispergit corpus," (inc. fab. 168 R.); "Ponti per freta Colchos delatus," (inc. fab. 182 R.); "Rapiunt per undas currus suspensos," (ib. 196); "Ardua per loca agrestia trepidante gradu nititur," (Pac. 272 R.); "Nunc per terras uagus extorris," (Att. 333 R.); "Multa siti prostrata uiam per," (Lucr. 6, 1262); "Transtra per et remos, &c." (Verg. A. 5, 663); "Unctós saluere (they ran) per utres," (Verg. G. 2, 384). Still, as the Latin language had three prepositions of the same origin, *per, trans,* and *super,* it was to be expected that the meanings would for the most part be distributed between them; so that the notion of "over" might with many writers be limited to *super.* Lastly, to the verbs compounded with *per* in the sense of "over" add *percurr-*, as used by Terence (Haut. iv. 4, 11) in "Curriculo *percurre*," run over, run across (to Charinus's).'

Page 119, *line* 10. Add as an additional paragraph:—

'The instances to which Diez refers are "Hygin. de condicionibus agrorum," p. 118, l. 6: *pos legem datam;* and M. Iun. Nissus, p. 294, l. 6: *ut pos te relinquas orientem;* to which may be added from the same class of writers, "Casae litterarum;" p. 329, l. 12: *Casa ... pos si* (= *post se*) *finem habet,* opposed to *finis ante se habentem* of line 3. So Munro in his Lucretius (4, 1186) writes *poscaenia,* and (4, 1252) in a foot-note prefers *pos sunt* to *post sunt,* the MSS. having *possunt;* but his reference to a solitary *posquam* as the reading of the sole MS. in Liv. (xlii. 10, 5) seems to have less weight, as *postquam* is a word of such frequent occurrence in Livy. Other instances are to be seen in Ribbeck's prol. to Vergil, p. 442, and Schuchardt's "Vokalismusdes Vulgärlateins, 1, 122." Few words then are better established in the Latin vocabulary than the form *pos.*'

Page 164, *line* 15. Add: '*mittere* scriptam solet (for so MSS.), Pseud. iv. 2, 46;' and to note 2 add: '*fore* (Pers. ii. 3, 6), *fore* (As. 214, 57).'

Page 165, *line* 2. Add: '*uiuere* (Glor. iv. 6, 60), *perdere* (Curc. iv. 2, 18), *adducere* (As. ii. 4, 32), *noscere* (Rud. ii. 3, 59);' and *l.* 10, add: '*reddere* (Amph. i. 1, 52).'

Page 167, *line* 14. Add: 'and the German particle *hin* of like meaning.'

Page 210, *line* 33. After Liv. xxvi. 9 add: 'postremis genu nixis, Liv. xliv. 9, 6.'

Page 211, *line* 14. For *inuenis,* read *iuuenis.*

Page 211, *line* 26. Add: '*clift,* as in *Netherclift* by the side of *cliff,* and perhaps *graft* by the side of *graff.*'

Page 212, *line* 25. For 'imperfect particles,' read 'imperfect participles.'

Page 213, *line* 1. After 7, 4, add: 'So too the Danish preposition is *i,* not *in.*'

ADDENDA, CORRIGENDA, ETC. 321

Page 215, *line* 2. Add: 'In the Dirae, v. 27, *uirectis* is the reading of two MSS. of the ninth century, D and Y of Ribbeck; and ought I think to have been admitted by the editor into the text. So in the Rosetum, l. 13, the same MSS. have *frutectis*, which is also found in the Cod. Harl. 2534.'

Page 217, *line* 11. Add: 'So also κρυβδα for κρυφα. Nor can the numerous adverbs in δον and δην in my opinion be opposed to this view, for in these also a γ seems to have disappeared from before the δ, just as a c has from such Latin adverbs as *cateruat-im*. Γδουπος too I should regard as older than δουπος.'

Page 236, *line* 13. Add: 'Of course this theory assumes that such adverbs as *breuiter* ended at first in ēr. A change of this kind would be parallel to what has occurred in *pater, mulier, &c.* It is with some confidence too that I venture to assert that I have met with many cases in which old writers give a long e to the adverbs in er, although at the present moment I can only point to the Rudens (ii. 3, 65): "Vt lépide, ut liberālitēr, ut honēste atque hau grauāto;" the Epidicus (iii. 4, 49), "Reór, peccatum lárgitēr. Immo haéc east;" and the Eunuch (ii. 1, 24), "Fácie honesta; mírum ni ego me túrpitēr hodie híc dabo."'

Page 247, *line* 18. For 'Hast.' read 'Haut.'

Page 262, *note* 1. Add: 'Because *āmi* is to be claimed for the suffix in *bhar-āmi*, to take this as an example, on the ground that the "dhatu" of the pronoun of the first person is *asmat*, and the plural forms of this pronoun, *asmā-kam* and *asmā-bhis*, point to the same result. But this admitted, a so-called causal verb, as *vēd-ay-āmi* (ich mache wissen) must have *ay* for its suffix, a form which corresponds with all accuracy to *ag* or *ac*, the suffix of Latin verbs, and to *αχ* of the Greek ταρασσω (ταρ-αχ-), for a guttural between vowels would readily slip into a *y*. The usual doctrine of Sanskritists, that the *â* of *bhar-âmi* is a mere connecting vowel, offends by its very extravagance. For such a purpose a short vowel alone can be admissible.

INDEX.

The English Alphabet is here adopted, so that for Greek words φ, χ, θ are considered as representing our ph, ch, th; while words with an initial asperate fall under A, and those commencing with ῥ under Ar (not rh). Latin words are commonly given in the crude form with an appended hyphen, in other cases are marked L; while A.-S. denotes Anglo-Saxon, BOH. Bohemian, BRET. Breton, DAN. Danish, F. French, G. German, GA. Gaelic, GO. Gothic, L Italian, IR. Irish, LITH. Lithuanian, N. Norse, S. Sanskrit, SC. Scotch dialect of English, SP. Spanish, SW. Swedish, W. Welsh. O is in some cases prefixed to denote Old.

A, 275.
a = ava, 11, 84.
a-, A.-S. 33, 34, 84.
a-, GA. 58.
-a- of L. vbs. 220.
a ενιτατικον, 128.
a, priv. 127, 294.
ab, L. 62, 292.
abaft, 119.
abasil, sc. 240.
abend, G. 218.
abici-, 110.
abiet-, 75.
aboard, 84.
abolesc-, 12.
absorbe-, 110.
acced-, 12, 14.
accend-, 13.
acci-, 14.

acclini-, 12.
accresc-, 12.
accumb-, 12, 23.
accumula-, 12.
scourr-, 14.
achtem, G. 211.
acknow, 34.
acknowleg 34.
acquiesc-, 13.
actotum, L. 112.
ac ualuti, 157.
ad-, 12, 15, 53, 57, 292.
ad-, W. 19, 33, 177.
adaequa-, 12.
adaestua-, 12.
adapari-, 13.
adaresc-, 13, 52.
adbib-, 52.

addormisc-, 13.
adesuri-, 13.
adh-, IR. 21.
adhinni-, 13.
adi-, 14.
adim-, 13, 52.
adimple-, 12.
a-dining, 29.
adiuua-, 12, 14.
adminiculo-, 14.
admira-, 13.
admisce-, 13, 52.
ado ! GA. 58.
adole-, 13.
adolesc-, 12.
adopari-, 12.
aduesperasc-, 13.
aeghväder, A.-S. 82.
æt, A.-S. 24, 31, 51.

Y 2

324

aeditno-, 216.
aaue-, 127.
af, oo. 62, 102.
aâl, v. 147.
afana, oo. 62.
afar, oo. 121.
afara, oo. 121.
affie-, 13.
affig-, 110.
afoot, 84.
aft, 102, 119.
aftana, oo. 120.
after, 117, 119.
aftra, oo. 119.
ag, ad. 58.
aggar-, 12.
aggredi-, 14.
-agh, κελτιο suff. 230.
agita-, 76.
agnito-, 279, 296.
agnoso-, 11, 13.
a-going, 213.
agresti-, 214.
agu 1 ad. 59.
x at times short, 183.
aime-l-il, r. 205.
aippan, ∞o. 179, 181.
al-, 73, 199.
αλδαο-, 217.
alder, o. 180.
alder, 217.
alderfirst, 217.
aldiza, oo. 133.
ali-, 171.
alio-, 170.
aliqui-, 172.
αλληλο-, 172.
Allen, 142.
aller, r. 219.
allena-, 10.
alliga-, 10.

allium, L. 228.
alloqu-, 10.
alt, a. 72.
alt-ero, 212.
altar-uter-, 168, 182.
αλθ, 220.
altiro, o. a. 123.
αλοχο-, 128.
aloft, 121.
along, 33.
αλωττα-, 305.
am, L. 61, 292.
ama-, 61.
amillo-, 136, 146.
amatum iri, 261.
ambed-, 10.
αμβροτο-, 127.
ambula-, 19, 223.
ambar-, 10.
-ami, a. suff. 321.
ammono-, 10, 13.
amputa-, 10.
an, ad. prefix, 132.
an, o. 23, 55.
an, L. 170, 183.
an, a. 290.
αν, priv. 127.
ara, 2, 3, 4, 8, 24, 73,
  293.
ana-, ad. 132, 146.
αναελστο-, 146.
αναετιμαι, 12, 23.
anakumbj-, oo. 23.
anaout, BRET. 20.
αναρροιβδε-, 216.
αναστεναζ-, 6, 22.
αταηρε-, 8.
ancient, 213.
andare, L. 219.
ander, a. 171.
ανθρπο-, 21.

Andrews's Lexicon, 10.
ανδροε, 217.
ανεfεδρο-, 146.
ανκλε-, 22.
ανηρ, 139, 301, 307.
anfangen, o. 30.
anbang, a. 21.
anbela-, 9.
anima, 285.
ανισο-, 55.
ankouna, BRET. 21, 27.
annar, H. 171.
anne, L. 169, 183.
anno-, 61, 260.
annulo-, 260.
anochd, IR. 296.
ανοιειζ-, 22.
anquir, 9.
anser-, 222.
antara, a. 170, 177.
αρθιε-, 220.
antidea, L. 125.
aniras, LITH. 177.
any, 171.
anya-, a. 172.
αωρο-, 127.
apama, a. 121.
apara, a. 121.
aperi-, 110.
apium, L. 228.
απο, 62, 292.
apple, 147.
appon-, 110.
apprehend-, 12, 29.
aqua-, 258.
arbusto-, 214.
arde-, 13 n., 199, 219.
arduo-, 13 n., 73, 219.
arise, 298.
aroma, 258.
arti-, 213.

ἀρθρο-, 221.
ascend-, 11.
asi, a. 304.
asperate, 313.
aspire, 11.
asudeso-, 11.
asurg-, 11.
asta-, 11, 297.
ἀστεροντ, 121.
astraindra, F. 219.
astru-, 11.
advānām, a. 303.
at, 57, 60.
-at-, L. suffix, 229.
στεντο-, 129.
αθανατο-, 127.
atque, 149, 151.
atque adeo, 153.
atque utinam, 154.
atting-, 12.
auf-, o. 103.
aufdecken, o. 26.
auflösen, o. 26.
Aufrecht, 124, 206.
augment, 205.
aul, PROV. 137.
αυλας-, 305.
αυττο-, 127.
aut, L. 170, 180.
αυξαν-, 222.
aveindra, F. 218.
avol, PROV. 137.
Avon, 138.
awake, 34.
axt, o. 216.
-ay-, a suff. 262,
321.
Ayenbite of Inwyt,
103, 104, 115.

Bao, 183.

βαλλ-, 294.
-bam, L. suff., 299.
βαν, 298.
Banerges, 201.
bay, 183.
bd, 216.
behind, 119.
bai, o. 252.
beinicht, α. 212.
ballicus, L. 229.
βελτιον-, 212.
beneath, 68.
βενθος-, 129, 220.
βαντιστο-, 212.
Bergk, 208.
berry, 216.
bet, 115, 180.
bey, o. 16.
biga-, 192.
Bindsell, 206, 271.
bis, L. 59.
bis, o. 59.
bit-, 298.
blb, BOH. 275.
Blindeisen, 12.
-bo, L. suff., 300.
bodkin, 190.
bo-in, GA. 304.
Bopp, 119, 120, 122,
125, 146, 172, 178,
184, 204, 241, 257,
260, 261, 276, 289,
291, 293.
bore, 190.
Bosworth, 32, 33, 34,
105.
bottom, 228.
bov-, 257.
bow, 183.
braggart, 213.
Brahmanas, 250.

break, 95.
brid, 274.
broach, 95.
t urden, 219.
burn, 224.
buttock, 228.

CAD-, 166.
caduceo-, 219.
caed-, 166.
caelesti-, 214.
caelitus, L. 246.
calamitas-, 167.
calf, 232.
Camps, 91.
cand-, 218.
carectum, L. 206.
carp-, 259.
case-endings, 287,289.
cami-, 193.
casto-, 189.
castra, L. 185.
castra-, 187, 189.
castro-, 188.
catervatim, 321.
cātus, L. 279.
causals, 261.
-ce, L. 161, 292.
candra, F. 216.
climec-, 232.
cis, L. 242.
citra, L. 280.
chambre, F. 223.
chez, F. 294.
chi, IT. 243.
chi-ket-mi, a. 280.
chin, 197.
chin, sund, 280.
chit, a. 280.
chordae uocales, 272.
χθ, 222.

INDEX.

claustro-, 185.
clift, 320.
cognito-, 279.
cognomentum, L. 212.
cognosc-, 152.
col-, 90.
combler, F. 223.
commigo, SP. 154.
comparatives, 34, 338.
concilia-, 16.
connecting vowel, 206.
contigo, SP. 154.
contra, L. 120, 212.
cord-, 219.
Cormen, 166, 209, 211.
corolo-, 217.
cunde, F. 217.
coward, 213.
craindre, F. 218.
crastino-, 213.
crawl, 259.
creep, 259.
crow, 250.
cs, 222.
ct, 207.
cubi ? 158.
cum, L. 222.
cunde ? 158.
curr-, 195, 269.
curru-, 194.
Curtius, 117, 119, 124, 202.
custod-, 215.
cut ? L. 150.
cuter ? L. 156.
Czermak, 272.

D of Latin neuters, 212.
dagger, 213, 226.
δαφνη, 159.

βαρβαρ-, 221.
Davis, 148.
de, L. 55.
declension, 287.
δεδουκα, 158.
defenstric-, 215.
degen, G. 225.
δευε, 123.
δειδ-, 158.
δεινο-, 158.
δείαμες, F. 205.
Δεμητερ, 217.
demonstrative roots? 278, 286.
Devon, 138.
dextero-, 214.
dhâtu, 292.
διχθα, 222.
Diez, 137, 204, 205, 217.
discrib-, 55.
distrent, F. 210.
diutius, L. 208.
diximus ? L. 205.
do, GA. 58.
do, IR. 54.
doce-, 264.
domestico-, 214.
Donaldson, 176; vii. xii.
domo-, 66.
dos, F. 65.
dosso, L. 65.
du, GO. præfix, 57.
dumectum, L. 208.
durch, G. 294.
dyn, MANX, 59.
dys, MANX, 59.

E of Lat. infin. 163, 164.

-e of Lat. adv. 235.
earth, 257.
Ebel, 112.
ecce, L. 281.
eccum, L. 281.
εχ-, 114.
ed, A.-S. 24, 31, 177.
eft, 60.
eigentlich, G. 212.
εικαθ-, 174.
einliver, N. 175.
einig, G. 174.
einst, G. 216.
εις, 222.
either, 168, 182.
εκεινο-, 181.
-els-, L. suffix, 229.
ελαφο-, 257.
ηλεκτρον, 305.
ελευθερο-, 221.
ελεξα, 300.
eller, DAN. SW. 179.
elope, 34.
εμαθον, 220.
emmet, 75, 227.
empfangen, G. 30.
empfehlen, G. 30.
emprise, 47.
en = inde, 167.
en-, G. 24.
επερπερο-, 63.
εραφθιν, 63.
ετερο-, 63.
Engonasin, L. 211.
ενι, 62.
ent, G. 24, 53, 512.
enterprise, 48.
entertain, 48.
entfallen, G. 18.
entgegen, G. 212.
ενθεν, 220.

INDEX. 327

entlassen, a. 37, 52.
entnehmen, a. 47.
entrebaiser, v. 40.
entteprendre, v. 46.
entreprise, v. 40.
entretenir, v. 46.
entsagen, a.37, 47, 52.
entsinnen, a. 28.
entstehen, a. 29.
entweder, a. 182, 212.
entzwei, a. 212.
-en- of Lat. adj. 230.
epenthesis, 301; 303.
επι, 121, 124, 292.
eppich, a. 228.
er-, a. 78.
-er of comp. 120, 124.
-er of Lat. adv. 335, 321.
ersm, L. 300.
ερικτθο-, 305.
-eri-, of Lat. adj. 230.
erkennen, a. 79.
erlösen, a. 80.
-erno-, of Lat. adj. 229.
-ero-, of Lat. adj. 230.
erschliessen, a. 80.
ersinnen, a. 79.
εσθλο-, 221.
et, L. 149, 166, 167.
εταθηρ, 129.
être, v. 216.
ε-τυπτ-ον, 295.
etwas, a. 175.
Ευριπιδης, 66.
evil, 138.
extero-, 214.

Faci-, 264.
facinos-, 220.
fall, 180.

fall-, 187.
falte, a. 212.
far, 105.
farbroder, Dan. 181.
farther, 105.
fechten, a. 211.
fell, 186.
fer-, 7.
fertili-, 213.
fessel, a. 225.
fetter, 228.
fight, a. 211.
figures, 301.
filia-, 202, 316.
find, sq. 31.
finger, 213.
Finn, 243, 245, 314.
Fleckeisen, 209.
flect-, 207.
fod-, 190.
fodica-, 75.
folli-, 193.
for-, 108.
Forcellini, 16, 18, 51, 210.
forcep-, 191.
fordo, 108.
forfee-, 191.
forget, 108.
forpec-, 191.
forswear, 108.
forti-, 262.
foxel, 307.
frago-, 216.
frang-, 230.
fratello, L. 234.
Friem Barnet, 205.
fresher, 213.
frodoza, oo. 123.
frutectum, L. 208, 214.
ft, 211.

fundo-, 228, note.
furca-, 190.
furche, a. 91.
Furlanetto, 18.

Gaffer, 181.
γαια, 275.
γαλarr-, 207.
gambol, 233.
gammer, 181.
γαμφηλαι, 197.
ganache, v. 197.
gander, 218.
Ganges, 258.
gane, a. 222.
Garnett, 89.
gav, a. 257.
gd, 216.
γδουπο-, 321.
ge-, a. 2.
geindre, v. 218.
gelächter, a. 211.
Gellius, 144.
gens-, 197.
γινυμαι, 197.
genetric-, 305.
γενε, 197.
genuine-, 197.
ghost, 285.
gimblet, 75, 227.
gingiua-, 197.
gmd, a. 257.
γραθο-, 197.
gnose-, 161, 296.
go, a vb. signifying, 268.
Goldstücker, 254.
gon, coan. 280.
Gothic, 24.
gownd, 207.
Graff, 260.

INDEX.

γραφ-, 231.
Grimm, 1, 24, 26, 38, 32, 35, 42, 43, 44, 57, 60, 61, 63, 74, 78, 79, 84, 120, 175, 179, 181, 204.
gᵃ, 222.
guarder, F. 210.
Guest, 244.
guma, 197.
γυναικ-, 305.
gwaeth, w. 181.
gwell, w. 181.
gyn, MANX, 59.
gys, MANX, 59.

HAGGARD, 212.
αἱμο-ω, 214.
haldit, o. N. 240.
Haldorson, 36, 141.
hammer, 213.
haufa, GO. 306.
haou, a. 197.
hare, 257.
hau, L. 77.
Haupt, 154, 155.
hazel, 217.
heart, 213.
ὕδωρο-, 216.
Hebrew roots, 277.
ἑσπερο-, 159.
hen = hence, 107.
hence, 167.
Hendrick, 218.
hennen, O. ENG. 167.
hennes, O. ENG. 167.
hert, o. 223.
ἕτερο-, 166, 175, 176.
hethen, O. ENG. 167, 220, 246.

heus, L. 161.
hiatus, 125, 202.
hic, L. 172, 247.
hiempa, L. 223.
hin, o. 320.
hin-a, L. 167.
hind, 119.
hirn, DORSET, 195.
hits, MALAGASH, 280.
holl, so. 96.
Holmboe, 68.
ὁμαλο-, 136.
homon-, 139.
ὁρα-, 215.
ὑψο-, 260.
ῥαβδο-, 216.
ῥαχι-, 76.
ῥεγ-, 216.
hridl, a. 287.
ῥοχθο-, 222.
ῥοφι-, 216.
hl, 211.
hu-cusque, L. 150.
humble, F. 223.
Humboldt, 140, 284.
bumo-, 139.
ὑπατο-, 42.
ὑπερχ-, 95.
ὑπιρ, 41.
ὑφιστημι, 46.
ὑπο, 44, 45, 293.
ὑποδιχ-, 45.
ὑπολαμβαν-, 45.
ὑπολιστ-, 38.
ὑψοσ-, 41.
hurl, 194.
hurry, 195.

I, a. 294.
ἱ, DAN. 321.
-i-, L. suffix, 229.

iecur-, 14.
ignominis-, 145.
ignora, 22.
ignosc-, 17, 22, 27.
uriσo-, 207.
ila, a. 257.
-ili-, L. suffix, 229.
-illa- of L. vbs. 229.
illo-, 156, 165, 170, 172, 247.
illinc, L. 245.
imberi-, 15.
imbu-, 16, 223.
imo-, 63.
impall-, 19.
impotenti-, 145.
in, 'down,' 63.
inare-, 18.
inardesc-, 16.
incalesc-, 18.
incandesc-, 16.
incend-, 16.
inati-, 19, 52.
incipi-, 18.
incita-, 16.
inclina-, 64.
incoha-, 18.
inconcilia-, 16.
increse-, 16.
incurvo-, 64, 317.
indaga-, 16.
inde, 'down,' 218.
indige-, 217.
insuscame, L. 231.
infami-, 145.
infecto-, 55.
inferi, L. 65.
infind-, 18.
inotiss-, L. 18.
infla-, 16.
inflamma-, 16.

INDEX. 329

inflect-, 16.
informa-, 18.
informi-, 145.
infra, L. 65.
infring-, 19, 48 n., 52.
ingemina-, 16.
ingrandesc-, 16.
inhibe-, 16.
inhorre-, 16.
innutri-, 16.
insepulto-, 55.
insequ-, 21, 146.
insolenti-, 16.
instaur-, 16.
instinct, 283.
institu-, 16.
insimula-, 17.
insurg-, 16.
insula, 66.
intabesc-, 19.
intelleg-, 29, 47.
intemperie-, 145.
intepesc-, 18.
inter, L. 48 n., 53.
interareso-, 48, 52.
interbib-, 48, 52.
intercid-, 48.
intercid-, 49, 52.
intereluud-, 49.
interds-, 51.
interdic-, 47.
interfic-, 49.
interfod-, 51.
interfrigesc-, 48.
interfring-, 48, 52.
interfug-, 51.
interfulge-, 51.
interi-, 49.
interim-, 49, 52.
interiung-, 47.
interluce-, 51.

interluce-, 51.
intermina-, 47.
intermisc-, 47, 152.
intermitt-, 48.
intermor-, 48.
interneca-, 48.
internosc-, 49.
interpella-, 49.
interpola-, 49.
interpung-, 49.
interquiesc-, 47.
interroga-, 50.
interrump-, 48.
interscind-, 49.
intersepi-, 49.
interspira-, 51.
interstingu-, 48.
intertenere, L 46.
interter- ? L. 48.
intertrigon-, 48.
interturba-, 47.
intervart-, 48.
intervis-, 51.
intumesc-, 16.
intus, L. 246.
inuestiga-, 16.
inuido-, 145.
innocato-, 55.
-io- of Lat. adj. 230.
ioco-, 14.
ion-, L. suff. 229.
ionga, ia. 307.
irai, F. 298.
isto-, 201.
-ita- of Lat. vba. 75, 229.
itara, a. 177.
iterum, L. 176, 177.
itidem, L. 167.
-itie-, L. suff. 229.
-ium, L. n. suff. 229.

iung-, 218.
iunio-, 305.
-iuo- of Lat. adj. 230.
iusticior-, 236.
iusum, L. 86.
iuus-, 14.

JAMIESON, 72.
jeder, G. 182.
Jefferson, 60.
jus, a. 296.
Johnson, 233.
jungoro, o. c. 123.

K, suffix, 305.
sai, 149.
kárava, a. 266.
karóka, 219.
kat, LITH. 280.
ker, 161.
ken, base of pronouns, 244, 279, 286.
-kin, suffix, 226.
kueval, 306.
know, 245.
krk, BOH. 275.
krt, BOH. 275.
κρύβδα, 321.
kship-ra-, a. 146.
κτα-, 207.
κτιπ-, 207.
Kuhn's Zeitschrift, 112, 113, 260.
Kühner's Gr. 2, 4.

L, initial, lost, 14.
Lachmann, 154.
lact, 207.
laeuo-, 121.
lamb, 223.
λαμβαν-, 220.

Lapp, 245, 314.
largitēr, L. 321.
lauch, a. 228.
laugh, 231.
laughter, 211.
lauru-, 189.
ld, 216.
lead, 216.
left, 121.
leg-ê-bam, L. 295.
leng, 180.
λεοντ-, 212.
lepos-, 257.
lesser, 147.
-let, suffix, 226.
λεξω, 300.
liberalitēr, L. 321.
libero-, 221.
Libystino-, 213.
lictor-, 194.
Liddell & Scott, 48, 54, 130, 174.
light, 211.
Ligustico-, 213.
limen-, 194.
linen, 245.
-ling, suffix, 226.
lira-, 91.
liters-, 193.
little, 138, 227.
lo, 281.
-lock, suffix, 226.
lointain, F. 212.
lording, 227.
lovest, 216.
loveth, 220.
ly, a vowel, 274.
lt, 212.
λθ, 220.
luc-s, L. 287.
lumbo-, 19, 221.

lz, 221.

Madvig, 228, 318.
magis, L. 122.
magistero-, 214.
maior-, 146.
male-, 202.
μαλακο-, 199.
Malden, 273.
male, L. 129, 130.
malle, L. 180.
malleo-, 182.
malmen, a. 199.
mīlo-, 138.
mīlo-, 147.
mand-, 198.
mande-, 217.
manduca-, 198.
manner, 202.
manoir, F. 202.
mant, w. 198.
Mantras, 250.
Marriott, xii.
μασα-, 202.
μασσ-, 202.
Massmann, 78, 83.
μασθαλιδ-, 221.
Matthiae, 2.
maxilla-, 202.
mb, 223.
μη, 294.
μεγεθει-, 174.
Meissner, 78, 81.
μεζον-, 146.
μεμβλωκα, 223.
men, Umb. suffix, 291.
menton, F. 198.
mentum, L. 185, 198.
Merkel, 173.
μεσημβρια, 223.
messer, a. 213, 226.

metathesis, 306.
metuculoso-, 303.
mickle, 138, 227.
μεγλα, 217.
might, 211.
ministero-, 214.
minor-, 122.
misce-, 222.
μισγ-, 222.
mix, 222.
mo, 180.
μογις, 202.
mol-, 199.
mola-, 198.
molesto-, 214.
μολις, 202.
μολυβδο-, 216.
Mommsen, 117, 144, 156, 208, 269.
mondenlicht, a. 304.
more-, 202.
morast, a. 119, 216.
morde-, 119.
mordre, F. 217.
Morris, 104, 147.
mortario-, 192.
morti, 213.
mos-, 202.
motion, 273.
mould, 199.
mourn, 224.
mouth, 198.
mp, 223.
mrid, s. 198.
mulce-, 199.
mund, a. 198.
murder, 219.
murec-, 191.
μυλη, 198.
Müller, C. O., 17.
Müller, Lucian, 160.

INDEX. 331

Müller, Max, 251, 253, 255, 257, 258, 278, 281, 299, 308, 309, 310, 315.
μυστακ-, 198.

N, paragogic, 162.
ν, interchanged with θ, 174.
ν = s of L, 163.
n of a. gen. 205.
n of ENG. gen. 205.
n, silent, 304.
na, SLAV. 57.
naitre, F. 216.
namentlich, G. 212.
navel, 68.
nd, 216.
nē, L. 170, 183.
ne, L. 294.
near, 124.
neath, 68.
necs-, 43 n., 66, 67.
nect-, 207.
ned, DAN. 68.
ηιFs-, 68.
neif, 304.
neither, 168.
nello, L 63.
νεο-, 72.
νεφελη, 68.
nequin-, 102.
νερθε, 60.
νεφ-, 68.
newt, 68.
ng, 224.
ni, CHIN. 68.
ni, a. 67.
nid, o. NO. 68.
nidr, o. NO. 68.
Niebuhr, 140.

nieder, G. 68, 293.
niemand, G. 218.
night, 211.
nit-, 210, 320.
niz, RUSS. 67.
nobis, L. 290.
noct-, 207.
nombre, SP. 223.
non, L., omitted, 160.
nonce, 178, 227.
nor, omitted, 168.
North American Review, 310 et seq.
noso-, 153.
noulaidmo-, 67.
nouo-, 68.
nt, 212.
-θ, 220.
nu-, 68.
nŭ, LITH. 67.
νυχ-, 62.
νυχ-α, 297.
nūg, LITH. 68.
νυκτ-, 99, 207.
'nunner, 125.
nutri-, 306.

OB, L. 60.
ober, G. 43.
obl-, 110.
obs, L. 200.
obsoleso-, 200, 220.
obsordeso-, 201, 219.
obst, G. 147.
obter-, 110.
occid-, 110.
oculo-, 161.
oeno-, 176.
of, 61, 292.
of, N. 115.
off, 62.

ofgnaing, 115.
ofmickill, S. 116.
of-serve, 104.
of-take, 104.
often, 121.
oftyened, 115.
ουρτορ-, 236.
ομφαλο-, 68.
on, 64.
on = of, 61.
on-, A.-S. 24, 30, 31, 40, 53.
onelifjan, A.-S. 30.
oncnavan, A.-S. 28.
ongitan, A.-S. 52.
ονομασ-, 225, 301.
onsecan, A.-S. 52.
ονυχ-, 66, 303, 307.
ονυματ-, 227.
operi-, 110.
opfel, G. 147.
αππρυ-, 302.
opinion-, 226.
οπισω, 122.
οπισθο, 221.
ορωπα-, 147.
oppet-, 110.
opple-, 147.
opprim-, 110.
or, 179, 181.
-or-, L suff. 238.
ord, DAN. 142.
ordi-, 219.
ordon-, 204.
opsy-, 84.
οπεχθι-, 222.
Orelli, 130.
οργυια-, 305.
ori-, 84.
origin of language, 282.

INDEX.

orm, Dan. 142
ορθο-, 220.
ορθρο-, 220.
θσ-, 213.
oss, 213.
ost, s.s. 94, 31.
other, 174.
ōsrum, N. 175.
otium, L. 206.
our, omitted, 162.
ουλα, 192.
ουθαρ, 222.
over, 44.
Ovid, 173.

Palast, o. 119, 216.
Paley, 173.
παλλας-, 231.
palo-, 203.
palumbe-, 96.
pand-, 218.
Pāṇini, 253.
ταομαι, 207.
ταρα, 293.
paragoge, 301, 305.
παρακαλυττ-, 113.
παρασθε-, 113.
παρασσγο-, 114.
παρατηθε-, 113.
παραφημι, 113.
παρασσων, 114, 203.
παραθερμο-, 114.
παρηλικ-, 113.
ταρορα-, 113.
Parry, 63, n.; xiii.
parti-, 213.
passives, 201.
patēr, L. 64.
paulo-, 202.
pect-, 207.
ped-, 217.

paior-, 148.
pellec-, 191, 231.
pend-, 218.
περθερ-, 129.
par with adj. 109.
par with sb. 318.
par with vb. 108, 319.
percell-, 109.
percurr-, 319.
perd-, 262.
peremni-, 61.
parendie, L. 111.
perfuge-, 112.
perfund-, 109.
perg-, 96.
parinde, L. 96.
parlin-, 109.
permagno-, 109.
persuastric-, 215.
peruert-, 109.
peruide-, 109.
perung-, 109.
petrifaction, 291.
pf, 223.
pfad, &c. a. 222, 223.
φερομεν, 295.
φιν, suffix, 290.
'phonetic types,' 283.
φθ, 221.
φθιγγ, &c. 221.
pignos-, 226.
pitpit, osc. 96.
plang-, 230.
plaustro-, 185, 189.
pleat-, 207.
plorabundo-, 233.
plumbo-, 216.
plural suffix, 291.
poden-, 191.
Poggendorff, 272.
poli- 50.

pollice-, 75.
polling-, 75.
pomo-, 122, 147.
pon-, 118.
popina-, 96.
porca-, 90.
porro, L. 74.
πορθμο-, 220.
pōs, L. 118, 123, 319.
poshac, L. 118.
posilla, L. 119, 123.
posmeridiano-, 118.
posquam, L. 118.
post, L. 117, 214.
poste, L. 125.
postempus, L. 117.
posterganeo-, 118.
postidea, L. 125.
ποτερο-, 242.
ποθιν, 245.
Pott, θ, 119, 140, 148, 257.
prebend-, 217.
prentili, a. 204.
πριν, 122.
Priscian, 145.
pristino-, 123, 213.
pro, L. 74, 92.
προ, 293.
procell-, 93.
procul, L. 157.
prod, L. 77, 93.
profano-, 94.
profundo-, 94.
prōm-, 93.
prono-, 92.
pronominal roots, 27 p
291.
προς, 123, 293.
προσω, 122.
τανοθι, 162.

προσίνεσις, 301.
προτερο-, 77.
provectiou, 177, 227.
pt, 213.
πτελαμο-, &c. 213.

QUADRIGA-, 193.
quaerita-, 75.
Quarterly Journal of Education, 147.
quattuor, L. 187.
que, L. 149, 159, 167.
questo, L. 243.
quien, sp. 243.
quinque, 187.

R, a vowel, 274.
rapi-, 264.
Rask, 26, 31, 93, 115, 121, 125, 126, 186.
rastro-, 192.
rd, 219.
re, L. 74, 97, 293.
recenti, 89.
recidiuo-, 97, 99.
reciproco-, 75, 90.
recita-, 88.
recuba-, 88.
recubitu-, 88.
recumb-, 99.
recupera-, 75.
recuruo-, 87.
red, L. 74.
refell-, 97.
rēg-, 95.
rĕg-, 95.
remane-, 38.
rep-, 259.
repando-, 87.
repon-, 89.

reside-, 88.
resoudre, F. 217.
retorque-, 98.
retro, L. 74.
Rheinisches Museum, 164.
Ribbeck, 298.
ricochet, 99.
ridge, 76.
rig, 76, 90.
rise, 95.
Ritschl, 97, 117, 118, 123, 125, 166.
-ro-, n. suffix, 229.
roga-, compounds of, 50.
roll, 194, 195.
rostro-, 185.
rouse, 95.
rt, 213.
ρδ, 220.
rtick, o. 76.
rz, 223.

SA, s. 289.
maculo-, 260.
saft, o. 121.
sale, F. 202.
sali-, 269.
salictum, L. 208, 214.
salt, 212.
sals, o. 223.
Sanders, 140.
Sanskrit asperates, 276.
sap, 121.
sarmin, a. 289.
sat, L. 115.
Saturday Review, 308.
sa, 222.
scala-, 198.

Scaliger, 151.
-schaft, a. suff. 211.
schlange, a. 259.
Schweizer, 209.
sci-, 233.
scribando-, 218.
scribenti-, L. 212.
secus, L. 123, 209.
segel, a. 203.
sepeli-, 110.
septentrion-, 195.
sarp-, 259.
serpenti-, 259.
sesqui-, 209.
σητις, 289.
setius, L. 209.
sg, 222.
si, L. 'so,' 158.
si-cut, L. 158.
siluestri-, 214.
Simplicius, 148.
sinistero-, 214.
sist-, 297.
sister, 215.
sitte, o. 202.
situ-, 201.
σταυρθμο-, 221.
στεν-, 234.
στερρο-, 222.
sluggard, 213.
slush, 201.
smure, sc. 181.
soll, 201.
sole, 202.
soleil, F. 234.
solemni-, 61, 260.
sorbe-, 216.
sordi-, 200.
sorex-, 181.
σωφροσυνη, 225.
soror-, 215.

sorti-, 213, 202.
souiller, F. 201.
soul, 285.
sparrow, 234.
spec-, 234.
σφαλλ-, 187.
spirit, 285.
spiritual words, 285.
sr, a. 259.
srp-, a. 259.
st, 213.
St. Edmund, 180.
St. Kenelm, 182.
sta-, 233, 297.
stamp, 223.
Stewart, Dugald, 282.
stern, o. 224.
sti, 221.
στίστε-, 221.
stinge-, 223.
Stokes, W., 177.
στομαr-, 213.
strag-, 230.
'Study of Words,' 264.
stump, 223.
sub, L. 38, 41, 42, 44.
submerg-, 45.
submitt-, 45.
subsist-, 48.
subter, L. 105.
subtus, L. 213.
suffod-, 45.
sullage, 201.
sully, 201.
sunimo-, 42 n.
sumpsi, L. 223.
super, L. 43.
superlatives, 238.
superné, L. 111, 210.
supparo-, 114.

T of Eng. neuters, 242.
tailleur, 238.
talo-, 202.
tars, a. 196.
rs, 149.
rt, 158.
tegumentum, L. 212, 227.
τεινω, 129.
tnla-, 203.
τεμνεσ-, 226.
temere, L. 310.
templo-, 223.
tumpos-, 223.
tund-, 217.
τρεβινθε-, 220.
terebra, 231.
terion-, 106.
terrestri-, 214.
τερθρο-, 221.
τετελεσμαι, 300.
that, 179.
that oon, 178.
θυτερον, 177.
the tone, 227.
thence, 179.
thet, old form of 'the,' 178.
third person pronouns, 179, 242.
thorough, 77.
Thorpe, 26.
θορυβε-, 231.
through, 77, 274.
θυγατερ-, 202.
thumb, 221.
rur-, 157.
tither, so. 177.
tithing, 227.
to-, o. ENG. prefix, 54, 102.

to, 57.
tobreak, 102.
tocalion-, 213.
toll-, 7.
toner, 175.
toustrio-, 215.
tonstrina-, 215.
topinch, 102.
tordre, F. 219.
tospend, 102.
tother, 177.
tranquillo-, 111.
trans, 111.
Trench, 284.
tres, F. 111.
tribunicio-, 234.
τριχθα, 222.
tristicior-, 236.
truc-, 235.
tuft, 211.
τυπτομεσθα, 221.
τυπτω, 295.
turf, 232.
turn, 224.
tarpi-, 200.
turpiter, L. 321.
tyrant, 213.
tz, 222.

-U, L. suff. 229.
uad-, 319, 298.
uas, L. 143.
uallo-, 186.
uanno-, 144.
uano-, 143.
uber, L. 222.
über, G. 43.
ue-, L. 143, 148.
uecord-, 148.
uegrandi-, 143.
uehament-, 143.

INDEX. 335

Ucion-, 144.
ael, L. 160.
uellica-, 75.
aelo-, 114, 203.
uelum palati, 206.
uend-, 262.
ueni-, 261.
uento-, 296.
uepallido-, 143.
uerbar-, 216.
uermi-, 259.
ueru-, 81.
ueuno-, 143.
uespertino-, 213.
uestl-, 215.
uide-, 21, 216.
uirectum, L. 208,
321.
-ula- of L. vbs. 229.
uld, DAN. 142.
ullo-, 170.
uls, L. 242.
ultra, L. 170, 212.
ulv, DAN. 142.
um, L. suff. 228.
um, o. 61.
umbilico-, 66.
umbra-, 66.
un, 26, 27, 51.
unart, o. 139.
unbild, o. 139.
undergitan, s.-s. 52.
undermine, 49.
underscan, s.-s. 52.
understand, 37.
understanding, vbs. of,
29.
undertake, 38.
undertaking, vbs. of,
28.
undienst, o. 139.

unding, o. 139.
-undo-, L. suff. 229.
ungestaltet, o. 145.
ungethler, o. 139.
ungewitter, o. 139.
ungezogen, o. 139.
ungott, o. 139.
ungross, o. 140.
ungui-, 66.
un-ion-, 226.
unkrant, o. 139.
unkub, o. 140.
unloose, 6.
unlust, 142.
unmensch, o. 139.
unrest, 142.
unter, o. 36, 38, 53.
unterarbeiten, o. 38.
unterbauen, o. 37.
unterbleiben, o. 38.
unterbrechen, o. 48.
unterdrücken, o. 38.
unterellern, o. 38.
unterfangen, o. 37.
untergehen, o. 49.
untergraben, o. 38, 45.
unterhalten, o. 36, 46.
unterhöhlen, o. 38.
unterjochen, o. 38.
unterkeilen, o. 37.
unterklässen, o. 40.
unterlassen, o. 37, 48,
52.
untermauern, o. 37.
untermengen, o. 38.
unterminen, o. 38.
untermischen, o. 38.
unternehmen, o. 36, 46.
unterrichten, o. 37.
untersagen, o. 37, 47,
52.

unterschneiden, o. 42.
unterschreiben, o. 38.
unterschwären, o. 38.
untersiegeln, o. 38.
unterstpilen, o. 38.
unterstehen, o. 37.
unterstützen, o. 37.
untersuchen, o. 37.
unterwaschen, o. 38.
unterweisen, o. 37.
unterwerfen, o. 38.
unterwühlen, o. 37.
unterzeichen, o. 38.
unterziehen, a. 36.
unthat, o. 140.
unthier, a. 140.
untiefe, o. 140.
untrust, 142.
untyme, 142.
-uo- of L. adj. 230.
uoca- = uaca-, 143,
208.
uocino-, 208.
uolnes-, 226.
uoloelle-, 192.
Upanishads, 250.
upper, 44.
upplöss, sw. 26.
upptäcka, sw. 26.
uptake, so. 28.
-urno- of L. adj. 229.
urt, DAN. 142.
urvocale of Bopp, 271.
ualukan, oo. 80.
ustula-, 214.
-ot- of L. sb. 229.
utero-, 179, 242.
utrum, L. 169.
uxor-, 215.

Va, F. 298.

INDEX.

vā, a. 296.
van, 307.
Varro, 75.
ver, a. 101, 106, 293.
verachten, a. 112, 211.
veralten, a. 106.
verbluten, a. 107.
verbrüoken, a. 106.
verfechten, a. 112.
verhören, a. 114.
verjähren, a. 100.
verkehren, a. 108.
vernehmen, a. 106.
versehen, a. 106.
vertheidigen, a. 112.
voilà, r. 281.
von, a. 61.
vowel-assimilation, 273, 274.
vowels, infinite, 273.

Wagner, G., 153, 155.
Wagner, W., 194.

wan-, a. sra. 142.
wanhope, 142.
wantrust, 142.
ward, 218.
waur, 146.
wax, vb. 222.
Westminster Review, 251.
Weymouth, 12, 206.
what, 179.
whence, 179, 245.
where = whether, 181.
where = whither, 181.
whether, 169, 242.
whirl, 194, 195.
whom, 244.
wider, o. a. 35, 119.
Willis, 271, 273.
Wilson, H. H., 263, 266, 268.
wind, 296.

winnow, 296.
wit, 21.
with, 35.
withstand, 120.
womb, 223.
wot, 21.
-wr-, w. suff. 238.

Ξγεσ-, 222.
ξυν-, 222.
ξυνο-, 222.

Y4, a. suff. 262.
-yana, a. suff. comp. 122.
year, 260.
yellow, 235.
yonder, 119.
yman, a.-a. 195.
yun-aj-mi, a. 219.

Zenn, 274.
ser, 102.
Zu, o. 57, 223

THE END.

www.ingramcontent.com/pod-product-compliance
Lightning Source LLC
Chambersburg PA
CBHW030312240426
43673CB00040B/1139